Turkey, the EU and the Middle East

This book focuses on the dynamics of Turkey's relationship with Europe in the context of the "Arab Spring" and analyses Turkish behaviour vis-à-vis foreign policy cooperation with the EU.

Süsler explains the complexity of Turkey-EU relations by looking beyond membership negotiations and examines informal foreign policy dialogue between Turkish and EU officials. The book discusses the reactions of the Turkish government to the uprisings in Libya, Syria, and Egypt and cooperative opportunities between Turkey and the EU. The analysis finds that although cooperation varies across cases, foreign policy dialogue has become a main driver of the Turkey-EU relationship. A counter-intuitive finding of the research is that the EU has often been the actor seeking Turkey's cooperation, rather than the other way around, clearly challenging the original power asymmetry between Turkey and the EU.

Based on interviews with diplomats and policy makers and extensive documentary research, this book will be of interest to political scientists, students, policy makers and researchers focusing on Turkish foreign policy and Turkey-EU relations. This book is also about exploring inventive ways of maintaining a complex working partnership with the EU and will be of interest to scholars working on the EU's relationship with "outsiders".

Buğra Süsler is a Visiting Postdoctoral Fellow at the LSE IDEAS, the foreign policy think tank of the London School of Economics and Political Science (LSE) and a Teaching Fellow at the University College London (UCL) Department of Political Science. His research focuses on foreign policy analysis, international cooperation, and global conflicts. He holds a PhD in International Relations and an MSc in Politics and Government in the European Union from the LSE as well as a BSc in Politics from the University of Bristol.

Routledge Studies in Foreign Policy Analysis

Series Editors:
Christopher Alden
London School of Economics, UK
Amnon Aran
City University of London, UK

The Foreign Policy Analysis (FPA) series covers a broad intellectual canvass, which brings together scholars of International Relations, Area Studies, Politics, and other related fields such as Political Psychology and Administrative Studies. It also engages with a wide range of empirical issues: from the study of the foreign policy of individual countries, to specific aspects of foreign policy such as economic diplomacy or bureaucratic politics, through germane theoretical issues such as rationality and foreign policy. The Series aims to specialize in FPA as well as appeal to the wider community of scholars within International Relations, related fields, and amongst practitioners. As such the range of topics covered by the Series includes, but is not be limited to, foreign policy decision-making; the foreign policy of individual states and non-state actors. In addition it will include analytical aspects of foreign policy, for instance, the role of domestic factors; political parties; elites. Theoretical issue-areas that advance the study of foreign policy analysis, for example, FPA and Gender, Critical FPA, FPA in a new media landscape, Ethics and FPA, are also be welcomed.

Colombian Agency and the Making of US Foreign Policy
Intervention by Invitation
Alvaro Mendez

Power, Perception and Foreign Policymaking
US and EU Responses to the Rise of China
Scott Brown

Intercultural Dialogue in EU Foreign Policy
The Case of the Mediterranean from the End of the Cold War to the Arab Uprisings
Pietro De Perini

America's Allies and the Decline of US Hegemony
Edited by Jonathan Paquin and Justin Massie

Turkey, the EU and the Middle East
Foreign Policy Cooperation and the Arab Uprisings
Buğra Süsler

www.routledge.com/series/RSIHR

Turkey, the EU and the Middle East

Foreign Policy Cooperation and the Arab Uprisings

Buğra Süsler

Routledge
Taylor & Francis Group

LONDON AND NEW YORK

First published 2020
by Routledge
2 Park Square, Milton Park, Abingdon, Oxon OX14 4RN

and by Routledge
52 Vanderbilt Avenue, New York, NY 10017

*Routledge is an imprint of the Taylor & Francis Group, an informa
business*

British Library Cataloguing-in-Publication Data
A catalogue record for this book is available from the British Library

Library of Congress Cataloging-in-Publication Data
Names: Süsler, Buğra, author.
Title: Turkey, the EU and the Middle East : foreign policy cooperation and
  the Arab uprisings / Buğra Süsler.
Description: First edition. | New York : Routledge, 2020. | Series:
  Routledge studies in foreign policy analysis | Includes bibliographical
  references and index.
Identifiers: LCCN 2019050838 (print) | LCCN 2019050839 (ebook) |
  ISBN 9780367236137 (hardback) | ISBN 9780429280788 (ebook)
Subjects: LCSH: Turkey—Foreign relations—European Union countries. |
  European Union countries—Foreign relations—Turkey. | Turkey—
  Foreign relations—Middle East. | Arab Spring, 2010—Influence. |
  Middle East—Foreign relations—Turkey.
Classification: LCC DR479.E85 S87 2020 (print) | LCC DR479.E85
  (ebook) | DDC 327.56104—dc23
LC record available at https://lccn.loc.gov/2019050838
LC ebook record available at https://lccn.loc.gov/2019050839

ISBN: 978-0-367-23613-7 (hbk)
ISBN: 978-0-429-28078-8 (ebk)

Typeset in Times New Roman
by Apex CoVantage, LLC

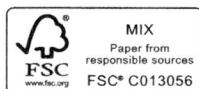

MIX
Paper from
responsible sources
FSC
www.fsc.org   FSC® C013056

Printed and bound in Great Britain by
TJ International Ltd, Padstow, Cornwall

To My Parents

Contents

Tables

Figures

Acknowledgements

This book is a product of my research at the London School of Economics and Political Science (LSE), and I would like to express my gratitude to everyone who contributed to the conception, development, and completion of this project.

First and foremost, I would like to thank my publisher. The Routledge team has been very supportive in the publication process. Special thanks to editors Rob Sorsby and Claire Maloney, the series editors Professors Amnon Aran and Chris Alden, and the two anonymous reviewers who provided very useful feedback on my work.

I am grateful to Professor Chris Alden for his invaluable support and motivation. I have learned a lot from him and it has been a privilege to work with him.

I also owe special thanks to Dr Ulrich Sedelmeier for his guidance and feedback as well as to Professor Ziya Öniş for his contributions.

I would like to express my gratitude for the financial support I received from the LSE – the LSE PhD Studentship and the LSE Middle East Centre Emirates PhD Award.

I completed the manuscript as a visiting postdoctoral fellow at the LSE IDEAS, and I would like to thank Professor Christopher Coker and Dr Emilia Knight for their support.

I would like to thank all of the interviewees who shared their valuable views with me and helped me during my fieldwork in Turkey and Belgium, and all of my colleagues and friends who gave me feedback on my work in conferences and workshops.

Lastly, I would like to thank my mum and dad, İlknur and Ferdi, to whom I dedicate this work, for their loving support.

1 Introduction

Turkish foreign policy has attracted considerable attention in the Justice and Development Party (AKP) era due to Turkey's increased engagement with the Middle East and has often sparked debates about Turkey's ambitions as an emerging power. How can we understand the way in which the transformation of Turkish foreign policy has affected the dynamics of Turkey's relationship with Europe and how the Turkish government has approached foreign policy cooperation and partnership with the European Union (EU) in the Middle East and North Africa?

The stalemate in Turkey's EU accession talks and security threats emanating from regional conflicts have significantly transformed the nature of Turkey-EU relations and subsequently made cooperation in the area of foreign policy the main driver of the relationship. Despite political tensions and spats between Turkish and EU leaders, the Turkish government has worked with the EU on key security issues, such as curbing illegal migration and tackling transnational terrorism. How can we explain why the Turkish government has agreed to cooperate with the EU and what cooperation implies for Turkey-EU relations? To analyse the complex evolving nature of Turkey's relationship with the EU, foreign policy cooperation during the Arab Spring needs particular examination.

The relationship between Brussels and Ankara entered into an exceptional era when the Arab Spring began. On one hand, there was a deadlock in Turkey's EU membership bid; on the other hand, the turmoil in the Middle East and North Africa brought about urgent foreign and security challenges for both the EU and Turkey regarding their immediate neighbourhood, where they both had vital strategic interests.

There was a clear distinction in the way the EU and Turkey responded to the uprisings, which became apparent as the tension escalated in the region. The Turkish government was generally reluctant to criticise the incumbent regimes and avoided jeopardising its relationships, while the EU harshly criticised the same regimes and imposed sanctions. Over time, the Turkish government adopted a hawkish stance against the regimes in Libya, Syria, and Egypt to a point that it even criticised the EU for not taking effective steps.

The disagreements between the EU and Turkey about how to react to the uprisings attracted considerable attention and led analysts to call for foreign policy coordination to be established parallel with the membership talks in order to improve their effectiveness regarding foreign policy issues of mutual interest (see e.g., Barysch, 2011a, 2011b; Grabbe and Ülgen, 2011; Lecha, 2011; Sandrin, 2012). The idea was that they would come to an agreement that would achieve mutual gains from cooperation. The three biggest issues at hand were how to deal with the turmoil in Libya, Syria, and Egypt.

Such renewed emphasis on increased cooperation appeared also in the context of membership negotiations. There were voices in the European Council and European Commission that clearly wished to avoid a deadlock in Turkey-EU relations, especially since there was a threat to stability from the Middle East. For instance, the European Commission launched the "Positive Agenda" in May 2012, aiming to intensify cooperation in the area of foreign policy. Commenting on the initiative, the EU Commissioner for Enlargement specifically underlined that the EU wanted to address common challenges in the neighbourhood together with Turkey and that the initiative was a tool to give new momentum to the relationship (Füle, 2012). The initiative was supported by the member states who declared that Turkey and the EU were "stronger together", drawing attention to "Turkey's importance in supporting stability in the Middle East" (Ažubalis et al., 2012). Similarly, the European Parliament issued statements promoting the "advantages for the EU of working more closely with Turkey on foreign and neighbourhood policy priorities such as the Middle East" (European Parliament, 2012).

In Turkey, policy makers also emphasised that foreign policy cooperation during the Arab Spring would be a "win-win" for both actors (Davutoğlu, 2012) because developing a closer relationship would be "mutually beneficial for both parties" given the "common objectives" in the region (Bağış, 2012a). For example, in the 51st session of the EU-Turkey Association Council, held in Brussels on 27 May 2013, Turkish Foreign Minister Davutoğlu (2013) explicitly stated that "in view of the Arab transformations which are at a critical juncture, the urgency for a genuine partnership between the EU and Turkey has become even more manifest". There was a mutual interest in working closely to tackle foreign policy problems in the shared neighbourhood and a belief that the EU and Turkey were stronger together (Bağış, 2012b). However, despite the recurring rhetoric of closer foreign policy cooperation, Turkey's cooperation with the EU was limited and it varied considerably, especially taking into account the way in which Turkey had differences of views with the EU regarding the crises in Libya, Egypt, and Syria.

This book asks: "To what extent did the Turkish government cooperate with the EU regarding the uprisings?" The empirical investigation is complemented by a second question, which makes a theoretical contribution: "What determined the degree to which the Turkish government cooperated with the EU in the area of foreign policy during the uprisings?" To what extent and why the Turkish government included cooperation with the EU in its foreign policy decision-making process, as identified here, raises theoretical implications.

This book is not about Turkey's EU membership bid, which has been the main focus of the vast majority of studies examining Turkey-EU relations. It contributes to our understanding of Turkish foreign policy and specifically Turkey's alliance with the EU in the area of foreign policy, considering both as important actors in a region in which they both have strategic interests. From this perspective, Turkey's EU candidacy is one factor, among many others, that can potentially influence Turkish decisions about whether to cooperate with the EU, as this book will unpack.

The main point that needs to be made regarding the foreign policy relationship between Turkey and the EU during the Arab Spring is that the EU had a strong interest in Turkish cooperation in order to be able to handle the turmoil and contain instability in the region. The EU was the "demandeur"; therefore, this book investigates whether and why Turkey provided, or agreed to, cooperation (i.e., the EU wanted something from Turkey; hence the focus is on Turkey).

Turkey's cooperation with the EU

The analysis presented here requires a discussion of what cooperation means and how it can be operationalised. The key questions that need to be addressed are: What is cooperation as a concept? What forms of cooperation can be identified? And methodologically, how can we identify cooperation empirically? As Keohane (1984: 12) explains, cooperation requires active attempts to adjust behaviour. If there is a harmony of interests, explaining cooperation is obvious; it is more important to be able to observe cooperation in the absence of a harmony of interests, when it involves an adjustment of behaviour and is thus more difficult to achieve. In such cases, cooperation is more in need of analysis. Therefore, it can be claimed that an integral part of Turkey's cooperation with the EU in the area of foreign policy concerns the extent to which Turkish decision makers adjusted their behaviour to accommodate EU positions and whether the Turkish government reached out to the EU in coordination.

It is possible to distinguish between different degrees of Turkey's cooperation (or the absence of it) with the EU. This book will use a scale from no cooperation to co-decision to make such a distinction, which will be unpacked in the next chapter. Figure 1.1 lays out the framework for analysing cooperation by summarising the different stages that will be used to analyse Turkey's cooperation with the EU during the Arab uprisings. Using this classification of different degrees of cooperation, this book will assess which of the following terms best describe Turkey's cooperation with the EU during the uprisings and will then move on to analyse the underlying reasons based on the theoretical framework.

Turkey's cooperation with the EU increases as the relationship moves towards the co-decision point on the right-hand side of the line:

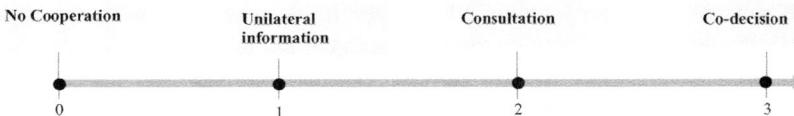

Figure 1.1 Degrees of cooperation

The term "no cooperation" describes no contact with the EU whatsoever in the Turkish foreign policy decision-making process and involves unilateral action without any information or consultation. The EU is not taken into account when foreign policy is made.

At the "unilateral information" (1) point, the Turkish government only informs the EU of its intended actions but then goes on to carry out these intentions without giving the EU an opportunity to make comments or explain its position. The EU has no opportunity to provide its own assessment of Turkish decisions due to a lack of consultation.

At the "consultation" (2) point, the Turkish government reaches out and consults the EU before acting. The EU has a chance to provide feedback on Turkish positions. This does not necessarily lead to a change in Turkish policy.

Co-decision (3) describes Turkey consulting the EU, and, if necessary, modifying its behaviour according to feedback. Therefore, there is a possibility of adaptation to the EU position and an accommodation of an EU policy. This does not necessarily mean a complete shift to EU preferences.

Explanatory factors

The explanations for cooperation can be divided into two broad camps using rationalist and constructivist approaches. Rationalist approaches assert that purposeful and goal-oriented actors follow the "logic of consequentialism" (March and Olsen, 1989: 160–62), make cost-benefit calculations, and engage in strategic bargaining to maximise their utility. On the other hand, constructivists argue that actors follow the "logic of appropriateness" (ibid.) and that the main motivations of actors are not costs and benefits but instead norms, values, identities, and "appropriate behaviour".

From a rationalist standpoint, the degree of cooperation is a consequence of a cost-benefit calculation and strategic behaviour. Rationalist approaches hypothesise: "For Turkey, if there are greater benefits from cooperation than from unilateral action, then Turkey will seek cooperation with the EU". Specific factors that come into play include, in the short term, concerns related to border security and domestic order, and, in the long term, economic gains from making Turkey a more influential regional actor.

From a constructivist perspective, factors such as norms of appropriate behaviour and identity need to be taken into account when explaining the degree of Turkey's cooperation with the EU. Constructivist approaches hypothesise: "If cooperation is seen as an appropriate behaviour, then Turkey will move towards the cooperation end of the spectrum". Specific factors include norms of appropriate behaviour the long-standing Turkey-EU alliance may have produced and potential cultural obstacles to cooperation with the EU.

The discussion requires a more specific identification of relevant factors that determine what the costs and benefits were and whether cooperation was appropriate. These include general factors regarding cooperation with the EU as well as specific factors tailored to the case studies. The next chapter will focus on the theoretical framework and unpack relevant factors in more detail.

Research design and methodology

This book focuses on three country cases during the Arab Spring. These are the uprisings in Syria, Egypt, and Libya. These countries were selected because they were major foreign policy issues for both the EU and Turkey during the course of the turmoil, and they present more empirical material than the uprising in Tunisia to assess the degree to which foreign policy cooperation took place. As the book will discuss, the need for foreign policy cooperation became more manifest as the protests in Tunisia spilled over to other countries and inspired a region-wide upheaval. In this respect, the book focuses on the wave of political instability that swept across the Arab world and the ways in which the EU and Turkey dealt with it.

The empirical analysis is disaggregated into "cooperative opportunities" (COs), selected as key instances in which the Turkish government took the initiative to act and had a chance to cooperate with the EU. These separate instances of cooperative opportunity are cases in their own right and provide a good picture of Turkish behaviour during the crises and therefore help to make an assessment of Turkish attitudes towards cooperation with the EU. Table 1.1 lists the specific COs (11 in total) this book will analyse. The COs will be analysed in the corresponding

Table 1.1 Cooperative opportunities examined

Uprisings	Cooperative opportunities (COs)
Egypt, including post-Mubarak era (Chapters 4 and 7)	• Anti-Mubarak uprising on 25 Jan 2011 (CO1) • Killings in Port Said on 26 Jan 2013 (CO9) • Removal of Morsi on 3 Jul 2013 (CO10) • Rabaa massacre on 14 Aug 2013 (CO11)
Libya (Chapter 5)	• Decision to support the opposition in Libya on 1 Mar 2011 (CO2) • Evacuation operation in Libya on 20 Feb 2011 (CO3) • Participation in NATO intervention on 24 Mar 2011 (C04)
Syria (Chapter 6)	• Sanctions against Assad on 30 Nov 2011 (CO5) • Participation in Friends of Syria Group after UNSC veto on 4 Feb 2012 (CO6) • Record refugee influx 6-9 Apr 2012 (CO7) • Downing of Turkish plane on 22 Jun 2012 and Akçakale shelling on 3 Oct 2012 (CO8)

country-specific chapters. Because leaders were ousted twice in Egypt, there are two chapters focusing on Egypt, examining the anti-Mubarak uprising and the removal of Morsi.

The qualitative investigation will be based on document analysis and interviews with diplomats and policy makers. The degree of cooperation will be assessed through examining a variety of sources, including statements made by Turkish and EU officials as well as interview data. The fundamental aims of the document analysis and interviews were to find whether consultations took place prior to policy action and to find evidence of EU preferences being incorporated into Turkish policy. For each case of policy action, interactions with the EU are analysed and assessed.

Methodologically, interviews and document analysis provided essential information regarding the kinds of interactions that took place between the EU and Turkey during the uprisings. In order to observe cooperation empirically and to identify the forms that it took, this analysis will examine interactions between the EU and Turkey after each CO and assess whether consultation with the EU took place prior to Turkish actions. Typical empirical evidence for information exchange would point to the provision of information through ad hoc meetings in which the Turkish government briefs the EU on its intended actions or preferences, or personal communication whereby Turkish officials inform EU officials about Turkish positions. More is needed as evidence for consultation. Ideally, there needs to be evidence indicating that the Turkish government took the initiative to contact the EU, that is, evidence that it requested and scheduled meetings with the EU or liaised with the EU Delegation in Ankara; moreover, the evidence should suggest that the Turkish government offered the EU an opportunity to comment on its positions. As for co-decision, empirically observable implications of cooperation could additionally involve policy adjustment as a result of EU feedback and possibly adaptation to an EU position.

Structure of book

Chapter 2 unpacks the theoretical framework, discussing different factors that potentially shaped Turkish foreign policy behaviour. It explains that, from a rationalist perspective, the degree of cooperation is a consequence of a cost-benefit calculation and strategic behaviour; and specific factors that come into play include, in the short term, concerns related to border security and domestic order, and, in the long term, economic gains from making Turkey a more influential regional actor. From a constructivist perspective, by contrast, factors such as norms of appropriate behaviour and identity need to be taken into account when explaining the degree of Turkey's cooperation with the EU. This chapter also explains the research design in more detail, specifically focusing on data collection and case selection.

Chapter 3 provides an overview of the cooperative frameworks between Turkey and the EU and the "Political Dialogue" at different levels. It is useful to establish an understanding of the existing regular frameworks for foreign policy dialogue because cooperation can take place in or be facilitated by existing frameworks for cooperation as well as taking place ad hoc, and the subsequent country-specific chapters will refer to existing frameworks. Chapter 3 also identifies fundamental features of the Political Dialogue between the EU and Turkey, discusses its implications with regard to the nature of the EU-Turkey foreign policy relationship, and finds that the foreign policy dialogue remained largely informal during the course of the Arab Spring.

Chapter 4 examines the degree of cooperation during the crisis in Egypt. The first part of this chapter focuses specifically on the reaction of the Turkish government to anti-Mubarak protests starting on 25 January. The main argument is that, although there were contacts between the EU and the Turkish government, the relationship did not reach the consultation point. The main factor influencing the Turkish response was not the EU position but instead was the US response. Turkish foreign policy decision makers strategically followed the steps of the US and waited until the US had made a clearly critical statement against the Egyptian regime. The Turkish reaction was a strategic action particularly because the Turkish government regarded criticising the Mubarak regime and supporting the opposition too quickly as costly actions. Uncertainty about the uprising led the Turkish government to turn to the US to determine the Turkish stance. The Turkish behaviour can be better explained using a rationalist approach specifically because Turkish decision makers aimed to avoid marginalisation in the international arena when they prioritised their alignment with the US position.

Chapter 5 analyses cooperation during the Libyan uprising, examining reactions with regard to the imposition of sanctions against the Gaddafi regime, the evacuation of Turkish citizens, and international intervention as a result of a UN Security Council resolution. This chapter specifically focuses on the U-turn in Turkish policy towards Gaddafi and argues that it was essentially a strategic adjustment to changing circumstances. Major factors that shaped Turkish behaviour were the evacuation operation and the international response against the regime. Again, the reaction was based on costs and benefits of action rather than on appropriateness. While there were frequent contacts with the EU, the EU was not a major actor involved in the foreign policy decision-making process in Ankara.

Chapter 6 moves on to examine the third country-specific case, the Syrian uprising, and analyses cooperative opportunities during the uprising phase of the crisis, specifically focusing on the initial reaction of the Turkish government to the turmoil and the way in which it developed its policy towards the Assad regime. This chapter argues that the Turkish government, through advocating a regional solution, prioritised cooperation with the Arab League over the EU, and there was no substantial "consultation" or "co-decision" with the EU, although it was informed and contacted by the Turkish government. Once more, the reaction of the Turkish government was based on costs and benefits of action rather than on appropriateness, because Turkish decision makers strategically adjusted their position to become amongst the harshest critics of the Assad regime, believing that President Assad would soon step down or be removed as Colonel Gaddafi of Libya had been. As the Turkish position regarding the Syrian regime shifted,

Turkish decision makers even pushed the EU to take more effective steps for a solution to the Syrian crisis, especially in the area of Syrian refugees.

In Egypt, leaders were ousted twice. So, it is possible to see the turmoil as having two episodes: a crisis involving uprisings against President Mubarak (Chapter 4) and a crisis involving the unrest against President Morsi, after which there was a military intervention led by General Sisi. As an extension to Chapter 4, Chapter 7 focuses on the second episode and analyses cooperative opportunities in post-Mubarak Egypt. Examining the second episode of turmoil in Egypt allows comparison of the reaction of the Turkish government across crises in Egypt. This chapter specifically analyses the reaction to anti-Morsi protests and the removal of Morsi and argues that there was hardly any substantial "consultation" between Turkish and EU officials, especially after the Turkish prime minister gave unequivocal support to the Muslim Brotherhood, siding with Morsi, even though his policies were leading to polarisation in Egypt. This chapter asserts that the Turkish leadership had strong preferences regarding the leadership in Egypt, favouring Sunni Islamists at the expense of other groups in the country's political spectrum. The Turkish leadership was closed to discussion with regard to its policies and often criticised those who did not share its perspective. As a consequence, Ankara even accused the West, and the EU, of legitimising a wrongdoing. Moreover, Chapter 7 argues that Turkish support for Morsi, after it had become clear that Sisi would stay, is difficult to explain as a purely strategic action, although the initial Turkish support for Morsi had strategic aspects. Political and cultural affinity between the AKP and Muslim Brotherhood were crucial factors in Turkish engagement in Egypt, constraining cooperation with the EU to the extent that they caused a divergence. Chapter 7 claims that substantial cooperation with the EU, in the form of "consultation" or "co-decision", would have been costly and that exchanging information without substantial consultation was the convenient action.

Overall findings

This book finds that there was generally a lack of substantial cooperation involving "consultation" because the Turkish government did not reach out to consult with the EU about its actions either before or after the public announcement of the Turkish position. EU feedback was not sought after and not taken into consideration in the decision-making process. However, in most cases, there was more than "unilateral information", and information exchanges between the EU and Turkish officials took place. Therefore, one way or another, the EU was always attached to the Turkish decision-making process. There was no substantial consultation or co-decision, but none of the Turkish decisions caught the EU by total surprise because the EU was informed about Turkish actions. As for the variation across COs, more cooperation can generally be seen where there was no direct threat to Turkish border security or to the political survival of the government.

A major factor that affected the degree of cooperation was the lack of convergence between the Turkish and EU positions, especially when the Turkish government adopted fundamentally different positions, such as its continuous support for

Morsi. Political and cultural affinity were both crucial to the Turkish foreign policy decision-making process in determining allegiance. However, although there was a correlation between the divergence of policies and the lack of a high degree of cooperation, it did not automatically lead to a complete absence of cooperation between the EU and Turkey. In all COs, there was at least "unilateral information", and it is possible to claim that cooperation improved the EU and Turkey's understanding of each other's policies.

The main argument of this book with regard to explaining the cooperation outcome is that rationalism better explains Turkish behaviour with regard to cooperation with the EU, particularly the general lack of high-level cooperation and the fact that there is not a complete absence of cooperation in the form of "no cooperation". Urgency of action and security concerns are specific factors that explain increased costs of cooperation. Although the Turkish government generally prefers the cost-effective outcome, there were some cases during the Arab Spring that cannot be fully explained in rationalist terms. For example, in Egypt after Morsi, the Turkish attitude to cooperation with the EU was dependent on the Turkish position with regard to the Sisi government: it is difficult to explain the Turkish government's behaviour regarding Sisi in Egypt as a purely strategic behaviour because of the cultural and political affinity between the AKP government and the Muslim Brotherhood, affinities which need to be taken into consideration in explaining why the Turkish government continued to regard Morsi as the legitimate leader.

Furthermore, another major point that this book makes is that the Arab uprisings marked a turning point in the foreign policy relationship between the EU and Turkey because often the EU needed Turkish cooperation rather than the other way around. The Turkish government was in the driver's seat, which meant a radical change in the traditional power asymmetry between these actors.

Moreover, the Turkish government was reluctant to criticise the incumbent regimes. The primary reason was persistence with the "zero problems with neighbours" policy that had been implemented before the Arab Spring. The Turkish government had established close ties with the governments of Libya, Syria, and Egypt, and the policy had been seen as a success story of the AKP government. When the crises started, Turkish foreign policy decision makers did not want to give up on the policy, and they did not anticipate that the unrests would snowball into a broader democratic upheaval in the region.

One of the key implications of the research presented here is that the foreign policy relationship between the EU and Turkey is not limited to the membership negotiations. The membership negotiations involve the foreign policy relationship, but they do not necessarily cover all aspects of the interaction. The foreign policy relationship is therefore a somewhat separate area of interaction that requires further attention. This research finds that informal foreign policy interaction continued and therefore can continue in the absence of progress in EU membership talks. This is especially important considering that the EU has continuously sought Turkey's cooperation after the uprisings to address important foreign policy challenges that EU member states have faced.

References

Ažubalis, A., Bildt, C., Erjavec, K., Garcia-Margallo, J., Hague, W., Lajcak, M., Marga, A., Martonyi, J., Mladenov, N., Paet, U., Portas, P., Rinkevics, E., Sikorski, R., Terzi, G., Tuomioja, E., and Westerwelle, G. (2012) "The EU and Turkey: Stronger Together", *EUobserver*, 28 June, http://euobserver.com/7/116780.

Bağış, E. (2012a) "Statement by HE MR Egemen Bağış in the 50th Session of Turkey-EU Association Council", Brussels, 22 June, http://register.consilium.europa.eu/doc/srv?l=EN&f=ST%204807%202012%20INIT.

———. (2012b) "Türkiye Avrupa'yı Kurtaracak", *TC Başbakanlık Basın ve Yayın Enformasyon Genel Müdürlüğü*, 21 November, www.byegm.gov.tr/turkce/haber/bai-trkye-avrupayi-kurtaracak/6703.

Barysch, K. (2011a) "Is Turkey Our Partner Now?" *Centre for European Reform*, 28 November, www.cer.eu/publications/archive/bulletin-article/2011/turkey-our-partner-now.

———. (2011b) "Why the EU and Turkey Need to Co-ordinate Their Foreign Policies", *Centre for European Reform*, 31 August, www.cer.org.uk/in-the-press/why-eu-and-turkey-need-co-ordinate-their-foreign-policies.

Davutoğlu, A. (2013) "Statement by HE Mr Ahmet Davutoğlu, Minister of Foreign Affairs of Turkey in the 51st Session of the EU-Turkey Association Council", Brussels, Belgium, 27 May, http://register.consilium.europa.eu/doc/srv?l=EN&f=ST%204807%202013%20INIT.

———. (2012) "The Changing Dynamics of the EU-Turkey Political Dialogue – New Opportunities and Challenges", Brussels, Belgium, 23 March, www.epc.eu/themes_details.php?cat_id=6&pub_id=1440&theme_id=29.

European Parliament. (2012) "Foreign Affairs Committee Wants Fresh Dynamic in EU-Turkey Relations", Brussels, Belgium, 1 March, www.europarl.europa.eu/news/en/pressroom/content/20120227IPR39344/html/Foreign-affairs-committee-wants-fresh-dynamic-in-EU-Turkey-relations.

Füle, S. (2012) "Speech at Turkey-EU Political Dialogue Meeting at Ministerial Level Press Conference", Istanbul, Turkey, 7 June, http://ec.europa.eu/avservices/services/showShotlist.do?out=PDF&lg=En&iref=I-073617-INT-1.

Grabbe, H., and Ülgen, S. (2011) "The High Price of Strategic Rivalry", *European Voice*, 20 April, www.europeanvoice.com/article/imported/the-high-price-of-strategic-rivalry-/70871.aspx.

Keohane, R.O. (1984) *After Hegemony: Cooperation and Discord in the World Political Economy*, Princeton, NJ: Princeton University Press.

Lecha, E.S. (2011) "The EU, Turkey, and the Arab Spring: From Parallel Approaches to a Joint Strategy?" in *Turkey and the Arab Spring: Implications for Turkish Foreign Policy from a Transatlantic Perspective*, German Marshall Fund Mediterranean Paper Series 2011, Washington, DC: German Marshall Fund of the United States, pp. 25–35.

March, J., and Olsen, J. (1989) *Rediscovering Institutions*, New York: Free Press.

Sandrin, P. (2012) "The Arab Spring and Calls for a Turkey-EU Foreign Policy Dialogue", *Political Reflection* 2(4): 34–40.

2 Explaining Turkey's cooperation with the European Union

This chapter establishes a theoretical framework for the analysis of Turkey's cooperation with the EU, using theories from mainstream international relations (IR) as well as analytical tools from foreign policy analysis (FPA) literature. Discussing various motivations behind Turkish actions, theories examined in this chapter lay the foundations of different explanations for Turkish behaviour regarding interaction with the EU. Broadly, there are two key explanations: Turkish behaviour follows either a strategic course of action taking into consideration costs and benefits, or appropriate behaviour. After having discussed key factors relevant to the two explanations for the degree of cooperation, the chapter details the research design focusing on the operationalisation of cooperation as well as data collection. Essentially, the theoretical framework establishes the basis for addressing the why question: "Why is there cooperation (or lack thereof) with the EU?" while the research design unpacks the methods used.

Table 2.1 specifies the key factors that rationalist and constructivist approaches identify in determining the costs and benefits or appropriateness of cooperation with the EU. For rationalist approaches, specific factors include low/high politics, mainly involving security concerns and economic repercussions of action; urgency of action, although this may overlap with security concerns depending on the issue area; and preference divergence from the EU. Security concerns and instances in which an action needs to be taken urgently generally indicate high costs in terms of cooperation with the EU. Economic factors and preference divergence from the EU are issue specific and can suggest both costs and benefits from cooperation, particularly depending on payoffs with regard to EU membership aspirations or regional leadership aspirations.

For constructivist approaches, specific factors include political and cultural affinity affecting the foreign policy decision-making process and Turkish identification with the norms of appropriateness prompting cooperation with the EU. Generally, the latter suggests that the degree of cooperation is directly proportional to the extent to which Turkey identifies with the norms of appropriate behaviour encouraging cooperation. The former is issue specific. Turkish attitude towards the EU, and foreign policy cooperation, may be affected across COs depending on the degree to which there is political and cultural affinity between the Turkish government and actors in the case study countries.

Table 2.1 Specific factors affecting cooperation with the EU

Rationalist approaches	• A combination of high and low politics, mainly involving security in the short term but also essential economic interests in the long term • Preference divergence from the EU • Urgency of action/response
Constructivist approaches	• Political and cultural affinity affecting foreign policy behaviour, including the attitude towards the EU • Identification with norms of appropriate behaviour prompting cooperation with the EU

Table 2.2 Theoretical approaches for analysis

	Rationalist approach		*Constructivist approach*
Logic	Consequences		Appropriateness
Core theory	Neoliberal institutionalism	Realism	Constructivism
Dominant motivation of cooperation with the EU	Welfare maximisation	Security maximisation and power politics	Norms of appropriate behaviour regarding cooperation
Favourable conditions for cooperation with the EU	When cooperation is cost effective		When cooperation is seen as appropriate behaviour

Fundamentally, rationalist approaches hypothesise: "For the Turkish government, if there are greater benefits from cooperation than from unilateral action, then the Turkish government will seek cooperation with the EU"; whereas, constructivist approaches hypothesise: "If cooperation is seen as appropriate, a higher degree of cooperation will take place" (Table 2.2). This analysis requires pinning down what constitutes the "costs and benefits of cooperation" and the "appropriate behaviour" regarding cooperation. This chapter will start by unpacking costs and benefits and then move on to examining appropriate behaviour. While doing so, it will also review the relevant literature. Costs and benefits are more complex, mainly because questions of identity and mutual community do not vary across cases. As will be discussed, costs and benefits vary depending on specific issues and domestic considerations. Therefore, this chapter will give more weight to elaborating on specific factors involved in rationalist calculations.

This book uses the distinction between rationalism and constructivism to situate itself in the broader IR literature. However, a competitive testing of these theories is not presented; rather, the main view here is that these approaches are complementary.[1] This study sets out to investigate how different factors affecting foreign policy making interact, not whether these factors matter. Take identity for example: in one way or another one would expect identity to be an important aspect of Turkish foreign policy making towards the Middle East and North Africa (once Ottoman territories), where the uprisings took place. In examining these regions, the key question for this book is not so much whether identity matters (one would expect it to matter) but how it interacts with other factors in the formation of Turkish positions in Ankara. That said, indeed, certain factors are more salient in certain case studies (more of which are discussed next).

The rationalist approach

Before moving on with the analysis, one needs to establish how the costs of cooperation vary across different forms of cooperation, and how specific factors laid out in Table 2.2 determine the costs and benefits of cooperation. This requires addressing the questions, "What kind of issues are generally most costly, and what kind of issue-specific costs and benefits are there?" and "How do costs and benefits vary depending on one's theoretical perspective?"

In addition, complementing the discussion of specific factors, this subsection will use insights from the FPA literature in order to focus on the domestic arena and the process of foreign policy decision making, rather than solely focusing on policy outcomes. This is important mainly because using FPA in light of rational-choice theories can provide a more accurate picture of the interaction of different factors – international and domestic – from which Turkish preferences are formed. This subsection will discuss factors that might interfere with rational decision making (e.g., self-perceptions and cognitive biases) as well as poliheuristic theory as an approach that seeks to reconcile rational and non-rational approaches to decision making.

Variation of costs and benefits

The main point that needs to be highlighted is that cooperation typically always involves costs to one degree or another since it requires some adjustment to (otherwise preferred) unilateral behaviour. However, these costs vary depending on the situation and on the form of cooperation. A higher degree of cooperation that involves "co-decision" is generally more costly than a lower degree of cooperation. For example, policy divergence from the EU is a specific factor that affects the degree of cooperation with the EU, as this chapter will discuss later. It is a significant cost for "co-decision" since it is costly to cooperate and accommodate EU preferences when the EU takes a fundamentally different position. Yet, policy divergence is not a significant cost for "unilateral information". So, cooperation gets easier and costs are reduced when the degree of cooperation is lower.

There are general costs with regard to cooperation with the EU. It is generally highly costly to cooperate when the Turkish government needs to take urgent action. In these instances, unilateral action is more preferable than cooperating with the EU. Specifically, an immediate direct security threat qualifies as an instance in which the Turkish government needs to react promptly. Indeed, this does not concern only urgency of action but also security as an issue-specific factor increasing costs of cooperation. In this instance, cooperation as "co-decision" might mean constraints on unilateral action in the sense of compromising on one's preferences. "Unilateral information" might take time, which can be considered as a cost, but not as much as "consultation". The key points here are that there can be general costs of cooperation, typically threats against Turkish sovereignty, and that the costs may vary depending on the form of cooperation, for example, "co-decision" to one degree or another is always more costly than lower forms of cooperation.

Variation in costs and benefits can also depend on one's theoretical outlook: for example, what may be considered a high cost from a realist perspective may not necessarily be perceived as such from a neoliberal standpoint. Two theories under the umbrella of rationalism – neoliberal institutionalism and realism – can be used in order to elaborate on different ways of interpreting costs and benefits from a rationalist perspective. A realist perspective brings security and power politics to the forefront as the dominant drivers of Turkish behaviour; whereas, a neoliberal institutionalist perspective suggests that the dominant motivation is welfare and focuses on the long-term benefits of cooperative behaviour. For example, a realist perspective amplifies the benefits of unilateral action when there are national security concerns, or it may see a higher degree of cooperation with the EU as an erosion of sovereignty, whereas a neoliberal perspective focuses more on welfare maximisation and low politics when considering any costs and benefits of cooperation.

High/low politics considerations

As discussed earlier, realism underpins high politics and expects national security to be a significant factor in determining the costs and benefits of cooperation with the EU. A realist approach stresses power politics and the position of Turkey in the international arena, at which point the Turkish aspirations of becoming a regional power become relevant for this analysis. From a realist viewpoint, the main Turkish aspiration since the end of the Cold War is to play a role in the new world order through becoming a regional power (e.g., Davutoğlu, 2001; Sayarı, 2000). During the AKP era, especially after the AKP's second term in power (2007 onwards), the redefinition of Turkish foreign policy has attracted ever-increasing popular and academic attention due to the strong activism of Turkey in the Middle East (e.g., Kirişçi, 2009; Öniş, 2011; Öniş and Yılmaz, 2009; Özcan and Usul, 2010; Düzgit and Tocci, 2009), and commentators have argued that Turkey is ambitious to become a "benign regional power" (Öniş, 2003: 2).

A revision of Turkish foreign policy priorities also meant that EU accession was no longer the priority of the Turkish government. According to Öniş and Yılmaz (2009), disappointment with the EU membership process has pushed Turkey to retreat to what they term "soft Euro-Asianism", a policy that does not regard EU membership as the top priority but instead considers it one of many focal points for foreign policy. Turkey's ambition to become a regional leader became particularly prominent after the government's second term, and EU accession was then no longer seen as the primary foreign policy aim, or as a prerequisite to becoming a global actor. Over time, the Turkish government has sought to explore alternative alliances that would help its aim to become a regional leader. The most evident example was when the Turkish PM clearly portrayed the Shanghai Cooperation Organization as an alternative to the EU:

> Now, of course when things go such a negative way [referring to EU-Turkey relations], as the prime minister of 75 million, you inevitably begin a different search. Therefore, I said that to Putin the other day: let us into the Shanghai Five [Shanghai Cooperation Organization] and we will say 'farewell' to the EU. The Shanghai Five is more powerful and it is better.
>
> (Erdoğan, 2013a)

With such a power politics-oriented outlook, cooperation could be costly if it constrained Turkey's room for manoeuvre in its new hinterland. For instance, in order to extend and strengthen its sphere of influence, Turkey might choose cooperation with regional actors over cooperation with the EU if cooperation with the EU becomes detrimental to the Turkish aim of becoming a regional leader. Considering the public debate in Turkey about whether it could be a "model" for the Arab states in the post-Arab Spring era, it could be claimed that the main Turkish aim has been to influence the region in a way that facilitates its goal of becoming a regional leader (Interview TR01; for a critical account see also Kirişçi, 2013).

The term "soft power" has been popularly used to discuss the growing Turkish engagement in the Middle East (Walt, 2012; Oğuzlu, 2007). From a realist standpoint, Turkish foreign policy behaviour is based on the aim of increasing Turkish soft power, and any obstacles that stand in Turkey's way to achieving this goal can be interpreted as costs. For example, if cooperation with the EU were to limit Turkey's ability to pursue unilateral action regarding important security issues, or if it were to hinder Turkey's exercise of power, then the costs of cooperation would be higher. Here, the essential link between soft power and costs of cooperation concerns whether cooperation increases or decreases Turkey's attractiveness in the region, and, depending on the degree to which it is detrimental to Turkish soft power, cooperation can be seen as costly.

It should be made clear that the rationalist perspective does not always expect an absence of cooperation due to high costs. There could also be expected benefits of cooperation, especially when moving from a realist perspective to a more neoliberal one that emphasises low politics. A major potential benefit of cooperation is that the Turkish government, through cooperating with the EU, can show the EU its strategic value as a foreign policy partner, which could then bestow benefits considering the EU membership process and regional alliance with the EU.

One of the main aims of Turkish foreign policy has been to join the EU as a full member. However, within the AKP era, this desire has not been homogeneous and has differed considerably over time. It is possible to say that Turkish interest in becoming an EU member peaked around the time of the opening of negotiations in 2005; however, gradually this interest has declined, especially after the AKP consolidated power in the domestic arena and revised Turkish foreign policy priorities to place more emphasis on becoming a regional leader than becoming an EU member.

Arguably, one of the main reasons why the AKP government preferred to maintain good relations with the EU when it took power in 2002 was because the EU demands concerning civilian control over the military fit well with its preferences (Sedelmeier, 2011: 14). As the AKP consolidated power in the domestic arena, a close relationship with the EU lost its instrumental value in terms of the struggle against the military control of politics. This also demonstrates how domestic politics has been reflected in foreign policy behaviour with regard to relations with the EU and provides an explanation for the change in the Turkish attitude from a deep commitment to integration in the early 2000s to a foreign policy approach that does not regard membership as a top priority. The reason why this is particularly important is because the gradual degeneration in the relationship has had a fundamental impact on the attitude of the Turkish government towards the EU and its willingness to cooperate in order to deal with foreign policy problems.

Nonetheless, the objective of EU membership has remained a key aim of the Turkish foreign policy agenda because membership generally has a strategic value regardless of domestic politics in Turkey. For this reason, Turkish decision makers have always claimed that Turkey would make a successful addition to the EU, especially in the area of foreign and security policy. For instance, during his visit to Prague in February 2013, Erdoğan (2013b) clearly stated that the EU needed Turkey if it wanted to become a strong global actor and underlined that there was "absolutely no deviation on the part of the government from the objective of becoming an EU member". Similarly, Davutoğlu (2015) declared that EU membership was a "strategic aim" for Turkey and that "Turkey would definitely become a member, one way or the other". In 2018, Erdoğan reiterated that full EU membership remained of strategic importance for Turkey (*Cumhuriyet*, 2018).

Therefore, EU membership, to one degree or another, has always had strategic value for the Turkish government. Foreign policy cooperation with the EU could be beneficial in the sense that it could strengthen Turkey's hand in the accession process and make Turkey more attractive as a potential member. If, through cooperation, the Turkish government can prove that it is an important and reliable asset to the EU, and if this brings Turkey closer to its strategic goal of EU membership, then cooperation could have benefits.

Furthermore, since the neoliberal institutionalist approach focuses more on the long-term benefits of cooperation and emphasises welfare maximisation as one of the dominant drivers of Turkish behaviour, prioritising the improvement of economic relations with the immediate neighbourhood is also beneficial. The implication this has for cost-benefit calculation during the Arab Spring depends on whether preferred cooperation with the various regimes would impede cooperation with the EU. At this point, policy divergence from the EU becomes relevant for this analysis.

Policy divergence from the EU

Policy divergence from the EU is a factor affecting the costs and benefits of cooperation with the EU. The more pronounced the differences of policies between the
EU and Turkey are, the harder it is to see a high degree of cooperation involving
adjustments of behaviour, because of the high costs involved. One of the key
issues here is the way in which Turkey and the EU might have fundamentally
different preferences and, as a result, may choose to react in different ways with
regard to the crises. Policy divergence from the EU may overlap with high/low
politics considerations, particularly because it can be a result of the Turkish leadership acting on economic motives that might make it difficult to cooperate with
the EU. Conversely, when there is not much policy divergence from the EU, it
becomes easier to engage in cooperation, especially at lower levels, such as at the
"unilateral information" level.

With the aim of making Turkey an influential actor in the region, the AKP leadership has pursued a policy of "zero problems with neighbours" (see Davutoğlu,
2001) and prioritised its relationships with Middle Eastern and North African
regimes. As Öniş (2012: 46) explains, the AKP approach to the Middle East and
North Africa pre-Arab Spring was fundamentally based on "principles of mutual
gain through economic interdependence". What this means is that the Turkish
government had established close ties with the regimes in the Arab Spring countries, which made it difficult for the government to be critical of them. Preferences
can therefore diverge from the EU if the Turkish government hesitates to criticise
regimes due to economic reasons. In other words, it is more costly to cooperate when cooperation with the EU translates into potential economic losses for
Turkey, especially considering the AKP's relationship with the Arab leaders and
populations in the region. For instance, if cooperation with the EU puts Turkish
assets in a crisis zone in danger, then the Turkish government would avoid it. Such
a situation can potentially happen if the Turkish government feels the need to
distance itself from the EU in an attempt to appear friendly to incumbent regimes
across the crisis zone for strategic reasons.

An important factor Davutoğlu took into consideration when devising the policy
of "zero problems with neighbours" was EU membership because it was essentially based on the idea that "Turkey should expand its area of political manoeuvre
and be ready with alternative policies for any result the EU-Turkey relationship
might produce" (Davutoğlu, 2001: 509). In other words, what Davutoğlu advocated, and what later became AKP policy, was that Turkey needed to keep its
options open regarding the EU membership process and to realise its potential
to influence its neighbourhood. What this means for cost-benefit calculations is
that the Turkish government can prioritise maintaining good relations with Arab
states, regardless of whether this creates a conflict with the EU.

Many have described the new tendencies in Turkish foreign policy as "neo-
Ottoman" since it sought to re-establish a form of "Pax Ottomana" (Özcan and
Usul, 2010; Erhan, 2011). The term "neo-Ottoman" refers to an ethno-religious

(i.e., Turkic-Islamic) policy aimed at bonding peoples sharing a common Ottoman history (so including Syria, Libya, and Egypt). The term, although coined before the AKP's formation, has been associated with AKP foreign policy due to the AKP leadership's emphasis on the improvement of relations with Middle Eastern states. What needs to be underlined here is the fact that there was a re-orientation of foreign policy under the AKP leadership, and a fundamental aspect of this re-orientation was the aim to secure long-term economic gains. To spell this out, these economic gains were based on increasing international trade and supporting Turkish companies working in Arab states. The main aspect of this re-orientation of foreign policy was to have an increased engagement with the governments in Arab states and to have a policy of rapprochement with those who had previously been hostile, such as the Syrian government. Therefore, a neoliberal perspective would presuppose welfare maximisation as a priority when a decision regarding cooperation is being made, and the degree of cooperation then depends on whether it constrains Turkish aims or not.

For example, close trade relations with Middle Eastern and North African regimes have generated much wealth for Turkey. Figure 2.1 shows that Turkish exports to the Middle East and Africa rapidly increased in the AKP era, peaking in 2012. For all three cases, there was a rapid rise in the total value of Turkish exports, especially before and from the beginning of the Arab uprisings. For example, in the case of Libya, the total value of Turkish exports increased from $489m in 2006 to $1.9bn in 2010, just before the start of the unrest in 2011 (Turkish Statistical Institute, 2016). After the signing of the 2005 Free Trade Agreement, Turkish exports to Egypt increased from $687m in 2005 to $2.76bn in 2011

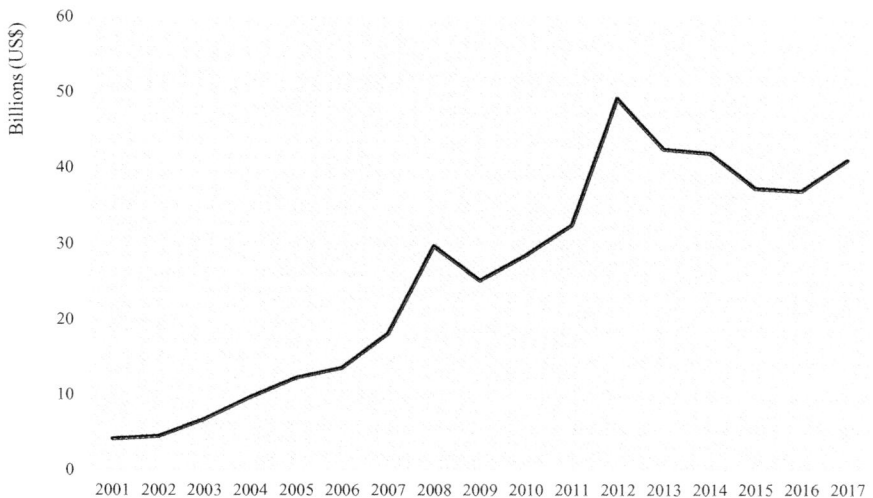

Figure 2.1 Turkish exports to the Middle East and North Africa region, 2001–2017

Source: (The World Bank, 2019)

(The Ministry of Trade of Turkey, 2019). Moreover, when the turmoil started, there were over 250 Turkish firms operating in Egypt with investments amounting to up to $2bn, most of which centred around Cairo and Alexandria (Davutoğlu, 2013; Kuburlu, 2011). Libya, Syria, and Egypt stand out as countries for which there was a steady increase in total export value until the beginning of the uprisings, which indicates that they were valuable economic partners for the Turkish government when the crises began (Turkish Statistical Institute, 2016). This therefore means that it would have been highly costly for the Turkish government to act in any way that could have brought potential harm to these economic gains.

Here, the costs of cooperation can also vary depending on the form of cooperation. For instance, co-decision with the EU may have required cutting relations with the incumbent regimes and imposing sanctions. In this case, it would have been highly costly for the Turkish government to cooperate. This is an example in which non-cooperation with the EU could have potential benefits, since the Turkish government acts to protect its vested interests and may choose to appear friendly to the incumbent regimes. If the EU takes certain measures against these regimes, the Turkish government may disagree or delay taking similar steps considering the damage such steps would have on their economic relations. In other words, because the costs of cutting trade relations for Turkey are higher, it might take parallel steps reluctantly and prefer not to accommodate EU preferences in its policy, which means cooperation with the EU can be costly. However, lower degrees of cooperation can have fewer costs since they do not involve accommodating potentially harmful EU preferences; for example, the Turkish government can still implement unilateral action in unilateral information as long as it informs the EU about what action it plans to pursue.

Therefore, policy divergence from the EU can be one of the factors determining the costs and benefits of cooperation depending on the CO. The costs of cooperation are higher and the degree of cooperation is lower when there is a greater divergence. That said, it should also be pointed out that the convergence of policies does not automatically lead to cooperation, although it would be easier to cooperate when there is a harmony of interests and policies.

Ideally, cooperation should be backed up by political will since the EU and Turkish officials need to be able to communicate for cooperation to take place. There can be practical problems inhibiting cooperation when there are tensions between leaders. For example, it is difficult for Turkish and EU leaders to gather around a negotiation table for "co-decision" a day after the Turkish leadership has accused the EU and the West of hypocrisy and imperialism. Officials may refrain from contact at higher levels to avoid criticisms and accusations, which was one of the issues making cooperation harder to achieve, as an EU diplomat at the EU Delegation in Ankara commented (Interview EU02). According to Marc Pierini, a former EU ambassador to Turkey (2006–2011), the real cause of the absence of cooperation was the transformation of Turkish foreign policy under the AKP government and, consequently, a lack of Turkish political will to cooperate with the EU, causing divergence from the EU (Interview EU03). So, policy divergence can make it both costly and difficult to achieve cooperation, especially when the views and preferences of actors are essentially different. Here, it is also important to take into consideration the evolution of Turkey-EU relations from a commitment to accession in the early 2000s to shallow cooperation with the EU in the post-2011 Arab Spring setting. The way in which the AKP government revised Turkish foreign policy priorities intensified policy divergence from the EU, especially due to Turkey's ambition to be accepted as a regional leader.

Urgency of action/response

Urgency is a factor determining the costs and benefits of cooperation. The costs of cooperation rise when the Turkish government needs to give an urgent response. This may overlap with the factors already discussed when/if other factors create an urgency for action. This especially applies to hard politics and security issues since these require a timely response. Cooperation can be costly because it almost always takes time to some degree and also because unilateral action might be preferable when there is an immediate threat to national sovereignty. A typical situation in which there is a high urgency of action is when there is a security threat to Turkish territorial integrity. An attack on Turkish soldiers or aircraft qualifies as a hard security threat, after which the Turkish government may prefer to avoid cooperation in order to respond with urgency, enacting immediate retaliation under the rules of engagement. Therefore, it is possible to claim that hard security issues and high politics usually require more urgent responses than do low politics issues.

The need to act urgently is not always due to hard security threats. Foreign policy issues might snowball and need urgent attention. Such issues often cause concern for the government in the domestic arena. For example, the Syrian refugee crisis gradually became an issue of greater urgency than the decision to freeze the assets of the Assad family. This was mainly because the refugee crisis had the potential to create greater concern for the government in the domestic arena. When the Syrian uprising began, only a few thousand Syrian refugees fled into Turkey, and it was easy for the Turkish government to accommodate them; however, when the numbers reached 100,000, it became a real concern for the government. They saw it as an issue needing an urgent response and immediately urged the UN to find a solution.

The costs of cooperation also depend on the type of cooperation. When the urgency of action is high, the costs of cooperation are greater for achieving a higher degree of cooperation. However, a lower degree of cooperation, such as "unilateral information", would have fewer costs and is therefore possible even if the government needs to take an urgent action.

FPA and the case of Turkey: domestic politics, Pax Ottomana and the "Sèvres Syndrome"

There are two specific ways in which FPA could help this analysis. First, an analysis of Turkish foreign policy behaviour would be incomplete without discussing domestic politics. The fundamental problem with the Rational Actor Model (see e.g., Allison and Zelikow, 1999) in analysing foreign policy is that it sees states as unitary actors, overlooking what goes on inside them. FPA's focus on the domestic environment is particularly useful when analysing the process of foreign policy decision making in its domestic setting. Second, a purely rationalist/game theoretical approach to any cost-benefit calculus tends to de-historise foreign policy problems. FPA offers useful insights into how history, as a factor potentially influencing foreign policy decision-making processes, informs any given context. Specifically, cognitive factors in interpreting the past are important when analysing the self-perceptions of decision makers. Here, history becomes relevant when it distorts rational decision making. The ultimate aim of using tools from FPA here is to achieve a more accurate picture of Turkish behaviour during the crises and Turkish cooperation with the EU.

When discussing the costs and benefits of action and Turkish foreign policy behaviour, it is important to clarify that the unit of analysis is the AKP leadership, which can be seen as playing a "two-level game" (Putnam, 1988). In other words, the costs of action can also be influenced by the domestic calculations of the leadership concerning its political survival, as this analysis will unpack.

The foreign policy decision making in Turkey under the AKP is a top-down process centred around a few individuals, namely Erdoğan and his closest advisors.[2] To some extent, until his resignation as the leader of the AKP in May 2016, Davutoğlu also had influence since he was recognised as the intellectual architect of the "new" Turkish foreign policy that prioritises engagement with former Ottoman territories, especially the countries of the Middle East and North Africa.[3] However, overall, there is not much collective debate or internal deliberation over critical issues within the AKP, and power is eventually concentrated in the hands of Erdoğan, to whom the founding members of the AKP granted supreme authority to run the party (Yavuz, 2009: 101; see also Tepe, 2005; Kutlu, 2003). One study observed a hegemonic type of authoritarianism within the AKP in the sense that the majority shows consent to the decisions of a minority led by the party leader[4] (Ayan, 2010).

As Öniş (2011: 53–55) mentions, economic and civil society interests have also become increasingly influential in the foreign policy decision-making process in Turkey during the AKP era. However, it could be claimed that these domestic interests are important only to the extent that they shape the foreign policy vision of the leadership. The implication this has for this study is that costs and benefits should not only be seen as costs and benefits for Turkey but also as costs and benefits for the political leadership. This is why the notion of a "two-level game" and the domestic environment are particularly relevant.

It should also be noted that the way in which President Erdoğan continued to be a highly influential figure in Turkish foreign policy, and rising authoritarianism in Turkey overall, indicate that the leadership is much less vulnerable to domestic pressures than usually is the case in democracies. Therefore, arguably, domestic politics matters increasingly less; however, it is still a relevant factor in this discussion.

Businesses can be considered as key domestic actors. For example, prior to the Arab Spring, Turkish construction companies had frequently operated in the Middle East and North Africa, and the Turkish PM had often invited business persons to join him on his official visits to the countries in the region to sign agreements, such as on his visit to Libya in November 2009, at which four ministers and 200 business persons accompanied him (*Sabah*, 2009). As a result of engagement in the region, economic interdependence had been established. It could be claimed that when making decisions at the onset of the Arab uprisings, Turkish decision makers took into account the consequences they could have on Turkish businesses in the region and tried to avoid upsetting actors involved in transnational trade relations. For example, for Libya, the Turkish government took into consideration the well-being of Turkish construction companies operating in the region. Cooperation with the EU can generally be seen as a costly action, considering the demands made in the domestic arena, especially if cooperation with the EU hurts Turkish economic interests.

Public opinion is another important aspect of a two-level game. Managing public support and satisfying voters are essential for self-interested decision makers who seek to ensure their re-election. Public opinion could also have had an impact on Turkish government reactions to the uprisings because, as Özcan (2008: 96) points out, Turkish public opinion is generally sensitive to developments that affect Turkic and Muslim communities around the world. The implication that this has on cost-benefit calculations depends on the kind of opinion the public adopts with regard to specific issues. For instance, when a Syrian bombshell hit the Turkish town of Akçakale in 2012, killing five civilians, the government passed a bill authorising unilateral military action against Syria. Many expressed concerns in Turkey, not just the public but also political parties, journalists, and lawyers, that this was in fact a "war bill" or a "license" to wage war against Syria, which was opposed by a considerable portion of the public (Peker and Malas, 2012). Quickly, the government responded to the claims and concerns, clarifying that they had no desire or intention to wage war but that they needed to show that they were capable of protecting Turkey's territorial integrity when there was a direct threat (NTV, 2012). In such instances, when unilateral action is not publicly popular, cooperation with the EU can generally have benefits. However, it could also have costs if the public favours unilateral action or dismisses cooperation with the EU. If the consensus of the public is that cooperation with the EU is redundant, especially considering the growing dissatisfaction with EU membership in Turkey, then having a closer foreign policy relationship with the EU can be costly.

It should be noted that public opinion is a potential contributing factor in the foreign policy decision-making process in Turkey. It would be misleading to claim that re-election concerns are among the main determinants of Turkish behaviour, especially considering the way in which the AKP has achieved successive landslide victories despite nationwide mass protests and growing public disapproval of its policies (e.g., the Gezi Park protests in 2013). So, public opinion is a relevant factor, but it should not be overstated.

A problem with a purely rationalist approach is that it tends to take history out of the picture. In the Turkish context, history is an important factor that needs to be taken into consideration when analysing foreign policy behaviour, especially during the AKP era since this party has often advocated the use of Ottoman history in foreign policy discourse. The primary way in which one could see the relevance of history in foreign policy decision making is by looking at the perceptions of decision makers. Self-perceptions, images, and schemas can be influential in foreign policy decision making, particularly through constraining rational decision making by distorting reality (see Boulding, 1956; Jervis, 1976).

The distinction made by Harold and Margaret Sprout between "operational" and "psychological" environments with regard to foreign policy decision making is useful here (Sprout and Sprout, 1956). By making this distinction, the Sprouts focused on the perceptions of decision makers and the way in which they can introduce significant distortions into foreign policy making. Similarly, Jervis (1976) wrote on "misperceptions" in foreign policy decisions and argued that leaders drew upon personalised understandings of history based on their own perceptions, rather than on the actual "operational environment" (see also Alden and Aran, 2012: 21). For Boulding (1956), foreign policy decisions are the products of the "images" leaders have of other countries, based on stereotypes, biases, and subjective beliefs, all of which introduce distortions to the "definition of the situation". The relevance these works have for this discussion is that they all highlight the importance of the self-perceptions of leaders when making analyses. The self-perceptions of the AKP government should therefore be taken into consideration when analysing Turkish foreign policy decisions so that the costs and benefits of cooperation with the EU can be better understood.

There are two important perceptions rooted in history that have affected modern-day Turkish foreign policy considerations. First, there is a perception that Turkey is surrounded by enemies, which leads to distrust towards the West, which is often termed the "Sèvres Syndrome" – the irrational fear, to the degree of paranoia, that Western powers are plotting to dismantle Turkey territorially, as they attempted to do via the abortive Treaty of Sèvres of 1920, which concerned the partitioning of the Ottoman Empire at the end of World War I (Hale, 2013: 162; Guida, 2008). Second, there is a perception that Turkey, as the successor of the Ottoman Empire, is the natural leader of former Ottoman territories (including the three country cases on which this book focuses), which creates numerous grey areas as to where the domestic ends and the foreign begins. These perceptions are relevant to the cost-benefit calculus in different ways, as this subsection will explain.

Increased distrust towards the West and the belief that Western powers are plotting against Turkey, to the degree of paranoia, can generally add to the perceived costs of cooperation with the EU. The traditional, or classic, Turkish foreign policy can be characterised by alignment with the West – a prominent early example is Turkish participation in the US-led coalition during the Korean War. The foreign policy outlook essentially reflected the psychology on which the modern

Turkish Republic was established and, to a large extent, it avoided engagement with Turkey's immediate neighbours, namely the Arab world, due to the perception that they had betrayed Turks at the beginning of the 20th century during the dissolution of the Ottoman Empire. Although Turkey aligned itself with the Western bloc, at the same time, it carried a certain mistrust towards the West (i.e., the Sèvres Syndrome), which has constituted a filter through which the world is perceived as well as a tool for the elite to manipulate public attitudes towards the outside world (Kirişçi, 2006: 32–37).

A clear example of how distrust in the West is reflected in politics is the time when Demirel, after assuming the presidency in 1993, referred to the Treaty of Sèvres and argued that Turkey would not gain the support of the West no matter how much progress was made in democratisation (Hale, 2013: 162). Using FPA language, it is possible to see that the treaty constitutes a historical analogy for leaders to express distrust towards the West and to appeal to the anti-Western emotions in Turkish society in a populist way. It affects Turkey-EU relations when public figures make references to the Europeans' or the West's alleged intentions to weaken or divide Turkey. To give a specific example, when there was a public debate in Turkey in 2002 on the adoption of reforms necessary to meet the Copenhagen criteria, public figures made statements implying that the West was trying to weaken Turkey (Kirişçi, 2006: 33–34).

Mistrust towards the West also peaked from time to time during the Arab Spring. For instance, during the Gezi Park protests in 2013, officials from the Turkish government and Islamist media outlets claimed there were foreign powers behind the unrest because they wanted to weaken Turkey. For example, the Deputy PM blamed the Jewish diaspora and the international press led by the West (Atalay, 2013), and one journalist, also a senior advisor to the PM, openly pointed to Germany and the UK (Bulut, quoted in *Akşam*, 2013). According to a former EU ambassador to Turkey, such statements significantly deteriorate Turkey's relations with the West and the EU (Interview EU03). The bottom line here is that the use of historical analogies, namely referring to the partitioning of the Ottoman Empire, and conspiracy theories reinforce a false reality that creates mistrust in cooperation with the EU. When the reality is distorted in such a manner in the perception of the public, cooperation with the EU becomes costlier. Especially considering the increased engagement in the Arab world during the AKP era and the idea of a "new" Turkish foreign policy, it is possible to say that the paranoia that Turkey is surrounded by enemies, expressed in the popular saying, "the Turk has no friend but the Turk", (see e.g., Oruçoğlu, 2014; Zeybek, 2007), has, to some extent, faded away. However, a certain degree of mistrust towards the West, rooted in history, remains and surfaces from time to time, thereby adding to the costs of cooperation with the EU.

The second perception rooted in history is that Turkey, as the successor state of the Ottoman Empire, can naturally restore the Ottoman order in the region, which is closely linked to the debates on whether Turkish foreign policy in the AKP era follows a neo-Ottomanist agenda. This perception also signifies a considerable departure from the traditional isolationist Turkish foreign policy since what goes on in former Ottoman territories is seen as closer to domestic politics.

Essential to this perception is the idea that Turkey is the political centre of the Ottoman order that it seeks to re-establish. This means that Turkey aspires to gain a broader area of influence, shape politics in its neighbourhood, and be recognised as a leader. The roots of this perception can be traced back to the conquest of Constantinople (*Konstantiniyye*) in 1453, after which Sultan Mehmed II declared himself to be the "Caesar" of Rome (*Kayser-i Rûm*). His desire to become the ruler of a world empire motivated him towards becoming the ruler of the Christian world as well (Kongar, 1998: 19–52). The conquest laid the foundations of the Pax Ottomana, the order under which Ottoman "millets" lived together, and it is possible to say that the Sultan wanted to hold on to the key characteristics of Pax Romana: eternity and universality (see Ortaylı, 2007: 11–24). What is important about the Ottoman order, besides its ambition to live up to its Roman predecessor, is that the multinational order consisting of Ottoman millets strengthened the central authority and the political nucleus that led the Empire. In other words, there was a hierarchical relationship between the components of the order that strengthened the central Turkish authority.

So, when in modern debates it is claimed that Turkey is following a neo-Ottoman agenda, it is meant that Turkey wishes to reinforce the idea of an order in which it is central. Answering questions about neo-Ottomanism in an interview, Davutoğlu stated: "If by order they mean *Pax Ottomana*, *Pax* in the meaning of order, we are trying to establish an order, it is not wrong to say such a thing" (Batur, 2009). This is crucial because it means that, for some issue areas, the boundary between foreign and domestic is blurred in the eyes of decision makers in the sense that they may see developments in former Ottoman territories as not entirely foreign or near equivalent to domestic politics in Turkey. This was especially noticeable during the Arab Spring because the Middle Eastern public was not seen as entirely foreign by the AKP elites. For example, when the crisis in Syria started, PM Erdoğan openly stated that he was concerned because he saw the situation in Syria as being equal to domestic politics in Turkey (*Hürriyet*, 2011). Another example can be the way in which he saluted former Ottoman territories along with Turkish cities in his speech after his electoral victory in 2011, during which he claimed they were the winners of the election as much as the Turkish public (Erdoğan, 2011).

Fundamentally, the way in which history specifically relates to the rationalist approach is through distorting rational decision-making processes. These perceptions, rooted in history – bias and scepticism about the intentions of the West, or the idea that Turkey is the natural leader of former Ottoman territories – can essentially affect how costs and benefits are seen. Specifically, distrust of the West may render cooperation more difficult, creating additional costs for cooperative behaviour. The self-perceptions of Turkish decision makers with regard to Turkish influence and capabilities in the region may lead the Turkish government to see the case study countries as not entirely foreign, which may affect the cost-benefit calculation regarding cooperation with the EU, especially if the government prefers to prioritise its relationship with the population of a region. The costs of cooperation with the EU may then increase if cooperation jeopardises the relationship the Turkish government would like to establish and maintain with post-Ottoman populations. The Turkish government has made it clear that it has a strategic interest in influencing the populations in these regions and establishing mutually beneficial relationships with whomever leads these populations. Cooperation with the EU, to the extent that it constrains the ability of the Turkish government to exercise power and to lead these populations, can be seen as costly.

It is important to point out that, in addition to offering a critique of the Rational Actor Model, the FPA literature offers approaches that integrate rational and cognitive schools of decision making. Poliheuristic theory (Mintz, 2004, 1993) is particularly useful in this respect and can potentially help explain the interplay between the rational and non-rational aspects of Turkish foreign policy decision making. This theory postulates a two-stage approach to decision making. In the first stage, decision makers narrow down policy options available through "simplifying complex foreign policy decisions," (Mintz, 2004: 7), and factors such as cognition and perception may come into play during the process. According to Mintz (1993: 601), leaders are affected by a variety of factors when narrowing down policy options, "including their past decisions, which may restrict their choice set due to increased sunk costs, cognitive investment, and so on". In the second stage, decision makers evaluate what is available to them from "the subset of 'surviving' alternatives" (Mintz et al., 1997: 554) and use rational decision making, including a "standard game-theoretic analysis" (Mintz, 2004: 7) in order to make a selection. Poliheuristic theory not only emphasises the importance of a domestic political setting in foreign policy decision making but also posits that decision makers use a mixture of decision-making strategies, which is an approach that is particularly useful when analysing complex decisions.

FPA approaches, and particularly poliheuristic theory, allow us to see that foreign policy decision making is by no means a straightforward process. Numerous factors may come into play during the decision-making process, these being not only regime survival and domestic politics but also personal factors, such as the personalities, perceptions, psychological dispositions, and cognitive biases of decision makers. The two-stage approach that poliheuristic theory posits is especially useful to harmonise the cognitive school of FPA with classic rationalist approaches. This study adopts the underlying principle of poliheuristic theory that there is a need to focus on the interplay between rational and non-rational factors in foreign policy decision making. However, the theory itself will not be applied as such because the main theoretical discussion in this book will be positioned in the broader theoretical debate in IR between rationalism and constructivism. In this respect, the insights and analytical tools offered by the FPA literature will be used mainly for examining the interplay between factors that affect foreign policy making in Turkey and for analysing how rational decision making can be distorted.

The constructivist approach

From a constructivist perspective, cooperative behaviour would stem from an actor's sense of what appropriate behaviour regarding cooperation might be. It is possible to distinguish between general cooperative behaviour in a democratic international community and issue-specific questions of appropriateness of cooperation on particular issues for which the level of appropriateness changes depending on the issue. Specific factors determining appropriateness can be identified as identification with norms of appropriate behaviour prompting cooperation with the EU, and political and cultural affinity affecting foreign policy behaviour, including the attitude towards the EU.

The argument Risse (1995) put forward in *Cooperation Among Democracies: The European Influence on US Foreign Policy* is particularly useful for this analysis. Examining NATO, he argued that smaller allies were able to influence US foreign policy because of the salience of a consultation norm within the transatlantic alliance (ibid.: 4). In his argument, the transatlantic community had established "alliance norms", which formed the appropriate behaviour for cooperation and led Europeans to influence policy making in Washington. According to Risse, it is not simply that NATO socialises members into its rules; the key for the argument is that the members are democracies, and their democratic identities make NATO a specific type of international organisation and give a specific meaning to the consultation norm. In this sense, it is not even necessary for the EU to socialise Turkey into a cooperation norm; shared democratic identities (and shared NATO membership) should mean that consultation on foreign policy is considered co-decision.

However, an issue with this argument is that, if taken seriously, it could also mean that Turkey has a democratic identity that is also, to some extent, internalised by the government. Considering the problems with democracy in Turkey during the AKP era and rising authoritarianism, especially after the second and third terms of the AKP government, the extent to which democratic values have been internalised is questionable, which might challenge any application of Risse's arguments to the Turkish context. Nevertheless, the principle is sound in the sense that cooperation in the form of co-decision can arise as a norm of appropriate behaviour.

It should be noted that the general appropriateness of cooperation in the international community is facilitated through international institutions where members exchange views about certain issues, such as the Arab uprisings. These platforms may not only create alliance norms but may also act as sources of socialisation. The general appropriateness of cooperation can be based on informing allies about actions that can potentially affect them and fulfilling roles in international organisations.

A constructivist argument could be made that a consultation norm between Turkey and the EU has been emerging as a result of foreign policy cooperation that might encourage cooperation as a norm. The appropriate behaviour for Turkey regarding cooperation with the EU would then be based on timely consultation that is at, or close to co-decision.

The constructivist use of the idea of Europeanization can also be useful for this analysis since it deals with the diffusion of norms. It could be claimed that over time Turkey has adopted "certain ways of doing things" that reflect on its foreign policy behaviour. Scholars writing in this tradition examine the way Turkey adopted EU norms. For example, Müftüler-Baç and Gürsoy (2010: 411) have pointed to Turkey's relations with Iraq and argued that the increased use of diplomatic and economic instruments versus military means to solve disputes was a sign that there had been a process of "adaptation to EU level norms". Essentially, from this perspective, the EU is a "normative actor" (see Manners, 2002) not only influencing the nature of foreign policy making in Turkey but also reinforcing the norms of appropriate behaviour regarding the Turkey-EU interaction. As a result of norm diffusion, Turkey might have adopted behaviour based on timely consultation and adaptation to EU norms. It should be noted that counter-arguments could be made claiming that norm adoption was a strategic decision, rather than socialisation.

It can be claimed that the long-standing interaction between Turkey and the EU is a potential source of appropriate behaviour. For this, the idea of "coordination reflex" is particularly useful. In the evolution of the Common Foreign and Security Policy of the EU, EU member states gradually adopted a general rule to consult each other prior to forming their final positions, and these consultations led to policy adaptations (de Schoutheete, 1980: 49). Aside from the institutional procedures of foreign policy coordination, there is an important normative dimension to the process that motivates EU members to cooperate when faced with a foreign policy problem. Even though Turkey is not in the institutional framework since it is not a member, similar norms might have emerged as a result of Turkey's lengthy aspiration to become a member of the Union. If there is "coordination reflex" between EU members today, then there is considerable potential that Turkey and the EU have developed a form of appropriate behaviour regarding their foreign policy interaction which might commit Turkey to cooperate with the Union. It is questionable if this reflex can be presumed to have emerged with non-members who are not part of the same routines as members, but the underlying logic may be useful.

To unpack this point, norm emergence could be a consequence of Turkey and the EU developing ways of maintaining their relationship. Cooperation would not take place simply because of benefits with regard to EU membership but because cooperation is considered the appropriate behaviour in the EU. Identification with the EU could lead Turkey to adopt cooperation as appropriate behaviour. However, the presumption is that there is identification, which, again, is questionable in the case of the AKP leadership.

As touched upon previously, it should be pointed out that the AKP era cannot be seen as homogeneous in terms of Turkish willingness to join the EU – especially considering that the AKP leadership, towards the second and third term in power, made it clear that Turkey could do without being an EU member. According to

Öniş (2008: 40), the "golden age of Europeanization and reform" in the AKP era was "from the end of 2002 to roughly the end of 2005", during which the AKP government pushed for full membership and democratic reforms. In the post-2005 era, however, there was a certain loss of enthusiasm and commitment to full membership, which he termed "loose Europeanization" (ibid.: 41).

The main point here is that, when taking into consideration the history of relations between Turkey and the EU in the AKP era, it is possible to claim that AKP interest in the EU fluctuated, which can also indicate that identification with the EU and commitment to reforms significantly changed over time. With the authoritarian turn in Turkish politics after the consecutive landslide electoral victories of the AKP, it can be argued that a sharp divergence has emerged with regard to identities of and norms adhered to by both actors, which would make cooperation on the basis of norms of appropriate behaviour more difficult.

Arguably, AKP identification with the EU has always been low due to its Islamist roots. The tradition in the Islamist section of the political spectrum is to see the EU as a Christian club, hence a community that Turkey should not join. To give an example, as a follower of *Milli Görüş*, a late 1960s Islamist political movement led by Necbettin Erbakan, Erdoğan stated:

> They [the European Community] won't accept us [as a member] but we must know the truth about it. The European Community is a Christian Catholic states club; we won't be a part of it. Why? Because, they won't see you as one of them as long as you don't adopt their religion. But, with God's will, we [the Welfare Party] are coming [to power in Turkey]; they won't take us into the European Community and we won't join.
>
> (Erdoğan, 1990)

Similarly, when he was an MP for the Islamist Welfare Party founded by Necbettin Erbakan, Abdullah Gül[5] argued against Turkish accession to the Customs Union in 1995, claiming that the EU wanted to take Turkey under control and clearly stated that Turkey had no place in the EU because the EU was a "Christian Union" (Gül, 1995).

When Turkey officially became an EU candidate in 2005 under the AKP, the discourse was different. The AKP position, as PM Erdoğan made clear, was that "the EU will either decide to become a global actor or it must accept that it is a Christian club" and that the Turkish candidacy was a "test for the EU" to decide whether it wanted to remain a "Christian Club" (Boland and Dombey, 2005). This argument has not changed since then; for example, in 2015, Erdoğan used similar words to describe the Turkish candidacy: "We are testing the EU, to see whether they will accept a country whose population is Muslim" (T24, 2015).

The main point is that, to one degree or another, Islamist politics in Turkey have maintained an identity-based worldview that assumes the West and the Muslim world are in opposition, and this has been especially salient since the Welfare Party rose to power in 1996 (Dalay and Friedman, 2013). Therefore, AKP identification with the EU is questionable given its Islamist roots.

It is important to point out that the degree of appropriateness may change depending on different issue areas. In some issue areas, such as those related to security threats to Turkey, cooperation may be more appropriate according to international standards. For example, when Syria shot down a Turkish plane, the Turkish government invoked Article 4 of the Washington Treaty for consultations in NATO. In such cases, the Turkish government may follow standard procedures because of its participation in international organisations and cooperation, particularly in the form of informing allies, which can be internalised as the appropriate course of action. However, for decisions that are less related to international procedures, such as the decision to take further restrictive measures or to impose additional economic sanctions, the degree of cooperation may be subject to the norms of cooperation developed between Turkey and the EU. So, there might be variation in terms of appropriateness across issue areas. When the Turkish government follows internationally appropriate behaviour as a consequence of its role in international organisations, then the appropriateness of cooperative behaviour might have less to do with its interaction with the EU.

It should be highlighted that constructivism does not always expect cooperation to take place. For example, there might also be cultural obstacles to cooperation. A key aspect of Turkish foreign policy during the AKP era has been cultural affinity with the Middle East (see Öniş, 2012: 46). Bilgin (2004) called this "a return to 'civilizational geopolitics'" and argued that the AKP views itself as "the emerging leader of its own 'civilizational basin' (consisting of the former Ottoman territories plus adjoining regions inhabited by Muslim and Turkic peoples)" (Bilgin and Bilgic, 2011: 173). Applying such a culture-based civilisational approach, it could be claimed that the Turkish leadership prefers prioritising cooperation with its own cultural/civilisational bloc. It is important to note that this can also mean that the government may tend to side with certain political actors in the case study countries who share similar cultural/political views.

At this point, the issue becomes more a question of identity-politics, contested identity constructions, and differences in identification for different elites. Since the unit of analysis here is the Turkish leadership, the focus should be on the identification of AKP elites, and it is possible to argue that their preferences generally lie within developing further ties with Arab states rather than with the EU. This is only one perspective; otherwise, it can also be argued that modern Turkey identifies itself with the Western bloc, especially considering its EU candidacy and NATO participation. The extent to which the transformation of Turkish foreign policy priorities is a consequence of problems with the EU membership process is questionable; however, it can be claimed that identity politics plays an important part.

A common perception, especially of the Islamist and far-right nationalist segments of the Turkish political spectrum, is that even though the Ottoman Empire collapsed, the order of the Turks lead could be restored and maintained. It could be restored and maintained not because of modern Turkey's achievements or prospects in the global arena but because of its past and the legacy of the Ottoman Empire. Davutoğlu (1989: 33) wrote: "Yes, the Ottoman Empire is dissolved in terms of international law but today the Republic of Turkey who declared this dissolution faces an obligation to fill the gap at the 'political centre' that emerged with the dissolution of the Ottoman Empire". According to his argument, the dissolution of the Empire is not complete; for example, in the Balkans, a continuing sense of Ottoman identity found in Muslim minorities adds to Turkey's sphere of influence (Davutoğlu, 1989, 2001). So, the implication that this has is that, again, the boundaries between foreign and domestic become blurry for Turkish decision makers when there is an issue having to do with Muslim or Turkic populations. From a constructivist perspective, such blurring could limit cooperation with the EU.

Furthermore, the appropriateness of cooperation also depends on the specific government behaviour. Again, the AKP elite may see the West/the EU as being in opposition to the Muslim world. Such a civilisational approach has been used by AKP decision makers. For instance, before he became a decision maker, Davutoğlu (1997: 10–15) wrote about the civilisational resistance of the Islamic world to Western dominance and assimilation and argued that the self-perceptions of civilisations allowed them to resist dominance. In this sense, Western civilisation may transform the formal and institutional sphere in Turkey, but as long as it fails to transform self-perceptions, there will inevitably be a civilisational resistance to Western dominance. The implication here is that Turkey fundamentally belongs to Islamic civilisation. In terms of policy preferences, such a civilisational approach could mean that the Turkish government does not see the EU as a legitimate actor in the region, and the AKP elite regard themselves as being closer to Middle Eastern people.

The key point here is that having a close relationship with Muslim people is not entirely a strategic behaviour – it is a result of shared identity and cultural affinity. For instance, considering the relationship between the AKP and the Muslim Brotherhood in Egypt, it can be argued that ideological affinity is a key aspect of the relationship, which motivates the AKP to side with the Muslim Brotherhood and to prefer the Muslim Brotherhood over other actors in the country's political spectrum. Therefore, this is beyond strategic opportunism and cannot be explained by simply using rationalist arguments. The tendency of the Turkish government to favour actors from a shared cultural background, such as the Muslim Brotherhood, can be an obstacle to cooperation, since cooperation becomes a matter of self-identification and preference. Constructivism can help explain, for example, why the Turkish government prefers coordination with the Arab League to cooperation with the EU, especially when the Turkish government emphasises finding a regional solution without involving other actors, such as the EU, whose involvement it sees as foreign intervention in the region. Again, the key constructivist point here is that the AKP prefers actors with which it shares a cultural and political affinity.

Essentially, the degree of cooperation with the EU rises when cooperation is seen as appropriate behaviour. Specifically, identification with the EU and norms that prompt cooperation with the EU would result in a higher degree of cooperation. Cultural and political affinity with Muslim states in the Middle East and the self-identification of AKP elites can also be influential factors because they might cause the Turkish government to prioritise its relations with these states and actors and make cooperation with the EU less appropriate. Ultimately, the constructivist perspective suggests that it is not costs and benefits that determine the level of Turkey's cooperation, but rather it is the appropriateness of cooperative behaviour.

Operationalisation of cooperation and data collection

Before moving on with the analysis, one needs to address in greater detail the questions of how to operationalise cooperation as the dependent variable and how to identify it in empirical research. Measuring cooperation is a matter of evaluating whether there was no cooperation, unilateral information, consultation, or co-decision with the EU based on the scale presented in Figure 2.1. This is done through examining indicators, where indicators are evidence that consultation has taken place before or after policy action. The data and evidence were generated from interviews and document analysis. Essentially, the book identifies the point to which the relationship corresponded and then asks the "why question", at which point the theoretical approaches discussed in this chapter come into play. Based on the theoretical approaches and empirical evidence, this analysis makes an assessment of underlying Turkish motivations with regard to cooperation.

The research examines Turkish actions and interaction with the EU after certain moments at which there was potential for cooperation. These were identified as "cooperative opportunities" (COs), key moments during the crises when the Turkish government could cooperate with the EU and instances in which the Turkish government took the initiative for policy action. Therefore, the cases in this book are not countries but specific COs because focusing on specific instances of cooperative opportunities makes it possible to systematically analyse and establish a better understanding of Turkish behaviour with regard to cooperation with the EU. COs help disaggregate the crises into isolated instances in which there was potential for Turkish cooperation with the EU. The empirical analysis focuses on the Turkish behaviour during each CO and Turkish interaction with the EU in order to assess Turkey's cooperation with the EU. The COs enable an analysis of Turkish behaviour vis-à-vis foreign policy cooperation with the EU and provide adequate empirical material to address the question of whether, and why, cooperation varied across cases. In terms of the timeframe of analysis, the book focuses on the uprising phase of the crises in Syria, Egypt, and Libya but also discusses the implications of political turmoil for Turkey's relationship with the EU.

Specifically, what this analysis seeks to establish is the extent to which Turkish decision makers consulted the EU, informed the EU of their decisions, and took EU preferences into account in their policies. To this end, data collection focuses on the nature of interaction between policy makers and the way in which they were in contact. In order to identify the degree of cooperation in empirical research, the analysis focuses on Turkish actions and Turkish interaction with the EU in the immediate aftermath of the crises.

Qualitative examination was based on document analysis and interviews. The document analysis focused on reports and statements published by the Turkish government and the EU. These include speeches, press releases, and briefings given by Turkish ministers and EU officials. Such primary sources are useful in investigating formal agreements and meetings between Turkish and EU officials. Turkish newspapers were used to learn about meetings Turkish decision makers attended and their public comments. These were checked against the official information that the Turkish Ministry of Foreign Affairs released on its website and on its Facebook and Twitter feeds. Facts used from Turkish newspapers were also cross-checked to avoid media bias.

Social media was also used as a source. A number of Turkish ministers, such as the EU minister of Turkey, have personal accounts on Twitter, through which they shared their opinions on developments during the Arab uprisings: such opinions were sometimes not reported or given much weight by conventional media. It was useful to gather information from various government officials to establish the inner workings of the government, and the personal messages (or tweets) of decision makers were helpful in revealing the government's attitude.

The essential questions were how the information found in sources should be used in identifying cooperation outcomes and how evidence for explanatory factors should be provided. In terms of cooperation outcomes, the focus will be on whether the Turkish government reached out to consult the EU regarding any course of action it planned to take, or informed the EU about its position. If the sources point to unilateral information, they will ideally include evidence that the Turkish government informed the EU about its position in the form of briefings, without giving the EU a chance to provide feedback. To identify consultation, the evidence will ideally suggest that the Turkish government reached out to discuss the crises with the EU before, and also after, the public announcement of a Turkish position. Some of this information is not available to the public. For example, newspaper articles can point to certain meetings taking place between the Turkish government and the EU; however, the content of the meetings may not have been revealed in much detail, which may make it difficult to establish whether there was unilateral information or consultation. Moreover, some meetings may not be reported, documented, or tweeted about, especially because of the informal nature of foreign policy interaction. At this point, interviews became key sources.

The foreign policy relationship between Turkey and the EU is mostly an informal area of interaction, which means that interviewing decision makers and diplomats involved in the relationship was necessary to establish the true nature of the interaction. Interviews were used to access information that is not available to the public, such as information about informal meetings with no public records and interactions between the EU and Turkey that were not documented. They were also used to establish who initiated meetings as well as the content and the overall tone of interactions. Therefore, interviews were a very valuable source of first-hand information.

It is both a disadvantage and an advantage for this research that the area of foreign policy cooperation is mostly informal in nature. It is a disadvantage because sources are limited and, sometimes, do not even exist. As Chapter 3 will explain, Turkey and the EU are not able to conduct high-level, regular, formal, and institutional foreign policy coordination meetings due to a lack of agreement and the course of Turkey's EU membership process. Because there is no institutional framework through which Turkey and the EU can formally cooperate, the issue area is limited to informal interactions between officials, and sometimes interactions are not traceable. For instance, the Turkish foreign minister made numerous telephone calls to the EU High Representative after the start of the uprisings. As this research reveals, the calls were made on an encrypted telephone line, and there is no actual record of the content of these conversations or even information on how many telephone calls were made. Often, the content of these dialogues, or the information that a conversation took place, is shared with the media; but if there had been formal interaction under an institutional framework, the content of interaction would be fully transparent (e.g., press statements, written conclusions, meeting minutes).

At the same time, it was an advantage for this research that the area of interaction is informal because only a very few people are involved in foreign policy cooperation between the EU and Turkey. There are a few officials directly involved because foreign policy cooperation has become an unusual and rather separate area that runs parallel with Turkey's membership process. Specifically, the EU High Representative's office at the EEAS led the conversation with the Turkish government during the Arab uprisings. When asked to comment on the foreign policy cooperation between Turkey and the EU, the Head of the Turkey Unit at the EU Commission, namely the Directorate-General for Neighbourhood and Enlargement Negotiations, directly referred to Ashton's team at the EEAS, saying they were qualified to comment and that the foreign policy relationship was different from the accession process (Interview EU07). Interviewed officials who were involved in the talks offered valuable insights into the nature of informal interaction that took place between Turkey and the EU, as they were able to provide information that was not available in the media or official documents.

The fieldwork took place in Brussels, Ankara, and Istanbul. Key decision makers and diplomats involved in the Turkey-EU foreign policy relationship during the Arab uprisings were interviewed. Interviewees included Turkish ministers, government officials, and diplomats, as well as EU diplomats working in Ankara and Brussels, and EU officials at the EEAS and European Commission.

The interviews were semi-structured and aimed to find evidence as to whether consultations took place between Turkey and the EU after certain incidents during the crises. Specifically, for "unilateral information", evidence should suggest that the Turkish government informed the EU about its decisions and actions but that the EU was not given the opportunity to give feedback. For instance, if the evidence suggested that EU diplomats in Ankara were called to the Ministry of Foreign Affairs for a briefing session about the planned action of the Turkish government but not given a chance to ask questions or to offer their perspective, this would indicate there was "unilateral information". For "consultation", there should be credible evidence that the Turkish government initiated the contact and requested the EU opinion on its intended actions. For "co-decision", the evidence should additionally include an indication that EU preferences were taken into account. In this case, policy adjustment and, if necessary, adaptation to EU policy may take place.

Most of the interviewees, especially the Turkish interviewees, did not wish for their names to appear in this study. Only the affiliation and position of certain interviewees will be specified in order to protect their anonymity. The guarantee of anonymity allowed them to make more honest comments and assessments and to reveal more than they normally would have revealed.

Interview codes will be used for in-text citations. These will include two letters (EU or TR), signifying whether the interviewee was giving information from the Turkish or EU perspective. Also, interview numbers are given which correspond to the list of interviews in the Appendix. So, for example, "EU04" indicates right away that the interviewee was associated with the EU. All the interviews with the TR code were conducted in Turkish. Quotes from these interviewees, and from other primary and secondary sources in Turkish, were all translated by the author.

The interviewees were also asked to identify further participants to interview, which was especially helpful, not only because their connections helped the arrangement of interviews but also because they were able to name officials within the bureaucracy who dealt with specific issue areas. For example, this book will examine the specific case of the evacuation of citizens from Libya, during which the EU's department of civil protection and humanitarian aid coordinated the EU's response. With the help of interviewees, I was able to identify and interview people working for that specific department in Brussels and in Ankara in order to obtain more information about EU interactions with Turkey at the time.

It should also be mentioned that any information gathered from interviews was not taken at face value. In order to triangulate my data and validate the information interviewees gave, I conducted secondary interviews with policy analysts and academics and fact checked with other interviewees as well as with document analysis.

Notes

1 See, for example, the study of Jupille et al. (2003) on "integrating institutions", which discusses complementarities between various institutionalisms, primarily between the rational and constructivist conceptions of institutions.
2 Some Turkish journalists even started to use "Erdoğan foreign policy" and "Turkish foreign policy" interchangeably (e.g., Çandar, 2015).
3 See e.g., Zengin (2010) who observed a "Davutoğlu effect" in Turkish foreign policy based on ideas such as "zero problems with neighbours" and "rhythmic diplomacy".
4 It should be pointed out that intra-party democracy was also an issue in the pre-AKP era, especially considering the populism of Erbakan and Özal, but this is out of the scope of this analysis.
5 Founding member of the AKP; Prime Minister 2002–2003; Foreign Minister 2003–2007; President 2007–2014.

References

Akşam. (2013) "Yiğit Bulut'a göre eylemlerin arkasındaki iki ülke" [Two States behind the Protests according to Yiğit Bulut], 19 June, https://www.aksam.com.tr/guncel/yigit-buluta-gore-eylemlerin-arkasindaki-iki-ulke/haber-217507

Alden, A., and Aran, A. (2012) *Foreign Policy Analysis: New Approaches*, Abingdon: Routledge.

Allison, G., and Zelikow, P. (1999) *Essence of Decision: Explaining the Cuban Missile Crisis* (2nd edition), New York: Pearson.

Atalay, B. (2013) "Press Conference in Istanbul", www.youtube.com/watch?v=Cc4h1HeP7Xg.

Ayan, P. (2010) "Authoritarian Party Structures in Turkey: A Comparison of the Republican People's Party and the Justice and Development Party", *Turkish Studies* 11(2): 197–215.

Batur, N. (2009) "Yeni Osmanlılar Sözü İyi Niyetli Değil" ["Using the Term Neo-Ottomans Is Ill-Intentioned"], *Sabah*, 4 December, www.sabah.com.tr/siyaset/2009/12/04/yeni_osmanlilar_sozu_iyi_niyetli_degil.

Bilgin, P. (2004) "A Return to Civilizational Geopolitics in the Mediterranean? Changing Geo-Political Images of the European Union and Turkey in the Post-Cold War Era", *Geopolitics* 9(2): 269–91.

Bilgin, P., and Bilgic, A. (2011) "Turkey's New Foreign Policy Towards Eurasia", *Eurasian Geography and Economics* 52(2): 173–95.

Boland, V., and Dombey, D. (2005) "EU Without Turkey 'Will Be Just a Christian Club'", *Financial Times*, 3 October, www.ft.com/cms/s/0/ca926e4e-33a9-11da-bd49-00000e2511c8.html-axzz4JzwuoPV1.

Boulding, K.E. (1956) *The Image*, Ann Arbor: University of Michigan Press.

Çandar, C. (2015) "Erdoğan dış politikası: Moskova'dan Brüksel'e dikiş tutmuyor", *Radikal*, 7 October, www.radikal.com.tr/yazarlar/cengiz-candar/erdogan-dis-politikasi-moskovadan-bruksele-dikis-tutmuyor-1446537/.

Cumhuriyet. (2018) "Erdoğan: AB'ye üyelik stratejik hedefimiz" ["EU Membership Is Our Strategic Goal"], 26 March, www.cumhuriyet.com.tr/video/video/948857/Erdogan__AB_ye_uyelik_stratejik_hedefimiz.html.

Dalay, G., and Friedman, D. (2013) "The AK Party and the Evolution of Turkish Political Islam's Foreign Policy", *Insight Turkey* 15(2): 123–39.

Davutoğlu, A. (2015) "TBMM Grup Toplantısı" [Parliamentary Meeting], Ankara, Turkey, 27 January.

———. (2013) "İstanbul Milletvekili Sayın Mustafa Sezgin Tanrıkulu'nun Yönelttiği 7/30664 Sayılı Yazılı Soru Önergesine Yanıt" ["Reply to the Parliamentary Question Raised by Istanbul MP Mustafa Sezgin Tanrıkulu, No. 7/30664"], 14 November, https://www2.tbmm.gov.tr/d24/7/7-30664sgc.pdf.

———. (2001) *Stratejik Derinlik* [*The Strategic Depth*], Istanbul: Küre Yayınları.

———. (1997) "Medeniyetlerin Ben-İdraki", *Divan* 1(1): 1–52.

———. (1989) "Balkanlar ya da Tamamlanmamış Bir Tasfiye", *Islam* 6(71): 32–33.

de Schoutheete, P. (1980) *La Coopération Politique Européenne* [*European Political Cooperation*], Paris and Brussels: Nathan/Labor.

Düzgit, S.A., and Tocci, N. (2009) *Transforming Turkish Foreign Policy: The Quest for Regional Leadership and Europeanisation*, Brussels: CEPS.

Erdoğan, R.T. (2013a) "Sansürsüz Özel", *24 TV*, Turkey, 25 January.

———. (2013b) "Speech in Prague, Czech Republic", 4 February.

———. (2011) "Speech After the 2011 General Election", Ankara, Turkey, 12 June.

———. (1990) "Speech in Sakarya, Turkey", 16 March.

Erhan, Ç. (2011) *Türk Dış Politikası'nın Güncel Sorunları* [*Contemporary Problems in Turkish Foreign Policy*], Ankara: Imaj.

Guida, M. (2008) "The Sèvres Syndrome and 'Komplo' Theories in the Islamist and Secular Press", *Turkish Studies* 9(1): 37–52.

Gül, A. (1995) "Speech at the Grand National Assembly of Turkey", Ankara, Turkey, 8 March.

Hale, W. (2013) *Turkish Foreign Policy Since 1774* (3rd edition), London, UK: Routledge.

Hürriyet. (2011) "Suriye Adeta İç Politika" ["Syria Is Almost Internal Politics"], *Hürriyet*, 15 May, www.hurriyet.com.tr/suriye-adeta-ic-politika-17790485.

Jervis, R. (1976) *Perception and Misperception in International Politics*, Princeton, NJ: Princeton University Press.

Jupille, J., Caporaso, J.A., and Checkel, J.T. (2003) "Integrating Institutions Rationalism, Constructivism, and the Study of the European Union", *Comparative Political Studies* 36(1–2): 7–40.

Kirişçi, K. (2013) "The Rise and Fall of Turkey as a Model for the Arab World", *Brookings Institution*, 15 August, www.brookings.edu/research/opinions/2013/08/15-rise-and-fall-turkey-model-middle-east.

———. (2009) "The Transformation of Turkish Foreign Policy: The Rise of the Trading State", *New Perspective on Turkey* 40(1): 29–57.

———. (2006) *Turkish Foreign Policy in Turbulent Times*, Chaillot Paper No. 92, Belgium: Institute for Security Studies.

Kongar, E. (1998) *21. Yüzyılda Türkiye* [*Turkey in 21st Century*], Istanbul: Remzi Kitabevi.

Kuburlu, C. (2011) "Mısır'daki 2 milyar dolarlık Türk yatırımı diken üstünde" ["$2 bn Turkish Investment in Egypt in Danger"], *Hürriyet*, 28 January, www.hurriyet.com.tr/ekonomi/misir-daki-2-milyar-dolarlik-turk-yatirimi-diken-ustunde-16871304.

Kutlu, Ö. (2003) "AKP'de Demokrasi Eksik" ["Democracy Is Missing in the AKP"], *Radikal*, 20 October, www.radikal.com.tr/haber.php?haberno=92669.

Manners, I. (2002) "Normative Power Europe: A Contradiction in Terms?" *Journal of Common Market Studies* 40(2): 235–58.

The Ministry of Trade of Turkey. (2019) "Trade Between Turkey and Egypt", https://ticaret.gov.tr/yurtdisi-teskilati/afrika/misir/ulke-profili/ekonomik-gorunum/turkiye-ile-ticaret.

Mintz, A. (2004) "How Do Leaders Make Decisions? A Poliheuristic Perspective", *Journal of Conflict Resolution* 48(1): 3–13.

———. (1993) "The Decision to Attack Iraq: A Noncompensatory Theory of Decision Making", *The Journal of Conflict Resolution* 37(4): 595–618.

Mintz, A., Nehemia, G., Steven, R., and Carnes, A. (1997) "The Effect of Dynamic an Static Choice Sets on Political Decision Making: An Analysis Using the Decision Board Platform", *American Political Science Review* 91(3): 553–66.

Müftüler-Baç, M., and Gürsoy, Y. (2010) "Is There a Europeanization of Turkish Foreign Policy? An Addendum to the Literature on EU Candidates", *Turkish Studies* 11(3): 405–27.

NTV. (2012) "Başbakan'ın danışmanı: Savaş istemiyoruz" ["PM's Advisor: We Do Not Want War"], *NTV*, 4 October, www.ntv.com.tr/turkiye/basbakanin-danismani-savas-istemiyoruz,eGK9nkoCMki2sFvwh-m5Wg.

Oğuzlu, T. (2007) "Soft Power in Turkish Foreign Policy", *Australian Journal of International Affairs* 61(1): 81–97.

Öniş, Z. (2012) "Turkey and the Arab Spring: Between Ethics and Self-Interest", *Insight Turkey* 14(3): 45–63.

———. (2011) "Multiple Faces of the 'New' Turkish Foreign Policy: Underlying Dynamics and a Critique", *Insight Turkey* 13(1): 47–65.

———. (2008) "Turkey-EU Relations: Beyond the Current Stalemate", *Insight Turkey* 10(4): 35–50.

———. (2003) "Turkey and the Middle East After September 11: The Importance of the EU Dimension", *Turkish Policy Quarterly* 2(4): 84–93.

Öniş, Z., and Yılmaz, Ş. (2009) "Between Europeanization and Euro-Asianism: Foreign Policy Activism in Turkey During the AKP Era", *Turkish Studies* 10(1): 7–24.

Ortaylı, İ. (2007) *Osmanlı Barışı* [*Ottoman Peace*], Istanbul: Timaş.

Oruçoğlu, B. (2014) "The Turk Has No Friend but the Turk", *Foreign Policy*, 14 November, http://foreignpolicy.com/2014/11/14/the-turk-has-no-friend-but-the-turk/.

Özcan, M. (2008) *Harmonizing Foreign Policy: Turkey, the European Union and the Middle East*, Burlington: Ashgate.

Özcan, M., and Usul, A.R. (2010) "Understanding the New Turkish Foreign Policy: Changes Within Continuity, Is Turkey Departing from the West", *Uluslararası Hukuk ve Politika* 6(21): 101–23.

Peker, E., and Malas, N. (2012) "Turkey Strikes Syria, Adds War Powers", *The Wall Street Journal*, 5 October, www.wsj.com/articles/SB10000872396390443635404578035822373395226.

Putnam, R.D. (1988) "Diplomacy and Domestic Politics: The Logic of Two-Level Games", *International Organization* 42(3): 427–60.

Risse, T. (1995) *Cooperation Among Democracies – The European Influence on U.S. Foreign Policy*, Princeton, NJ: Princeton University Press.

Sabah. (2009) "Libya'ya tarihi ziyaret" ["Historic Visit to Libya"], *Sabah*, 24 November, www.sabah.com.tr/siyaset/2009/11/24/erdoganel_mahmudi_gorusmesi_basladi.

Sayarı, S. (2000) "Turkish Foreign Policy in the Post-Cold War Era: The Challenges of Multi-Regionalism", *Journal of International Affairs* 54(1): 169–82.

Sedelmeier, U. (2011) "Europeanisation in New Member and Candidate States", *Living Reviews in European Governance* 6(1): 1–32.

Sprout, H.H., and Sprout, M. (1956) *Man-Milieu Relationship Hypotheses in the Context of International Politics*, Princeton, NJ: Center of International Studies, Princeton University.

T24. (2015) "Erdoğan: AB'yi şu anda test ediyoruz, bakalım halkı Müslüman bir ülkeyi hazmedebilecekler mi?" ["Erdoğan: We Are Testing the EU – Will They Accept a Muslim Country?"] *T24*, http://t24.com.tr/haber/cumhurbaskani-erdogan-cibutide-konusuyor,284861.

Tepe, S. (2005) "Turkey's AKP: A Model 'Muslim-Democratic' Party?" *Journal of Democracy* 16(3): 69–82.

Turkish Statistical Institute. (2016) "Turkish Exports by Country Group and Year", www.tuik.gov.tr/UstMenu.do?metod=temelist.

Walt, S. (2012) "Letter from Istanbul", *Foreign Policy*, 18 May, http://walt.foreignpolicy.com/posts/2012/05/18/letter_from_istanbul.

The World Bank. (2019) "Turkey Exports to by Country and Region, in US$ Thousand 2001–2017", https://wits.worldbank.org/CountryProfile/en/Country/TUR/StartYear/2001/EndYear/2017/TradeFlow/Export/Partner/ALL/Indicator/XPRT-TRD-VL.

Yavuz, M.H. (2009) *Secularism and Muslim Democracy in Turkey*, New York: Cambridge University Press.

Zengin, G. (2010) *Hoca: Türk Dış Politikası'nda 'Davutoğlu Etkisi'* [*Hoca: The Davutoğlu Effect in Turkish Foreign Policy*], Istanbul: İnkılap.

Zeybek, N.K. (2007) "Türk'ün Türk'ten başka dostu . . ." ["The Turk Has No Friend but the Turk"], *Radikal*, 23 October, www.radikal.com.tr/haber.php?haberno=236510.

3   Institutional framework for foreign policy dialogue between Turkey and the EU

The purpose of this chapter is to provide an overview of cooperative frameworks (i.e., institutional frameworks for the mutual exchange of information and cooperation on foreign policy) between Turkey and the EU because these will be relevant to the different issues and countries that the chapters will cover. The Political Dialogue is a formal institutional framework for the exchange of information and cooperation, and it takes place at different levels involving the highest-level officials from the EU and Turkey. This chapter will highlight the fundamental features of the Political Dialogue, as well as other formats of foreign policy dialogue, and discuss the scope it offers for general consultation on foreign policy and the nature of the EU-Turkey foreign policy relationship, leaving it to the following chapters to provide evidence as to what the implications for cooperation are. The main conclusion of this chapter is that, during the course of the Arab uprisings, the foreign policy dialogue remained largely informal, meaning that the standard frameworks, such as the Political Dialogue, were not particularly central in terms of the consultations that took place.

The institutional frameworks for foreign policy dialogue between the EU and Turkey partly exist due to the candidate status of Turkey but are mainly due to association (the Association Council). Some frameworks also apply to other third countries (Political Dialogue), although Turkey has a privileged role because the complex nature of the relationship has made the Political Dialogue particularly developed, as the next section will discuss. The fundamental aim of focusing on the institutional frameworks that the EU has created for foreign policy cooperation with non-members, although the main focus of the book is Turkish foreign policy, is that there are a number of potential frameworks in place that in principle can facilitate cooperation between Turkey and the EU due to Turkey's candidacy. Formal meetings can provide an opportunity for cooperation if there is a framework for regular meetings, although not much joint decision making takes place in these meetings. The next section presents the main features of the dialogue and other formats and discusses how these might increase the likelihood of cooperation.

Political Dialogue

The Political Dialogue has historically been the EU's main instrument for establishing formal relations between the Common Foreign and Security Policy (CFSP) and third countries (Sedelmeier, 2005: 157–58; Regelsberger, 1990; Monar, 1997). It is therefore not unique to Turkey, and the EU has similar frameworks in place for conducting structured dialogue on foreign policy with third countries. For example, before the Eastern enlargement of the EU in 2004, the Political Dialogue with Central and Eastern European Counties (CEECs) was developed into a multilateral format in which the dialogue was conducted at all levels of the CFSP decision-making hierarchy – heads of state/government, political directors, European correspondents, CFSP working groups – covering all areas of foreign policy and placing the pre-accession CEECs in a privileged position among non-members (Sedelmeier, 2005: 164).

In a similar way, the Political Dialogue with Turkey takes place at different levels. The highest-level decision-making mechanism is the EU-Turkey Association Council, which derives from the accession process and therefore covers a wide range of issues, including foreign policy. Strictly speaking, the Association Council can be considered separate from the Political Dialogue because the Political Dialogue can exist without an Association Agreement in place. In the case of Turkey, both are closely connected and integral to the ongoing dialogue.

Participants in the Association Council include the foreign minister of the EU member state that holds the EU presidency, the EU Commissioner for Enlargement, the EU Minister and Chief Negotiator of Turkey, and the Turkish foreign minister. As one of the interviewees, a senior bureaucrat at the Ministry of EU Affairs of Turkey, explained, the meetings are based on texts (Interview TR02). So, each side, both the EU and Turkey, reads and presents the texts that they have prepared. Decisions are taken unanimously, and both the EU and Turkey have one vote each. Through this meeting, the EU and Turkey formally assess their relationship and the membership process. The Association Council, as the highest-level decision-making framework between the EU and Turkey, can be seen as a platform for co-decision since leaders may make joint decisions about how to proceed with Turkey-EU relations, as well as with policies towards other countries and foreign policy actions.

The foreign policy relationship is discussed particularly when assessing developments under "Chapter 31: Foreign, security and defence policy", one of the chapters which is blocked relating to the Cyprus issue. Especially since the beginning of the Arab uprisings, the Turkish government started to reiterate its willingness to have regular and formal foreign policy consultations with the EU even though Chapter 31 was blocked; however, there was a lack of agreement, particularly among EU states, about having formal talks on foreign policy, as this book will elaborate on later.

Additional to the EU-Turkey Association Council, there is a dialogue framework that is called "ministerial dialogue" to which the EU High Representative, the EU Commissioner for Enlargement, the EU Minister and Chief Negotiator of Turkey, and the Foreign Minister of Turkey attend. It has a similar composition to the Association Council, but it is more focused on foreign policy matters. Since the start of the Arab uprisings and the Positive Agenda initiative of the

European Commission, which sought to intensify foreign policy dialogue with Turkey, foreign policy cooperation has generally been an important agenda item in these meetings. According to another interviewee, a senior bureaucrat at the Ministry of EU Affairs in Turkey, who attended all of these meetings from 2011 to 2015, the Turkish foreign minister was usually at the forefront in leading meetings because the EU wanted to obtain information from Turkey about developments in the region (Interview TR02). The Turkish foreign minister presents Turkish positions to the EU; however, it is not a decision-making platform and no joint decisions are made, rather meetings end with expressions of goodwill (Interview TR02). The meetings have not been regular; their arrangement tends to depend on whether ministers can commit their time, but they have been held at least once a year (Interviews EU01 and EU02). An EU diplomat in the Political Section at the EU Delegation in Ankara explained that the meetings generally help the EU to understand Turkish positions but suggested that these meetings should be held more frequently to engender effective foreign policy coordination, which is again one of the arguments of the Turkish government when proposing more frequent and regular meetings (Interview EU01). Ministerial dialogue meetings can act as fora for consultation in the sense that ministers can exchange information and ask for the EU's feedback on Turkish positions.

Another dialogue mechanism is called "Turkey-EU political dialogue at political directors' level". The participants are the undersecretaries of the Ministry of EU Affairs and the Ministry of Foreign Affairs of Turkey, the Deputy Secretary General of the EEAS, and the Director General for Enlargement. Again, these meetings are not regular. The participants aim to meet once a year depending on whether the officials have time to commit and the general aim of the meetings has been to discuss cooperation on foreign policy issues. For example, after the meeting in March 2014, the permanent delegation of Turkey in Brussels specified that the main objective was "to foster coordination and cooperation in bilateral relations and on foreign policy areas of common interest", and among the issues discussed was the situation in the Middle East, particularly in Syria (*The Turkish Herald*, 2014a). According to a former EU ambassador to Turkey, these meetings are based on an exchange of views, but they have never altered policy for either side (Interview EU03). This dialogue mechanism improves understandings but does not allow one party to influence the other's policy (Interviews EU03 and EU02). So, it is more about cooperation at the information stage without so much decision making taking place.

In addition to these levels of dialogue, there have been other occasions on which Turkish and EU officials have met and had a chance to talk. For example, after the Political Dialogue meeting at the ministerial level on 10 February 2014 in Brussels, the Turkish foreign minister attended the EU Foreign Affairs Council dinner at the EEAS where he expressed his views on a wide range of issues, including the importance of stability in the Balkans (*The Turkish Herald*, 2014b). Also, for a period of time, the Turkish foreign minister used to be invited to the informal gathering of EU foreign ministers in Gymnich, on which this book will elaborate more.

The case studies in this book will be used in an examination of whether, and to what extent, these contacts had any or much impact. Generally, it is possible to say that these institutional frameworks might improve the possibility of cooperation, especially if meetings take place frequently. In fact, a Turkish diplomat at the Permanent Turkish Delegation to the EU expressed that these sorts of contacts between the EU and Turkish ministers were very useful, but they needed to be more frequent and regular in order to create a functioning foreign policy dialogue (Interview TR04). The case study chapters will assess whether such contacts indeed encouraged cooperation.

At this point, it is useful to clarify that the main actor in the EU coordinating foreign policy dialogue during the Arab Spring was the EEAS, specifically the High Representative (HR) Catherine Ashton and her Turkey team. Since the aim of the mechanisms between the EEAS and the Turkish government is to foster cooperation, one could argue right off that the rate of Turkey's alignment with EU statements indicates whether cooperation mechanisms work or not. However, as explained earlier, cooperation does not necessarily mean alignment with EU statements and, in fact, the alignment rate is not a good indicator of cooperation at all. To clarify the way alignment works, once the EU agrees on a statement expressing its position, it contacts certain third countries, mainly candidates including Turkey, inviting them to join the statement. So, alignment is offered not just to Turkey. Other countries are invited as well, and on the same terms, which are "take it or leave it", that is, without room for negotiation to change the declaration. The main reason why Turkey's alignment with the EU is not a good indicator of cooperation is because the Turkish government is usually given very short notice, which leaves insufficient time to align, even if the Turkish government actually intends to align (Interviews EU01, EU02, EU03, TR02, TR03, TR04).

In addition to this, the Turkish government is generally resentful of being treated as "any other country". A senior Turkish bureaucrat in the EU Ministry expressed his discontent with the way Turkey was treated, saying, "I am Turkey, I am not a country like Egypt, I am a candidate state and I have had a partnership with you for more than 60 years. You cannot treat me like Egypt" (Interview TR02). The main discontent here also concerns the fact that Turkey has no say in EU statements and it cannot contribute in any way, similarly to other countries offered a chance to align with the EU. For instance, according to an interviewee at the EU section of the Ministry of Foreign Affairs of Turkey, the Turkish government was resentful because the EU did not consult Turkey regarding sanctions against Russia (Interview TR05). A senior Turkish bureaucrat at the Ministry of EU Affairs explains, on the same issue:

> They [the EU] impose sanctions against Russia without even talking about it with Turkey. Russia is your most important historical ally, most important trade partner. Why would you sign a text a couple of EU personnel wrote hastily in a couple of days there [in Brussels]? Then they wonder, 'Why didn't Turkey align?' blah blah blah.
>
> (Interview TR02)

This is also one of the reasons why it is important to analyse interactions between Turkey and the EU on a case-by-case basis to see the extent to which there is cooperation. This is because there is no straightforward indicator, such as the alignment rate, to assess the degree of Turkey's cooperation with the EU.

Another important point to note about the nature of Political Dialogue and the role of the EEAS is that, as the Turkey advisor to HR Ashton emphasised, the EEAS has tried to coordinate foreign policy cooperation in the area of foreign policy as defined by the interests of EU member states (Interview EU04). This means that, in order to achieve formal foreign policy cooperation with Turkey, the EEAS needs the approval of all EU member states. This is exactly the reason why informal dialogue has become the norm in the Turkey-EU foreign policy relationship, as the next section will discuss in detail. The fundamental issue here is that, although the majority of EU member states would like closer foreign policy cooperation with Turkey, there is no unanimous agreement on establishing formal consultations with the Turkish government, mainly due to problems with the membership negotiations in general. The most apparent obstacle to formal and regular contacts is the Cyprus issue, which has blocked the opening of chapters, including the one on foreign policy cooperation (Interview EU04). This is why the foreign policy relationship is an unusual area of interaction, because, as mentioned earlier, there is a general shared understanding that both the EU and Turkey need closer foreign policy cooperation, but in practice the formal establishment of such a platform has not been possible. So, the solution that the EEAS and the Ministry of Foreign Affairs of Turkey came up with was to conduct dialogue but to call it informal, as the next section will explain.

Ultimately, there are different levels in the institutional framework between the EU and Turkey that can potentially foster foreign policy cooperation. Although Turkey has a much closer relationship with the EU as a third country, the problems with the membership negotiations limit formal interactions, which is the main reason why the EU and Turkey have sought to establish a parallel relationship based on informal talks on foreign policy.

The informal nature of foreign policy interaction

The disadvantage of the institutional framework for cooperation was that it confined foreign policy interaction to the formal institutional setup in place. The emphasis in the interviews with the EU diplomats was that the EEAS was coordinating the best possible partnership with Turkey in the area defined by the preferences of EU member states. The problem was that the interaction was blocked related to the problems of membership negotiations, which created a need for informality. For instance, a diplomat at the EU mission in Ankara clearly stated that the Republic of Cyprus had blocked formal interactions on numerous occasions, and similar issues relating to the membership process affected the foreign policy dialogue during the uprisings (Interview EU6). In fact, according to the Turkish EU minister, this was precisely the challenge that the "Positive Agenda" initiative that the EU Commission launched in 2012 had sought to overcome (Interview TR01). He claimed that it was designed to bypass the veto of the Republic of Cyprus so that the Commission and Turkey could talk without "political obstacles" (Interview TR01). For this reason, even specifically agreed upon foreign policy meetings and discussions on thematic and regional issues were referred to as "informal" by both Turkey and the EU (Interview EU06).

Foreign policy cooperation between Turkey and the EU during the Arab Spring was greatly based on the informal dialogue between the EU High Representative Catherine Ashton and Turkish Foreign Minister Ahmet Davutoğlu. Interviews with EU and Turkish diplomats suggest that the dialogue was based on friendship and mutual concern over the turmoil in the Middle East and North Africa. Specifically, Ashton's Turkey advisor at EEAS describes the dialogue in the following way:

> The model of cooperation under Cathy Ashton was very much a personal relationship with Ahmet Davutoğlu. They were very close. They spoke very frequently. I think he was probably the person she spoke to the most on the phone. They constantly saw each other formally in the context of international meetings etc. And there was very close communication and information sharing. And what we tried to do at the official level was to try to support that through developing a wide range of consultation mechanisms with Turkey. I was on several occasions with her [Ashton] in Ankara and here [Brussels] seeing Davutoğlu and I can say that the Ashton-Davutoğlu relationship was based on close personal friendship. Their families even knew each other.
> (Interview EU04)

When asked how the dialogue worked during the crises of the Arab Spring, the interviewee responded, "there were very regular discussions between Davutoğlu and Ashton on the Arab Spring. I mean that has really been the key focus of our dialogue. So, real-time picking up the phone, discussing the situation in Egypt, Syria, and Libya" (Interview EU04). This also meant that they were able to communicate informally on the telephone regardless of when or whether dialogue meetings were scheduled to take place.

Commenting on the shortcomings of meetings, a senior bureaucrat in the Ministry of EU Affairs in Turkey described them as being mostly based on an exchange of information instead of being a forum for decision making. He said, "these meetings end with expressions of good will. It is not like we say, 'Okay, we are making such and such decision together'. As the name suggests, they are 'dialogue meetings' – not a committee or a council meeting, such as the EU-Turkey Association Council" (Interview TR02). Another EU diplomat in Ankara argued that the mechanisms were not sufficient for efficient foreign policy cooperation, which is also a Turkish argument for more institutionalisation of foreign policy cooperation. The diplomat said,

> We are trying to build cooperation on pure foreign policy, separated from the enlargement process. We have very intense consultations with Turkey including the 'ministerial dialogue' and the 'political directors' consultations'

but they can meet only when they can find time. There is a need to talk more [with regard to Egypt, Syria, and Libya] but these mechanisms are not sufficient for closer cooperation.

(Interview EU02)

As mentioned earlier, the ministerial and political directors' consultations were meant to take place at least once a year; however, this was not always possible, which is why the informal conversations between the Turkish foreign minister and the EU HR were particularly important for the exchange of information (Interviews EU01 and EU02).

Therefore, there are both advantages and disadvantages of the Political Dialogue in terms of fostering cooperation. The main advantage is that it is a formal framework involving the political leadership as well, which means that it can encourage co-decisions easier. The disadvantages are that the formal framework is affected by the problems of Turkey's accession process, the format is not designed for joint decisions, and it may be difficult to have informal meetings on short notice due to scheduling issues. In terms of their function, the existing frameworks help maintain a dialogue but generally do not go any further, although both the EU and Turkey have often reiterated the need for enhanced cooperation.

A good specific example of an informal meeting in which foreign policy is discussed is the Gymnich meetings to which Turkey attends when invited. As far as Turkey is concerned, Gymnich meetings, the biannual informal meetings of EU foreign ministers, do not go beyond mere talking. In fact, a senior bureaucrat at the EU Ministry of Turkey described the atmosphere in the meetings as "chit-chat at a large breakfast table" (Interview TR02). They are informal meetings that are held once a year. Turkey may or may not be invited depending on the decision of EU member states. When Turkey attends, the meeting can potentially contribute to cooperation since it, at least, provides a forum for the Turkish government to express its views and listen to those of the EU ministers. However, Turkey was not always invited during the Arab Spring because, as several EU diplomats claimed, the EU ministers were irritated by the "know-it-all attitude" of Turkish Foreign Minister Davutoğlu (Interview EU05). An EU diplomat claimed that there was a "fatigue" from listening to him speaking all the time (Interview EU02). "EU ministers have limited time there", he explained (Interview EU02). Another EU diplomat claimed that Davutoğlu spoke as if he were "lecturing" the ministers, thereby implying that "Turkey knows the Middle East the best" (Interview EU05). As a result of this "fatigue", interviewees claimed that the Turkish foreign minister, hence Turkey, was not invited on a number of occasions, such as the Gymnich meeting in the second half of 2012. It should be noted that the second half of 2012 was when the Republic of Cyprus held the EU presidency and when Turkey froze relations with the EU for this reason; so, it can be claimed that political reasons can also have an impact as well. Although the Turkish government apparently did not regard the meeting as having had much importance, the meeting had the potential to serve as a platform for the exchange of views that might have led to coordinated action.

This example is useful in two ways. First, it shows that there is a lack of agreement on Turkey's participation in these meetings, which means that Turkey might participate one year and not participate another. There is uncertainty about whether Turkey will be invited or not. Second, it demonstrates the degree to which the different preferences of EU member states can have an impact on channels of cooperation. In other words, the kinds of issues that affect the membership process, and even smaller issues, such as Davutoğlu's manner of speaking, can well affect the nature of the foreign policy relationship between Turkey and the EU. This is no surprise, but it is essential to note that this is one of the reasons why foreign policy dialogue largely remained informal and irregular. And, essentially, this was the major reason why Davutoğlu and Ashton were encouraged to discuss foreign policy issues personally during the course of the Arab Spring regardless of whether Turkish and EU positions converged or not.

In addition to the regular institutional frameworks for cooperation, there can also be ad hoc meetings and direct communication. A key aspect of the informal relationship during the Arab Spring was the telephone conversations between Davutoğlu and Ashton. It should be pointed out that the fact that telephone conversations took place does indicate some level of cooperation, but deeper empirical analysis in Chapters 4–7 will pinpoint exactly which channels were used and whether they led to cooperation. With regard to how such informal interaction took place, the overall consensus among interviewees, including the Turkish diplomats, was that there were frequent telephone conversations between the two. Ashton's advisor clarified that they talked on the telephone as events happened during the crises (Interview EU04). The interviewee also pointed out that FM Davutoğlu called HR Ashton regularly during the uprisings, even before the public announcement of the Turkish position and Turkish reaction (Interview EU04). For instance, in some cases the Turkish government did not make its position immediately public and waited for other actors in the international arena to take a stance. The interviewee claims that informal telephone conversations also took place during this period, which means that in some instances Davutoğlu was able to hear EU input while the Turkish position was being finalised.

Again, the issue-specific chapters will discuss these points in much more depth, but, generally, what the interviewees said in terms of the substance of conversations was that these informal conversations were based on information sharing. The Turkish government would share its take on the crises and inform about Turkish positions and impending actions. For instance, in some cases, the Turkish government not only informed the EU about what position it would take but also requested expressions of support and solidarity.

The informal dialogue was, of course, a two-way street. So, generally, when the interaction took place, the EU position was also communicated to the Turkish government. Again, this changed depending on the situation. For example, during the uprisings, there were cases in which Davutoğlu called Ashton, but there was no EU position at the time of interaction, as this book will discuss in detail later. In short, Ashton also had a chance to inform the Turkish government about what the EU intended to do and to express views. These conversations took place sometimes even before Turkish decisions had been made or actions had been carried out.

As a conclusion, the Political Dialogue and other formats of foreign policy dialogue take place at different levels. The Political Dialogue as a framework to maintain a foreign policy relationship has the potential to enhance the probability of foreign policy cooperation if more regular meetings take place. However, it had limitations with regard to fostering cooperation during the Arab Spring, particularly due to the politics of the Turkish membership bid. Ultimately, the channel of communication between the EU and the Turkish government was open informally in the area of foreign policy. The personal friendship of Davutoğlu and Ashton was at the centre of foreign policy cooperation during the Arab Spring. An aim was that cooperation would be developed without too much interruption from the developments in Turkey's membership process.

Two additional general observations can be made. First, in the aftermath of the Arab uprisings, informal dialogue has continued to be the norm in the Turkey-EU foreign policy relationship. Even at the presence of political tension between EU and Turkish leaders, the EU High Representative and Turkish Foreign Minister were frequently in touch to discuss foreign and security matters of mutual importance. For example, the Ministry of Foreign Affairs in Turkey has made it public many times that Turkish Minister Mevlüt Çavuşoğlu and EU High Representative Federica Mogherini have had telephone conversations to discuss developments in Syria, Libya, and Russia (Anadolu Ajansı, 2019; Ministry of Foreign Affairs of Turkey, 2016; DHA, 2019; *Hürriyet*, 2018). Second, disagreements and political tension between Turkey and the EU do not necessarily mean an absence of cooperation. Cooperation in the form of consultation or unilateral information can still take place even when Turkey diverges from EU positions. For example, following the 54th meeting of the Association Council between the EU and Turkey held in Brussels on 15 March 2019, Çavuşoğlu clearly stated that although they "did not share the same view on everything" the meeting was "very productive" (Bloomberg, 2019). Based on the institutional frameworks in place for foreign policy cooperation and considering the observations about the informal nature of foreign policy interaction, the case study chapters will evaluate the actual extent of cooperation that took place between the EU and Turkey.

References

Anadolu Ajansı. (2019) "Turkish Foreign Minister, UK, EU Officials Talk Libya", *Anadolu Ajansı*, 9 April, www.aa.com.tr/en/politics/turkish-foreign-minister-uk-eu-officials-talk-libya/1446830.

Bloomberg. (2019) "Çavuşoğlu: Her konuda hemfikir değiliz ancak çok toplantı verimli geçti" ["We Do Not Share the Same View on Everything but the Meeting Was Very Productive"], *Bloomberg*, 15 March, www.bloomberght.com/cavusoglu-her-konuda-hemfikir-degiliz-ancak-cok-verimli-gecti-2204833.

DHA. (2019) "Bakan Çavuşoğlu'ndan iki kritik görüşme" ["Two Important Meetings of Minister Çavuşoğlu"], *DHA*, 25 January, www.dha.com.tr/politika/disisleri-bakani-cavusoglu-mevkidasi-ile-gorustu/haber-1622783.

Hürriyet.(2018)"BakanÇavuşoğlu'ndanönemligörüşmeler"["MinisterÇavuşoğlu'sImportant Meetings"], *Hürriyet*, www.hurriyet.com.tr/gundem/bakan-cavusoglundan-onemli-gorusmeler-40960415.

Ministry of Foreign Affairs of Turkey. (2016) "Dışişleri Bakanı Sayın Çavuşoğlu'nun AB Dışilişkiler ve Güvenlik Politikası Yüksek Temsilcisi Mogherini ile Telefon Görüşmesi Hakkında Arka Plan Notu" ["Notes Regarding the Telephone Conversation Between Foreign Minister Çavuşoğlu and EU High Representative Mogherini"], Ankara, Turkey, 27 July, www.mfa.gov.tr/disisleri-bakani-sayin-cavusoglu_nun-ab-disiliskiler-ve-guvenlik-politikasi-yuksek-temsilcisi-mogherini-ile-telefon-gorusmesi-hk.tr.mfa.

Monar, J. (1997) "Political Dialogue with Third Countries and Regional Political Groupings: The Fifteen as an Attractive Interlocutor", in Regelsberger, E., Wessels, W., and de Schoutheete, P. (eds.), *Foreign Policy of the EU from EPC to CFSP and Beyond*, London, UK: Lynne Rienner Publishers, pp. 263–74.

Regelsberger, E. (1990) "The Dialogue of the EC/Twelve with Other Regional Groups: A New European Identity in the International System?" in Edwards, G. and Regelsberger, E. (eds.), *Europe's Global Links – The European Community and Inter-Regional Cooperation*, London, UK: Pinter Publishers, pp. 3–26.

Sedelmeier, U. (2005) *Constructing the Path to Eastern Enlargement: The Uneven Policy Impact of EU Identity (Europe in Change): The Uneven Policy Impact of EU Identity*, Manchester: Manchester University Press.

The Turkish Herald. (2014a) "The Turkish Herald Monthly E-Newsletter", *Permanant Delegation of Turkey to the EU*, Issue 23, April, www.theturkishherald.eu/t/j-5280D858A219C380.

———. (2014b) "The Turkish Herald Monthly E-Newsletter", *Permanant Delegation of Turkey to the EU*, Issue 22, March, www.theturkishherald.eu/t/j-4245893B750BCB26.

4 Turkey's foreign policy cooperation with the EU during the Egyptian uprising of 2011

Following the apparent success of demonstrations in Tunisia, a popular uprising began in Egypt in January 2011 and forced one of the region's longest-serving and most influential leaders, President Hosni Mubarak, from power. The turmoil presents a good case study to analyse how Turkey behaved considering its renewed interest for cooperation with the EU in the beginning of the Arab Spring. This chapter consists of a single cooperative opportunity focusing on the 18 days of crises, from the start of mass demonstrations on 25 January until Mubarak resigned on 11 February.

The main questions regarding potential cooperation for the EU and Turkey was whether and when to stand out against Mubarak and openly voice support for the opposition. Generally, cooperative behaviour would have ideally involved the Turkish government seeking consultation with the EU so that both could be well informed about each other's actions and support each other when they saw fit. Specifically, for this cooperative opportunity, cooperation would imply common support for the opposition and criticism of the Mubarak regime.

This chapter examines the Turkish reaction and the extent to which there was cooperation with the EU. The empirical investigation focuses on the timing and substance of the Turkish policy regarding the Mubarak regime and analyses the interactions between Turkish and EU officials.

Turkish interests in Egypt and reaction to the crisis

The Turkish policy towards Egypt in the AKP era had two prominent dimensions, which were also in line with Turkish policy towards the broader region and the idea of "new" Turkish foreign policy: the economic dimension of deepening economic interdependence through the fostering of transnational trade, which was helping Turkey to develop its economy, and the political dimension of developing closer and mutually beneficial political relations with the Egyptian regime. Turkish interests involved promoting investment and securing Turkish businesses in Egypt and complementing economic relationships through maintaining good political ties. The political dimension can be seen as having a wider regional aspect, which is related to the fundamental goal of the "new" Turkish foreign policy of becoming a regional power. Having Egypt's support was essential for the Turkish government to become an influential actor in regional issues. Therefore, both economic and political dimensions aimed to complement each other.

There is also a fundamental cultural component of the relationship that was used as a tool to maintain and promote stronger relations. The cultural component was based on cultural affinity and Muslim fraternity. A classic example of the way this works in practice is the way in which Turkish decision makers emphasise a common Ottoman history and that Egyptians and Turks are brothers, just as the Turkish President did after Mubarak's visit to Turkey in 2009 (e.g., *Cumhuriyet*, 2009). So, culture comes into play through an emphasis on shared identity. It should also be highlighted that cultural and political affinity can potentially motivate the Turkish government to prefer certain domestic actors in Egypt (e.g., the Muslim Brotherhood) over others.

Going before the AKP era and considering the history of relations, it is possible to say that the relationship had ups and downs. For example, Turkey and Egypt had a bitter relationship at the beginning of the Cold War, particularly due to the diplomatic crises of 1954 and tensions over politics around the Baghdad Pact. After the coup of 1952 against Egypt's monarchy, tension escalated between the Turkish ambassador in Cairo, who was married to a member of an Egyptian noble family, and the new President Abdel Nasser, and, as a result, the Turkish ambassador was declared persona non grata in 1954 (see Bardakçı, 2011). With regard to the Baghdad Pact, the Egyptian government strongly urged Arab nations not to participate and argued that the military alliance between Turkey, Iran, Iraq, Pakistan, and the UK served the interests of Israel and imperialists (Gürün, 1983: 137). According to Fırat and Kürkçüoğlu (2001: 620–21), the real issue was not the diplomatic crisis or the Baghdad Pact; the real issue concerned competition for political leadership in the Middle East at a time when Turkey was leading states closer to the West, whereas Egypt was leading the states who wanted to protect their political and economic independence against the West.

There was also additional tension between Turkey and Egypt because Turkey, due to its foreign policy outlook at the time, had a distant approach to former Ottoman territories, which include Egypt. This meant that the government avoided too much engagement with the country and prioritised its alliance with the West. Meanwhile, in Egypt, Arab nationalism peaked, and the country became one of the most prominent advocates of pan-Arab ideology. So, neither Turkey sought too much engagement with Egypt due to its foreign policy outlook, nor Egypt sought too much engagement with Turkey due to its ideological position as the leader of Arab nations. The 1950s can be seen as a time when the Turkey-Egypt relationship was particularly at a low point.

In the AKP era, Turkish engagement in Egypt gradually increased. Bilateral relations slightly improved during the period when Erdoğan and Mubarak were in power, particularly after both sides agreed to closer dialogue in 2007, signing the "Memorandum for a Framework for Turkish-Egyptian Strategic Dialogue" in Istanbul, which had the aim of "strengthening bilateral economic, political, and cultural cooperation between Turkey and Egypt" (Ministry of Foreign Affairs of Turkey, 2015). In the following years, until the start of the Arab Spring, the

Turkish foreign minister described Egypt as a "strategic partner", and there were high-profile visits, including Turkish President Gül's visits to Egypt in 2008 and 2009 and Mubarak's visit to Turkey in 2009 (ibid.).

A close look at the remarks of Turkish politicians during their visits and meetings with Egyptian officials demonstrates the Turkish approach to Egypt in the AKP era. For instance, after meeting with Egyptian President Mubarak in Istanbul in 2009, Turkish President Gül referred to him as a "brother" in a speech and said that bilateral cooperation was essential especially with regard to regional issues of mutual concern, such as the situation in Gaza. Moreover, he emphasised the importance of strengthening political and economic relations and specifically mentioned that Turkey welcomed the rise in trade volume that had almost doubled from $2.5bn in a short time (*Cumhuriyet*, 2009). Later in that year, during Mubarak's visit to Turkey, Gül even suggested lifting visas, reminding the Egyptian leader about the Free Trade Agreement that had been signed in 2005 (*Zaman*, 2009b).

When Turkish Foreign Minister Davutoğlu visited Egypt in the same year, he made similar remarks about the importance of cooperation, especially with regard to the situation in Gaza, and made clear references to the Ottoman Empire. In addition to meeting Mubarak, he also met journalists and academics and explained his vision of Turkish foreign policy by outlining the transformation that the policy had been going through since the AKP took office. In his speeches during his visit, he frequently used the phrases, "I am Ottoman" and "Nobody can get away from their history", emphasising that the Ottoman Empire had not been a Turkish state but rather a "mosaic of nations" (*Zaman*, 2009a). Both Gül's and Davutoğlu's remarks point to the economic and political aspects of the relationship since they underline the importance of intensifying trade and cooperation in the region.

Moreover, their words also indicated that the policy towards Egypt was consistent with Turkey's revised approach to the Middle East prior to the Arab Spring, particularly considering the arguments based on cultural affinity and regional trade. These arguments were in fact fundamentally based on the idea that Turkey needed to expand its area of influence using its geocultural potential, which was the central argument Davutoğlu made before he became a policy maker (Davutoğlu, 2001). Expanding Turkey's area of influence involved becoming a pivotal actor with regard to regional issues. One of the concerning issues on which Turkey wanted to be particularly influential was the Israeli-Palestinian conflict. To this end, Turkish officials frequently brought up this issue in their bilateral meetings, knowing that Egypt's support was essential. Ultimately, it is possible to say that, in line with Turkey's new engagement with the neighbourhood, the Turkish approach was based on promoting not only trade but also closer political ties, using the rhetoric of shared culture and history as much as possible.

At the onset of the crisis in Egypt, analysts in Turkey argued that the Arab Spring would be a good test for the "new" Turkish foreign policy. For instance, a report published by the Foundation for Political, Economic and Social Research (SETA) in Ankara argued that the "new" Turkey had changed the political dynamics in the region, especially with the "upright" policies that it had followed in the post-Davos era.[1] It stated "Turkey, which reaches out to the Arab people when talking to governments is not possible, has created a significant area of influence in the Middle East. . . . The crisis in Egypt has been the first important test for this area of attraction" (Bölme et al., 2011: 43–44). Maintaining this area of attraction and Turkey's legitimacy in the eyes of the Egyptian people was an important concern in Turkey's reaction to events, particularly at the very beginning of the uprising, as this chapter will proceed to examine. It could also be stated that creating an area of attraction was a strategic goal for Turkey, and risking it was a costly action.[2]

With the rhetoric that Turkey was with the people of Egypt, the Turkish government strongly supported pro-democratic forces in Egypt after the Turkish PM openly called the Egyptian President to step aside on 1 February. The Turkish government then frequently expressed its support during the political transformation, considering the will of the people and presenting the Turkish experience of democratisation as a model for Egypt.

After the uprising had started, the Turkish government was presented with a dilemma: should it protect its self-interest or support democratic movements in Egypt? (This dilemma also occurred in the other case studies that this book examines.) The main reason for this dilemma can be found in the uncertainty surrounding the political situation in Egypt. The end result was a balancing reaction that bought time until there was more certainty about the change of leadership.

To unpack this point, protecting interests meant maintaining a working relationship with the Egyptian government in order to reach strategic goals, such as becoming a regional power and maintaining a mutually beneficial trade relationship. Yet, there was also the issue of supporting democratic change for the people of Egypt. If the leadership would likely change, then it would be beneficial for the Turkish government to give support to the opposition. In this way, the Turkish government would not only support the promotion of democracy but would also start off on the right foot with whomever was going to be the new leader. However, if the leadership would likely stay, then it would be costly to support the opposition right away. At the same time, the Turkish government wished to avoid appearing as if it were supporting a leader who was oppressing his people. As a result, the safer policy option was to find a balance between protecting self-interests and advocating democratic change, at least until it became clearer as to how the crisis would unfold. For this reason, the Turkish government, as this analysis will discuss, did not wish to be the first to call for President Mubarak's resignation; instead, it waited to see the international reaction and especially whether the US was going to withdraw its historical support for President Mubarak.

It should also be noted that there was uncertainty about who would lead Egypt if regime change took place. In the case of Egypt, and also in the wider region, the Turkish government had a tendency to prefer the Muslim Brotherhood, as this book will discuss later in depth. Through conducting relations with Islamist actors, it was better able to use neo-Ottoman discourse with the aim of making Turkey a leader in the region. Specifically, this meant that when the Muslim Brotherhood seemed likely to take power after President Mubarak, the Turkish government happily supported it. This chapter will examine Turkey's response to regime change in detail, but, before proceeding, it reviews the EU's approach to Egypt to establish EU preferences with regard to Egypt and the extent to which these were compatible with, or contradictory to, Turkish preferences.

The EU's preferences and reaction to the crisis

What is important for this analysis, as in the cases of Libya and Syria, is the strategic importance of Egypt to the EU. In order to establish an understanding of the EU's preferences with regard to the crisis, first it is essential to consider EU-Egypt relations prior to the uprising.

Similar to the case of Libya in particular, it is possible to say that the EU had immense political and economic interests at stake in maintaining a mutually beneficial partnership with Egypt. These interests were clearly outlined, for example, at the 6th Meeting of the EU-Egypt Association Council in April 2010, right before the crisis in Egypt began. It is important to note that, as in the case of Turkey, the Association Council Meetings are one of the main mechanisms on which bilateral cooperation with Egypt is based, and the discussions at the meetings range from free trade regulations to cooperation with regard to migration. The first item in the statement made by the EU regarding the 6th Meeting of the EU-Egypt Association Council held in Luxembourg read: "The EU-Egypt partnership and its strengthening are based on common values, interests, and concerns. The EU and Egypt share the goal of building stability, peace, and prosperity in the Mediterranean and the Middle East regions" (European External Action Service, 2010). Emphasising the importance of mutual partnership, the EU reaffirmed its interest in maintaining close ties with Egypt, which indicated not only that Egypt was an economic partner but also a strategic actor in the Mediterranean and the Middle East region, where the EU was trying to establish itself as an influential actor. For example, one of the issue areas in which the EU thought it could benefit from a closer alliance with Egypt was the Middle East peace process. Acknowledging the "important role Egypt plays in promoting stability in the region", the EU made it clear that it sought a closer partnership with Egypt, particularly with regard to regional affairs (ibid.).

Therefore, it can be claimed that in addition to economic gains from partnership, the EU had political interests in line with its wider aim of establishing itself as an important actor in the region. To accomplish that, the EU prioritised stability in its approach, which meant that it favoured stable governments, open channels of dialogue with existing governments, and political stability in a country. A clear example of this, as this book will discuss later, was the EU's reaction to the Sisi government. Even though the EU was well aware that General Sisi had carried out a coup d'état, it was reluctant to admit to this and preferred to establish regular and normal relations with the government, keeping channels of dialogue open. It did not adopt a hostile attitude, as the Turkish government had done, but in speeches EU personnel emphasised the restoration of stability in the country (Interviews EU01 and EU02). When the crisis began in January 2011, the EU had immense economic and political interests at stake in a successful transition (Interviews EU01 and EU02). In terms of concrete policy choices, this entailed initially supporting the government against internal challenges, but once this had become untenable, the focus became promoting a smooth transition to what would most likely be stable governance.

The EU behaviour was criticised by analysts because it was problematic, ineffective, and incoherent. It was problematic because, related to the previous point on stability, to some degree it also had a dilemma between supporting a democratic movement and self-interest. For instance, Sadiki (2015: 561) points to Ashton's statement on 10 February in which she reminded Egyptian authorities that "full respect for human rights and fundamental freedoms is essential" (Ashton, 2011b) and claims that this statement was problematic since she qualified her words only two weeks later, saying, "this is the European Union wishing to support what is for Egypt to lead" (Ashton, 2011a). Sadiki (2015: 561) also points out that, two years later in response to President Morsi's (temporal) adoption of a presidential decree, which was supposed to put him above judicial control, Ashton (2013) underlined the need to have "strategic patience" with Egypt, whereas the European Parliament (2013) called for the suspension of any budgetary support to Egypt "if no major progress is made regarding respect for human rights and freedoms, democratic governance and the rule of law". Pinfari (2013) specifically focuses on Ashton's use of the expression "strategic patience" and points to the democracy versus stability dilemma that the European Neighbourhood Policy, as a foreign policy instrument of the EU, had long faced.

The EU's response was ineffective and incoherent because, when the uprising against President Mubarak started, the EU struggled to speak with one voice and failed to act in a timely manner (European Council on Foreign Relations, 2012: 101). As this chapter will discuss, there was generally more unity in the case of Egypt compared to the case of Libya, but, still, EU member states had a degree of divergence that prevented them from responding quickly to developments in Egypt. Arguably, a contributing factor to slow decision making and divergence in the EU in the onset of the crisis was the ongoing discussion on the EU's role in the Mediterranean with the revision of the European Neighbourhood Policy and how the EU could reinforce its engagement with its southern neighbours (see e.g., Pertusot, 2011).

Turkish reaction to anti-Mubarak uprising on 25 January

The initial reaction of the Turkish government to the demonstrations starting on 25 January can be studied as a cooperative opportunity. When the crisis started, the Turkish government, on one hand, felt the need to appear as a role model for the Egyptian people, which for actual foreign policy behaviour meant that the government needed to show a degree of support for their struggle, while, on the other hand, it sought to protect its essential interests by waiting to see whether the Mubarak regime was likely to fall. As mentioned in the previous section, such behaviour can also be seen across cases during the Arab uprisings, which this book will address later.

Turkish decision makers focused on securing Turkey's strategic interests, which included protecting Turkish assets and evacuating Turkish citizens, and avoided costly actions, such as adopting an anti-Mubarak outlook right away when the demonstrations began. Elements of religion and identity were present in Turkish foreign policy discourses, but as this analysis will unpack, the initial reaction was fundamentally defined by a cost-benefit calculation.

Cooperation with the EU was limited to information exchange and did not reach the point of consultation for a number of reasons. First, the EU position was finalised very late, after the Turkish position had been determined. So, while Turkish foreign policy was being made, there was no clear EU position to take into account even if Turkish decision makers had reached out to the EU to request feedback on their intended actions. This does not necessarily mean a complete absence of cooperation. In fact, there was cooperation in the sense that the Turkish government informed the EU about its position before the EU had a policy.

Second, there is evidence suggesting that there were informal contacts between the EEAS and the Ministry of Foreign Affairs of Turkey (Interviews EU02, EU04, EU05, EU06). Specifically, HR Ashton and FM Davutoğlu spoke informally in telephone conversations to exchange views. However, there is no conclusive evidence from interviews or the document analysis that contacts with the EU led to an adjustment of behaviour.

Third, the reason why the EU position was not a major factor in the Turkish reaction was because Turkish decision makers saw the US position as decisive in terms of whether the Mubarak regime would fall or not. So, their strategy was to wait until the US had taken a critical position against the regime, then to adopt a similar stance. This was beneficial for the Turkish government because, until the international response had become clearer and they could better ascertain whether President Mubarak was going to step down, they had time to evacuate a considerable number of Turkish citizens in Egypt, these citizens having established their presence over the preceding years as a result of the AKP's policy of developing economic interdependence with Egypt.

This analysis also finds that the Turkish government developed a renewed interest in a formal framework of foreign policy cooperation and attending foreign policy meetings in the EU. It is possible to say that the crisis in Egypt was the catalyst for this renewed interest. However, this interest remained a proposal: the fact that there was such an interest does not necessarily mean that there was a genuine interest in cooperating with the EU, but it does indicate that there was a failed attempt to develop a stronger and formal framework that foresaw more frequent ministerial contacts.

Formation of Turkish position

The Turkish position was made public on 1 February, on the eighth day of uprising, when the Turkish PM urged the Egyptian President to step aside and meet the demands of the people. This eight-day period needs to be examined to identify influential factors in the making of Turkish policy and whether and to what degree there was cooperation with the EU.

It should be noted that when demonstrations spread to Egypt at the start of the Arab Spring, the use of neo-Ottoman discourse in Turkish foreign policy was at its peak. The Turkish PM was visiting Arab states frequently and talked about political and economic unity. Most notably, on 12 January 2011, during his visit to Kuwait and Qatar, PM Erdoğan addressed the Arab people, saying, "we are self-sufficient! If obstacles are removed, the 57 states of Islam can become self-sufficient with their production, technology, and brainpower" (Ülsever, 2011; Berberoğlu, 2011). When asked, he denied wanting to be the leader of the Islamic world, but at the same time he led integrationist initiatives, such as the Schengen-inspired "Şamgen",[3] which was about creating a visa-free zone between Muslim states (Berberoğlu, 2011). In early January 2011, many commentators (e.g., Ülsever, 2011; Yetkin, 2011) criticised the way in which statements made by foreign policy makers were based on emphasising shared religion and called pan-Islamist claims in Turkish foreign policy "delusion". Meanwhile, the Turkish media was talking about how Turkey's popularity had increased in Egypt and in the Islamic world in general and debating whether Erdoğan could be the "new" Gamal Abdel Nasser (*Hürriyet*, 2010; Bilgenoğlu, 2010; see also Andoni, 2010). So, it is essential to examine Turkish behaviour with regard to the crisis in Egypt in light of these trends and self-perceptions. Overall, although there were elements of religion and identity in Turkey's foreign policy discourse towards Egypt, as this analysis will unpack, the Turkish government prioritised its fundamental interests in the face of unrest in Cairo. Because of the increased engagement with the country, there were a considerable number of Turkish citizens and businesses in Egypt that the Turkish government wanted to protect from harm when the uprising started.

In the immediate aftermath of the turmoil, Turkey's primary concern was to protect its essential interests as much, and as soon, as possible. These interests included the well-being of Turkish citizens and businesses in Egypt. Turkey's first response was to ensure the safety of its citizens, and evacuation was on the top of the agenda. The Turkish government successfully flew many Turkish citizens back to Turkey using state-owned Turkish Airlines, which was extensively covered by the Turkish media.

For example, stories that were in the national news included the ones about 25 Turkish nationals taking shelter in a school and a national sports team stranded in a hotel in order to avoid violence in Cairo (*Hürriyet*, 2011d). As an official working in the Turkish disaster management agency (AFAD) stated, evacuations were one of the main components of the Turkish reaction to the uprisings, including the one in Egypt, especially due to the high number of Turkish citizens in these zones, and they also helped evacuate a number of foreigners upon requests by other states (Interview TR06). An EU diplomat in Ankara specifically mentioned that the EU was thankful that EU citizens had also been evacuated by Turkey on additional charter flights (Interview EU06).

The majority of Turkish citizens had been successfully evacuated by the end of January, before Turkey had a clearer stance against Mubarak – about 1444 Turkish citizens had been evacuated by 31 January (*Hürriyet*, 2011c) – and it could be stated that the high number of Turkish citizens involved was one of the reasons why it could be costly for the Turkish government to openly criticise and upset the Mubarak regime right from the beginning. So, the bottom line here is that the Turkish position in the immediate aftermath of the unrest was to avoid openly critical statements against the regime.

Moreover, the Turkish government showed great concern for Turkish economic interests in Egypt. For instance, on 30 January – five days after the protests had begun – the Turkish Minister of Economy replied to a question on the turmoil, expressing his concern that the instability in the region could have negative consequences for Turkey and called for stability and democracy in the Middle East and North Africa. He underlined that Egypt was an "essential economic partner" and that Turkey had 6,553 Turkish firms exporting to Egypt and 1,500 Turkish workers as well as showrooms and branches of 34 firms in Egypt (Cihan, 2011b). In terms of policy choices, the emphasis on stability meant that the Turkish government did not necessarily want the regime to change and stayed neutral or made generic expressions of concerns about the situation in order to avoid risking relations with the existing government; however, when this became untenable and the leadership change appeared more likely, the Turkish government promoted a smooth transition to what would most likely become a stable government. A day after the statement by the Turkish Minister of Economy, PM Erdoğan held a cabinet meeting to ask ministers their views on Egypt before unequivocally asking President Mubarak to step down (Gürcanlı, 2011), and it is possible to claim that economic concerns were given much importance during discussions over the finalisation of the Turkish position.

Another important aspect of the formation of the Turkish position was the international response. The Turkish government avoided being openly critical of the Egyptian regime in the first week because it wanted to concentrate on the evacuation, until it had a better idea about how the international response was going to be shaped. The evacuation was particularly important because Turkey had a considerably large number of citizens in Egypt compared to many other states, which was also the case with Libya. In the meantime, the Turkish government especially waited to see the US response since it had been a major ally of the Mubarak regime.

When considering the timing of the Turkish decision (Figure 4.1), it is possible to say, as a Turkish journalist (Gürcanlı, 2011) noted, that Ankara was "silent" until the Turkish PM made a clear statement about the crisis on 1 February. Both the Turkish PM and FM had strong opinions, particularly about Egypt and its place in the new Turkish foreign policy; however, they preferred not to make any comments for a week. To give a specific example, FM Davutoğlu (2011a) did not post a single tweet on his Twitter page (@Ahmet_Davutoglu) during the uprising, although he used Twitter quite often, posting a total of 18 tweets in the month of January. Similarly, the Ministry of Foreign Affairs of Turkey (2011) (@TC_Disisleri) only tweeted updates about the evacuation of Turkish citizens during the uprising. When FM Davutoğlu was asked about Egypt in the first week of the crisis, he refrained from making direct statements, giving instead vague answers such as, "we are following the events closely" and "Egyptian people are

Monday	Tuesday	Wednesday	Thursday	Friday	Saturday	Sunday
24	25 Uprising starts	26	27	28 US position starts to become clearer	29 UK-France- Germany joint declaration	30 Obama- Erdoğan telephone call
31 EU Council Meeting	1 Turkish position public	2	3	4	5	6
7	8	9	10	11 Mubarak resigns	12	13

Figure 4.1 Timeline of events, January–February 2011

brothers", and emphasising that Turkey followed the principle of non-interference in domestic affairs (Hürriyet, 2011a). Therefore, it could be argued that the Turkish government was waiting for the right moment to make a clear statement.

Since Mubarak was one of the major allies of the US in the Middle East, the US position was important not just for Turkey but also for other actors in the international arena. Therefore, it is useful to examine the US reaction as well. The day the crisis started, US Secretary of State Hilary Clinton "urged all sides to refrain from violence", without making a harsh statement (Reuters, 2011). On 27 January, US Vice President Joe Biden (2011), in a TV interview, said that Mubarak was an "ally" of the US and that he would not refer to him as a "dictator" and disagreed when asked about whether Mubarak should step down. On the same day, answering questions during an online town hall with YouTube viewers, US President Obama emphasised the need for reforms in Egypt, noting Egypt's role as an ally of the US (Raddatz and Wong, 2011). So, it was somewhat unclear whether or not the US wanted Mubarak to resign at this point.

The US took a clearer stance on 28 and 29 January by defending the rights of protesters and signalling that the crisis in Egypt had passed a "critical turning point" (Lander, 2011). At this stage, it was clear that Washington supported the demands of the protesters and saw that the status quo in Egypt was untenable. The Turkish government, along with many other states, was observing the US position because Mubarak was an important ally to the US.

Aligning with the US, the big three EU member states, UK, France, and Germany made a joint declaration on 29 January, urging Mubarak to stop the violence and "embark on a process of transformation" (UK Prime Minister's Office, 2011). It became clearer at this point that the EU statement was going to be shaped more or less in line with their declaration. However, it should be stressed that the UK, France, and Germany were the first member states to issue such an open statement. Most other EU member states were also following a wait-and-see approach and, as a result, the EU position was not clear. In fact, there was no coherent EU position in the first week at all. On 27 and 28 January, HR Ashton released statements that did not go beyond a basic iteration of the need to stop violence and respect human rights (Ashton, 2011d). She also added that she would discuss the situation with her "colleagues in the Foreign Affairs Council Meeting on Monday [31 January] in Brussels" (Ashton, 2011c). Therefore, it is not possible to talk about an EU position on the weekend of 29–30 January, when the Turkish position was finalised and Turkish decision makers were getting ready to announce the position in the following days.

On the weekend of 29–30 January, having successfully evacuated a large number of citizens from Egypt, which was a concern for Turkish decision makers, there was an important telephone conversation between the Turkish PM and the US President, after which the Turkish government aligned with the US position and acted in coordination with the US, even helping US citizens escape the conflict zone.

It should also be noted that, at this point, the Turkish government was also under public pressure to break its silence, there having been much criticism in major newspapers. Critics had questioned the government's silence, especially considering how Turkey had started to engage in Egypt, frequently using neo-Ottoman discourse. For example, on 30 January, a columnist in the popular daily newspaper the *Hürriyet* asked:

> Doesn't Turkey have a single word to say? What happened to all the talk about 'we are closely interested in the Ottoman territories'? Ok, let's say Tunisia was far away but what about Egypt? . . . The US has this much to say about what is going on over here but Turkey has not a single word to say, is that so?
>
> (Berkan, 2011)

The issue here was not about having "a single word to say" but rather that the Turkish decision makers waited to align with the US and observe the international reaction before making a statement in order to avoid marginalisation.

The US President started making telephone calls to leaders around the world and called PM Erdoğan on Sunday 30 January (BBC, 2011). It was reported that during their lengthy conversation, President Obama asked PM Erdoğan to support the idea of a transitional government and that the two leaders agreed to cooperate with regard to the situation in Egypt (*Hürriyet Daily News*, 2011; *Hürriyet*, 2011b). So, 30 January was the exact date on which Turkish decision makers decided how they were going to react to the crisis. From this point onwards, Turkey broke its silence over the crisis and followed the US lead. Detailing the content of the conversation, a Turkish newspaper, the *Radikal*, reported:

> It was uncertain as to whom Turkey would support in Egypt. Until today, Turkey had made general comments talking about the stability of the region and the democratic rights of the people of Egypt. It was learned that the Turkish government adopted the view that 'Mubarak needs to go'.
>
> (Zeyrek, 2011)

On 1 February, the Turkish government made its first clear statement. PM Erdoğan openly called on Mubarak to step down, urging him to "meet the people's desire for change" (Cihan, 2011a).

The US position was one of the most influential factors in terms of the timing of the Turkish position. PM Erdoğan himself stated that their stance had been finalised after his conversation with the US President. He said, "I spoke to President Obama . . . and discussed the events in Egypt. . . . He got our views and we got his views. It is confirmed with this phone call that we agree that the legitimate demands should be met and stability should be restored" (Erdoğan, 2011). An interviewee at the Middle East section of the Ministry of Foreign Affairs also pointed to the US position as essential for the timing of the public announcement of the Turkish reaction (Interview TR07). Similarly, the former Turkish ambassador to the US and MP for the Republican People's Party (CHP), Loğoğlu, also claimed that the EU was absent in the decision-making process during the uprising in Egypt, and it was mainly the US that prompted the Turkish government to take a stance (Interview TR10). The way in which the Turkish government directly linked the Turkish position to the US position even caused a debate in the domestic arena. For instance, the leader of pro-Kurdish BDP, Selahattin Demirtaş, said, "this man [Mubarak] has been a dictator for the last 30 years. Erdoğan has waited to see the Americans' [stance] before acting. . . . We had to support the people in upheaval against a dictator" (*Hürriyet Daily News*, 2011).

It should be pointed out that the US position influenced primarily the timing of the public announcement of the Turkish decision. One could say that, in terms of the substance of the Turkish position, the Turkish government was going to align with the US anyway. In other words, there were other factors influential in the making of Turkish foreign policy with regard to the anti-Mubarak uprising, and another important aspect of the policy was the position of Israel. To unpack, the Israeli government did not want President Mubarak to leave and put pressure on the US to curb criticism (Ravid, 2011). As *Reuters* described, Israel was "shocked" by the US' insistence on supporting the protesters against Mubarak, and the US position was perceived in Israel as "Obama's betrayal of his ally Mubarak" (Hamilton, 2011). At that time, there was still tension between Turkey and Israel over the Gaza flotilla raid incident[4] which had taken place in 2010. The Turkish government was following closely the arguments put forward by the Israelis supporting Mubarak and wondering what Obama would decide. According to a Turkish journalist, Turkey had concerns before publicly making a statement against Mubarak that Washington would listen to Israeli PM Netanyahu and curb criticism against Mubarak (Zengin, 2013). Had the US government curbed criticism against Mubarak, it would have caused some degree of uncertainty about the future of Mubarak, which, therefore, can be seen as another reason for the Turkish government to wait for the US position.

The main point here is that when the US preferred a regime change, which led to the view in Israel that Obama "betrayed" his ally Mubarak, the Turkish government happily concurred. So, the issue was not only about the situation in Egypt but also about the question of whose preferences would prevail in the region. By calling for President Mubarak to step down, the Turkish government was not only siding with the US but also adopting a counter-position to Israel. This position was important for the new Turkish foreign policy, as it would allow the Turkish government to demonstrate once more that it was with the Arab people, advocating what they wanted. Such symbolism is important and convenient, considering the way in which the Turkish government had started to use neo-Ottoman discourse and the notion of brotherhood when talking to Arab nations. Pursuing policies that appealed to the Egyptian public and taking a stance against the preference of Israel fit well with Ankara's broader pursuit of regional influence.

Moreover, one of the reasons why Israel supported Mubarak was because of concern over Islamists taking office in Egypt. This was of concern to Israel because of the potentially hostile approach the Egyptian foreign policy could have gained, especially with regard to the conflict in Gaza. Israeli PM Netanyahu himself warned about the potential rise of Muslim Brotherhood, comparing the uprising to the Iranian Revolution and seeing it as a "tremendous threat" (Tankersley, 2011; *Haaretz*, 2011). The fall of President Mubarak meant that the opposition and the Muslim Brotherhood would play an important role in Egyptian politics, which had already been foreseen by politicians in Turkey (e.g., by the Vice Chairman of the Republican People's Party (CHP) in charge of foreign relations, Osman Korutürk, who underlined that this was a real possibility in the speeches that he made before Mubarak lost power (*Cumhuriyet*, 2011)). The potential rise of the Muslim Brotherhood was an opportunity for the Turkish government because, if it had come to power, the Turkish government would have been able to use discourse based on religion more effectively and turn the ideological kinship between the AKP and the Muslim Brotherhood into influence in matters of regional importance, such as the Israeli-Palestinian conflict.[5]

So, while in principle the Turkish government welcomed change in Egypt, it was reluctant to do so as long as it was unclear whether there was going to be a change in power, for fear of alienating Mubarak in case he retained power. The Turkish government had its own interests at stake with regard to the post-Mubarak era, and this is essentially why, when the US had a clear stance against Mubarak, and when the international reaction was clearly against the regime, the Turkish government happily became one of the harshest critics of Mubarak, since this was also in line with its interests. In this sense, the US endorsement of "change" did not require much adjustment of Turkish preferences, but it could be claimed that it was influential in the timing of an openly critical Turkish position against Mubarak.

The tendency to support the Muslim Brotherhood also explains why the Turkey-Egypt relationship had its "golden era" when the Muslim Brotherhood was in power after Mubarak. The Turkish government believed that it would be able to present itself as a natural "model" for Egypt in the post-Mubarak era. In order to give an idea about how Egypt was perceived by the Turkish government, for example, the Minister of EU Affairs and Chief Negotiator of Turkey, Egemen Bağış, replied to a question on Turkish foreign policy after the fall of Mubarak, arguing that Turkey was the "only" model for Egypt and pointed to the way in which Erdoğan's speech against Mubarak had been aired live in the Middle East (Interview TR01).

As a result, there are a number of factors one must take into account when considering the formation of the Turkish position in the first week of the crisis. Overall, it could be claimed that it was a result of a cost-benefit calculus in terms of the content and the timing of the public announcement of the Turkish position. In order to assess cooperation with the EU in the first week and in the subsequent days of the crisis, Turkish interactions with the EU need to be examined in depth.

Interactions with the EU

There was potential for cooperation with the EU both before and after the public announcement of the Turkish position. The EU did not have a united policy when the Turkish position was finalised after consultation with the US. However, before the public announcement of Turkish policy on 1 February, potential cooperation could have involved the Turkish government informing the EU of its intentions with regard to the stance it was about to take. Cooperation could also have taken place after the announcement of the Turkish position in the second week of the crisis until Mubarak resigned.

There is no specific evidence that the Turkish government informed the EU about the position it planned to take before publicly announcing it on 1 February. The position was then communicated through diplomatic channels as soon as it became official Turkish policy (i.e., through communication with the EU Delegation in Ankara (Interview EU05)). So, there was at least "unilateral information" when the position was public. Again, there was no coherent EU position when Turkish decision makers were liaising with the US. So, the EU was not in a position to give feedback on the Turkish policy even if it had been asked to do so when the Turkish position was being finalised; therefore, "consultation" did not take place.

There is evidence from the interviews with EU diplomats that there were frequent informal telephone conversations between the Turkish FM Davutoğlu and the EU High Representative Ashton throughout the crisis in Egypt, which involved information exchange (Interviews EU04, EU05, EU06). So, it is likely that the Turkish position did not catch the EU by surprise when it was publicly announced, and that there was informal exchange during the crisis until Mubarak left, especially after both the Turkish and EU positions had become clearer.

Overall, the interaction can be described as lacking "consultation" because it is not possible to say that the Turkish government reached out to the EU to seek its feedback. However, the EU was informed about Turkish policy, especially after the position had been finalised after the first week of the crisis. To unpack this point, as previously mentioned, the EU struggled to make a statement, and the High Representative was heavily criticised for this reason. EU ministers were only able to meet on 31 January (on the seventh day of the crisis) and finally made a statement "recognising the legitimate democratic aspirations" of the Egyptian people (The Council of the European Union, 2011). In the meeting, there were disagreements over how to react, which also slowed the EU down. For instance, ministers failed to agree on the condemnation of sectarian attacks because of a disagreement over the use of the word "Christian", and the talks ended angrily when Italy accused the High Representative of "excessive political correctness" when she refused to specify religious groups as victims of attacks over Christmas (Waterfield, 2011). When the EU finally published a statement about the crisis on 31 January, the Turkish government had already decided during consultation with the US that it would support the regime change in Egypt. So, in this case, the Turkish position was finalised before the EU was even able to meet and comment on the situation. Therefore, consultation with the EU, or adjustment of policy after consultation with the EU, was out of the question. There is also no evidence that the intention of the Turkish government to support regime change was specifically communicated to the EU before it was announced.

It could be argued that one of the main reasons why the EU was not seen as an actor that the Turkish government wished to consult was due to its limitations in acting in a timely or effectively manner, which was also one of the points made by the Turkish FM Davutoğlu when criticising the EU during the Arab uprisings. In the case of Egypt, there was not much difference in terms of the timings of the announcements of positions: it seems that the Turkish government was also "late" in taking its position, until prompted by the US. However, the important difference here is that the Turkish government purposefully waited to take a stance, whereas the EU was simply unable to formulate a common position at once. For instance, FM Davutoğlu criticised the EU in a speech at the London School of Economics, in which he referred to the Arab uprisings:

> If today, at this moment, we were far away from, in an area, let me say in Finland, Scandinavia, if there is crisis in any country right now, I got information, in one hour latest, I will collect all the information and I will make an analysis and I will produce a solution or an approach or a policy. Then I will consult with my Prime Minister, with my President by phone and in two hours latest we will have a national position regarding to this crisis. My plane is waiting in 20-minutes distance, I will take the plane, I will land to that country in up to the distance in three-four hours, but latest in six-seven hours we will be part of this process. This way or the other we will have a position. But if you want to develop a position, first all of you will get your national information. Then Brussels will ask all of you, 'what is your national position?' Each of you will have different positions, most probably, at least three or four positions will emerge and Brussels tries to bring them together in one policy. If there are three-four positions and if you try to make a compromise out of four positions, it means you will have a position of no position. Because in order to make a compromise you will cut some parts of these policies. After three-four days, maybe sometimes a week, you will make a joint statement. This time that crisis will be over, another crisis will start [Quoted Verbatim].

(Davutoğlu, 2013)

There are two contradictions in this statement that are helpful for the analysis presented here. First, what FM Davutoğlu said contradicts the Turkish behaviour with regard to the anti-Mubarak uprising, since it took more than "six-seven hours" for the Turkish government to adopt a position. The government was even criticised internally for indecisiveness. This contradiction is helpful because it clarifies that the Turkish government purposefully waited to announce its position, and it was not because of a particular indecisiveness or an inability to formulate a position.

Second, the statement reveals that the EU is a weak and ineffective actor, as far as the Turkish government is concerned. It is sometimes not even seen as an actor at all due to its failure to act timely. Therefore, based on a general Turkish perspective of the EU, it could be argued that the EU was not an actor that the FM Davutoğlu wanted to consult, which applies not only to the crisis in Egypt but also to other case studies in this book. With regard to the case of the anti-Mubarak uprising, this Turkish take on the EU's role in the region could be considered as one of the factors explaining the absence of "consultation" with the EU. However, this would be a contradictory statement, because if the Turkish government did not see the EU worthy of consulting, then why did it, on an institutional level, seek to strengthen consultation mechanisms as a result of crises in the region, especially in Egypt?

The second point needs unpacking further. When the Arab uprisings started, the Turkish government revised its proposal to strengthen foreign policy cooperation with the EU (Interviews TR04, TR05, TR09, EU03, EU06). The uprising in Egypt demonstrated that the instability had the potential to spread across the Middle East, which was one of the main reasons why the Turkish government brought up the issue of enhanced foreign policy cooperation in meetings with the EU.

A senior Turkish diplomat who was personally involved in EU-Turkey negotiations explained that Turkey had approached the EU for foreign policy coordination shortly after the start of the Arab Spring but that the EU had been reluctant. He said:

> We have had consultations [with the EU] on every subject with regard to foreign policy but these were very informal because of Cyprus. When ministers gather and talk they usually discuss Egypt, Syria and Libya. . . . At the beginning of the Arab Spring, I was in Ankara and I was the first one to propose it [formal foreign policy cooperation]. I said [to the EU], 'let's do something together'. We were eager; they were not.
>
> (Interview TR09)

The Turkish ambassador to the EU, Selim Yenel, explained this at a public event in Brussels when discussing foreign policy cooperation with the EU regarding the Middle East:

> We [Turkey] have offered the EU to work closely on many occasions. We are basically talking to each other at a high level but not as a whole. We are talking to Lady Ashton but we would like to have the whole of the 27 working with us and I think that would be more influential or have some backbone to it [Quoted Verbatim].
>
> (Yenel, 2012)

Marc Pierini, who was the EU ambassador in Ankara at the start of the Arab Spring shed more light on the content of Turkey's proposal to work closely: "The idea was we would draw up a list of countries in Africa where it would be good to coordinate then we would exchange views and cooperate on Libya, Egypt, and Tunisia" (Interview EU03).

To see an example of how this interest is reflected in official documents and to make an assessment of why there was such an interest from the Turkish side, the foreign policy section of Davutoğlu's statement at the 49th Meeting of the Turkey-EU Association Council, which gathered on 19 April 2011, is useful to examine. Davutoğlu's speech both explains Turkey's motivation and demonstrates that Turkey was eager to develop closer foreign policy cooperation. He explained the need for enhanced foreign policy cooperation in the following way:

> The EU has to be strategically relevant, economically competitive and culturally inclusive to be a global player and to cope with the future challenges in a strong position. In this respect, Turkey's accession will be an added value rather than being a burden to the EU [Quoted Verbatim].
>
> (Davutoğlu, 2011b)

He did not neglect to emphasise that Turkey would contribute to EU foreign policy. This is crucial in the sense that he used this point with regard to Turkey's accession when building his argument about how useful foreign policy cooperation would be, because it shows that the Turkish government wanted to use foreign policy cooperation to strengthen its hand with regard to the accession process and ultimately to prove to the EU that it would be a reliable member. In other words, Davutoğlu was not only talking about foreign policy but also trying to sell the EU on the idea that Turkey should become a member state. He continued:

> We believe that, given our shared objectives for common neighbourhood and beyond, Turkey and the EU have so much to gain from closer cooperation and coordination in foreign policy. In particular, Turkey's increasing soft power assets in a wide geography converges with and complements those of the EU to benefit all [Quoted Verbatim].
>
> (Davutoğlu, 2011b)

Here, he reveals Turkey's primary motivation, which concerned increasing their influence in the region. Ambassador Yenel also put this emphasis on soft power during his speech. He stated that on many occasions Turkey had reached out to the EU for cooperation:

> [Turkey] offered them [the EU], let's work together. We [Turkey] have limit to our own soft power. There is a limit to our influence and I am sure there is a limit to the EU's influence as well but we do have comparative advantages and if we can work together, we can achieve much more and we can do it in a very soft way [Quoted Verbatim].
>
> (Yenel, 2012)

Therefore, there was a frequent emphasis on working together in order to increase soft power

While talking about the Gymnich meetings that FM Davutoğlu attended, an EU diplomat claimed that EU ministers felt Davutoğlu spoke like a lecturer with the attitude of "we know the region the best and therefore Turkey is a valuable partner" (Interview EU05). The lecturing tone was obviously not welcomed, but what is important here is that the overall argument was based on the idea that cooperation was needed to increase soft power in the region. In other words, the Turkish government was asking for cooperation to increase its influence. Therefore, Turkey's motivation when talking about foreign policy cooperation was to maximise its influence in the region, and, while doing that, Turkey also wanted to use the opportunity to prove to the EU that it was a valuable ally who should be accepted as a member, not only for Turkey's good but also for the EU's good.

After claiming that Turkey would contribute to EU foreign policy at the 49th Meeting of the Turkey-EU Association Council, Davutoğlu moved on to the main point of the proposal, which included his participation in Council meetings:

> It was with this understanding that I have put forward certain proposals to enhance Turkey-EU strategic dialogue during the first Turkey-EU Political Dialogue Meeting in Istanbul on 13 July 2010. These proposals included my participation in relevant Foreign Affairs Councils at ad hoc basis for consultations on regional and international issues of mutual concern. Since then we have been waiting for concrete steps to be taken [Quoted Verbatim].
>
> (Davutoğlu, 2011b)

Then, he continued on talking about how the uprisings during the Arab Spring could have been an opportunity for cooperation. What actually happened was that, as the EU ambassador at the time, Pierini, explained, Turkey renewed its proposals to establish foreign policy coordination after the start of the Arab Spring (Interview EU03). So, Turkey was interested in closer foreign policy cooperation even before the Arab Spring, which confirms the argument that Turkey's primary motivation was in line with its new objective of increasing its soft power in the Middle East. In the face of the Arab Spring and the reshuffling of power in the region, this interest intensified, which explains why this issue was a major item in Davutoğlu's speech.

Why it was an unsuccessful initiative, or a proposal, is a different issue. For Pierini, it was mainly the Ministry of Foreign Affairs bureaucracy who wanted cooperation, but it did not sit well with the political leadership (Interview EU03). One could also say that such an initiative could never have been implemented anyway because of the potential Cyprus veto. The important point here is not why it failed; it is the Turkish attitude towards cooperation, which also explains the nature of interaction during the anti-Mubarak crisis.

The Turkish proposal for enhanced cooperation was a strategic response to the uprisings, especially after the turmoil started to spread following the unrest against Mubarak. The fact that the Turkish government had a renewed interest in coordination after the start of the uprisings indicates that it wanted to increase its influence in the region while leading the EU's foreign policy. Therefore, rationalism better explains the Turkish attitude towards cooperation, as the renewed interest was caused by increasing turbulence and the need to be more effective in the region rather than norms of appropriate behaviour regarding cooperation.

The Turkish government saw the uprisings, especially starting from the anti-Mubarak uprising, as an opportunity to prove to the EU that it was a valuable asset and that it could help EU foreign policy to be more effective, which was essentially one of the main reasons why Turkish decision makers repeatedly underlined that the EU was weak and that Turkey had a lot to offer. If they had been involved in the EU foreign policy decision-making mechanisms, they could have had the chance to shape and contribute to EU decisions. If the EU had turned down such contributions, then they could have had the chance to hold the EU responsible for the failure. Either way, it was beneficial for the Turkish government to propose enhanced cooperation with the EU at the beginning of uprisings and shortly after the fall of Mubarak.

As a result, it is possible to say that there was no genuine will to coordinate, even though there was a Turkish proposal that foresaw frequent consultations between Turkish and EU ministers. This also explains why there was an absence of substantial cooperation during the unrest against Mubarak, which would have involved the Turkish government specifically informing and consulting the EU before and after the announcement of the Turkish position.

Conclusion

Analysing the timing and the substance of Turkish policy, it is possible to claim that the main factors influential in the Turkish decision-making process were Turkey's substantial interests in Egypt, including its citizens in the conflict zone, and the US position regarding the Mubarak regime. Turkish decision makers wanted to wait for the international reaction to become clearer, especially the US reaction, before supporting the opposition.

The Turkish decision to give support to democratic change was finalised on the weekend of 29–30 January after a telephone conversation with US President Obama. Arguably, the main reason to support the US position was because at that time it was clearer that Mubarak would not be able to retain office without US backing. The US specifically influenced the timing of the Turkish decision but not so much the substance of it, since supporting the opposition that was led by the Muslim Brotherhood was already in line with the interests of the Turkish government.

Considering the Turkish preference formation, it is possible to say that the reaction was based on a cost-benefit calculation. Specifically, the Turkish government avoided costly actions, which would have been criticising the Mubarak regime and supporting the opposition too quickly while there was uncertainty about the uprising.

The second part of the empirical analysis presented here focused on Turkish interactions with the EU to assess the degree of cooperation and identify underlying reasons for any such cooperation. The EU and the Turkish government, especially the EU HR and the Turkish FM, held informal talks during the course of the Egyptian uprising, which suggests that there was an exchange of views. Information exchange with the EU was useful in the sense that it allowed the Turkish government to keep up with developments at the EU's end with regard to transition in Egypt that would involve the Islamist Muslim Brotherhood.

The EU position was not clear when the Turkish government formulated its reaction, which is one of the main reasons why there was no consultation. Moreover, the Turkish government considered the EU to be an incapable actor and did not prefer reaching out to the EU in order to specifically inform or consult about the position that it was planning to take. The Turkish position, once it was finalised and announced, was communicated to the EU. So, there was at least "unilateral information" and possibly information exchange that involved the EU presenting its take, once it was formed. It is hardly possible to say that there was "consultation" but, based on the fact that there were informal telephone conversations between HR Ashton and FM Davutoğlu, it can be argued that the Turkish position did not catch the EU by surprise.

Another essential finding is that the Turkish government renewed its proposal for closer foreign policy cooperation with the EU at the start of the uprising, especially when the Turkish decision makers thought that the instability was likely to spread after the fall of Mubarak. So, the uprising against Mubarak triggered a strategic response to deal with the rising instability in the region. Although there was a proposal to seek consultation with the EU, it is not possible to claim that there was a genuine will to cooperate. It was beneficial for the Turkish government to propose more institutionalisation of foreign policy cooperation because Turkish decision makers were trying to sell the idea that Turkey was an asset to the EU that could make it more effective. The Turkish attitude to foreign policy cooperation with the EU at the time also explains the absence of "consultation" or "coordination" during the anti-Mubarak uprising, which would have involved the Turkish government reaching out to the EU and discussing its policy both before and after the public announcement of the Turkish position.

As for the specific factors determining the costs and benefits of cooperation with the EU, it can be claimed that Turkish decision makers prioritised long-term economic gains through seeking to establish good relations with post-Mubarak Egypt and supporting the opposition, which had a potential to become a strategic supporter of the Turkish government on regional issues. Once it had become clear that Mubarak had lost US support, which made it unlikely that he would retain power, supporting the opposition was immediately beneficial; however, achieving a higher degree of cooperation with the EU, such as "co-decision" or "consultation", was not a priority.

As a result, it is possible to say that the interaction during the CO can be described as lacking "consultation". However, there was at least "unilateral information", which means that, on the spectrum, the relationship was between the "unilateral information" and "consultation" points.

Notes

1 Referring to the incident between the Israeli President and Turkish PM at the Davos World Economic Forum in 2009. The Turkish PM stormed off the stage after a heated debate on the Israeli-Palestinian conflict. What the analysts emphasise is that after the incident, PM Erdoğan gained popularity among the Arab people for defending Gazans.
2 For example, in his address to the Arab League in Cairo in September 2011, PM Erdoğan reiterated that Turkey stood in solidarity with the Arab world against Israel. As a journalist observed, the Turkish PM used this speech to strengthen Turkey's campaign to become a more influential actor in the Middle East (Black, 2011).
3 This is a word play on Schengen using the word *Şam*, which is Turkish (and also Arabic: *ash-Sham*) for Damascus, Syria.
4 An Israeli military operation against civilian ships of the Gaza Freedom Flotilla killed Turkish citizens in 2010, resulting in a crisis between Israel and Turkey.
5 The potential rise of the Muslim Brotherhood also fit well with the Turkish government's use of neo-Ottoman rhetoric. The AKP elite believed that the uprisings could create a newly emerging regional order which Turkey could lead – for instance FM Davutoğlu (2012) stated, "A new Middle East is born. We will continue to be the owner, the pioneer, and the servant of this new Middle East." This view was heavily criticised by the opposition in Turkey. For example, the Vice Chairman of the CHP in charge of foreign relations, Osman Korutürk, criticised the government, saying that an irredentist rhetoric could undermine Turkey's relations with Middle Eastern states, who are not willing to follow the AKP in the long run (Interview TR08).

References

Andoni, L. (2010) "Erdogan 'Is No Gamal Abdel Nasser'", *Al Jazeera*, 20 June, www.aljazeera.com/focus/2010/06/201062093027892694.html.
Ashton, C. (2013) "Statement on the Current Situation in Egypt", Strasbourg, France, 13 March, http://europa.eu/rapid/press-release_SPEECH-13-221_en.htm?locale=en.
———. (2011a) "Remarks Following the First Part of Her Visit to Egypt", Cairo, Egypt, 22 February, http://europa.eu/rapid/press-release_SPEECH-11-116_en.htm.
———. (2011b) "Statement by EU High Representative Catherine Ashton on Egypt Following the Speech of President Mubarak", Brussels, Belgium, 10 February, www.consilium.europa.eu/uedocs/cms_Data/docs/pressdata/EN/foraff/119255.pdf.
———. (2011c) "Statement by the EU HR Ashton on Egypt", Brussels, 28 January, www.consilium.europa.eu/uedocs/cms_data/docs/pressdata/EN/foraff/118992.pdf.
———. (2011d) "Statement by the EU High Representative Catherine Ashton on the Events in Egypt", Brussels, 27 January, www.consilium.europa.eu/uedocs/cms_Data/docs/pressdata/EN/foraff/118963.pdf.
Bardakçı, M. (2011) "Kahire'deki unutulmuş skandal" ["The Forgotten Scandal in Cairo"], *Haberturk*, 23 September, www.haberturk.com/yazarlar/murat-bardakci/672257-kahiredeki-unutulmus-skandal.
BBC. (2011) "Egypt Protests: ElBaradei Tells Crowd 'Change Coming'", *BBC*, 30 January, www.bbc.com/news/world-middle-east-12320200.
Berberoğlu, E. (2011) "İslam Dünyası Kendine Yeter ama AB'ye Alternatif Değil" ["The Islamic World Is Self-Sufficient but Not an Alternative to the EU"], *Hürriyet*, 12 January, www.hurriyet.com.tr/islam-dunyasi-kendine-yeter-ama-ab-ye-alternatif-degil-16739292.
Berkan, İ. (2011) "Emperyalizmin uzun gölgesi" ["The Long Shadow of Imperialism"], *Hürriyet*, 30 January, www.hurriyet.com.tr/yazarlar/16888449.asp.
Biden, J. (2011) "Exclusive | Biden: Mubarak Is Not a Dictator, but People Have a Right to Protest", *PBS Newshour*, Interview with Jim Lehrer, 27 January.

Bilgenoğlu, A. (2010) "Arap Medyası Erdoğan'ı Hangi 'Darbeciye' Benzetiyor?" ["To Which 'Coupist' Does the Arab Media Compare Erdoğan?"] *Odatv*, 10 June, http:// odatv.com/arap-medyasi-erdogani-hangi-darbeciye-benzetiyor-1006101200.html.

Black, I. (2011) "Turkey Plays High-Stakes Game Positioning Itself at Heart of Arab World", *The Guardian*, 13 September, www.theguardian.com/world/2011/sep/13/ turkey-recep-erdogan-cairo.

Bölme, S.M., Küçükkeleş, M., Ulutaş, U., Özhan, T., Yılmaz, N., and Ensaroğlu, Y. (2011) *25 Ocak'tan Yeni Anayasa'ya: Mısır'da Dönüşümün Anatomisi* [*From 25 January to a New Constitution: The Anatomy of Transformation in Egypt*], Ankara, Turkey: Foundation for Political, Economic and Social Research (SETA).

Cihan. (2011a) "Başbakan Erdoğan, Mısır olaylarına değindi: Halktan gelen değişim arzusunu tereddüt etmeden karşılayın" ["Prime Minister Erdoğan: Meet the People's Desire for Change with No Hesitation"], *Cihan*, 1 February, www.cihan.com.tr/tr/basbakan-erdogan-misir-olaylarina-degindi-halktan-gelen-degisim-arzusunu-tereddut-etmeden-karsilayin-1-246325.htm.

———. (2011b) "Bakan Çağlayan: Mısır'a 6 bin 553 firma ihracat yapıyor" ["Minister Çağlayan: 6553 Firms Export to Egypt"], *Cihan*, 31 January, www.cihan.com.tr/tr/ bakan-caglayan-misira-6-bin-553-firma-ihracat-yapiyor-245682.htm.

The Council of the European Union. (2011) "Press Release. 3065th Council Meeting, Foreign Affairs", Brussels, Belgium, 31 January, http://europa.eu/rapid/press-release_ PRES-11-16_en.htm.

Cumhuriyet. (2011) "AKP oyun kurmaya çalışırken oyuncak oluyor" ["While Trying to Become a Pivotal Actor, the AKP Is Becoming Easily Influenced"], 30 January, www. cumhuriyet.com.tr/haber/diger/217572/_AKP_oyun_kurmaya_calisirken_oyuncak_ oluyor_.html.

———. (2009) "Müşterek çalışma içerisindeyiz" ["We Are Working Jointly"], *Cumhuriyet*, 11 February, www.cumhuriyet.com.tr/haber/diger/41266/_Musterek_calisma_ icerisindeyiz_.html.

Davutoğlu, A. (2013) "Transformation in World Politics: The Challenges for Global and Regional Order", *Contemporary Turkish Studies Lecture*, 7 March, London School of Economics and Political Science (LSE), London, UK.

———. (2012) "Speech at the Grand National Assembly of Turkey", Ankara, 26 April, www.mfa.gov.tr/disisleri-bakani-sayin-ahmet-davutoglu_nun-tbmm-genel-kurulu_nda-suriye_deki-olaylar-hakkinda-yaptigi-konusma_-26-nisan-2012.tr.mfa.

———. (2011a) "Twitter Page of Ahmet Davutoglu", https://twitter.com/Ahmet_Davutoglu [Accessed 12 April 2019].

———. (2011b) "Statement by HE Mr Ahmet Davutoğlu Minister of Foreign Affairs of Turkey in the 49th Session of the EU-Turkey Association Council", Brussels, Belgium, 19 April, http://register.consilium.europa.eu/doc/srv?l=EN&t=PDF&gc=true&sc=false &f=ST48052011INIT.

———. (2001) *Stratejik Derinlik* [*The Strategic Depth*], Istanbul: Küre Yayınları.

Erdoğan, R.T. (2011) "AK Parti grup toplantısı konuşması" ["Speech at AKP Group Meeting"], Ankara, Turkey, 1 February, www.akparti.org.tr/basbakan-erdoganin-ak-parti-grup-toplantisinda-yaptigi-konusmanin-tam-metni_7846.html.

European Council on Foreign Relations. (2012) *European Foreign Policy Scorecard 2012*, London, UK: European Council on Foreign Relations.

European External Action Service. (2010) "Statement of the European Union on the 6th Meeting of the EU-Egypt Association Council", Luxembourg, 27 April, http://eeas. europa.eu/egypt/aa/2010_eu-egypt_statement_en.pdf.

European Parliament. (2013) "Situation in Egypt: European Parliament Resolution of 14 March 2013 on the Situation in Egypt [2013/2542(RSP)]", Brussels, Belgium, 14 March, http://eur-lex.europa.eu/legal-content/EN/TXT/?toc=OJ%3AC%3A2016%3A0 36%3ATOC&uri=uriserv%3AOJ.C_.2016.036.01.0118.01.ENG.

Fırat, M., and Kürkçüoğlu, Ö. (2001) "Ortadoğu'yla İlişkiler", in Oran, B. (ed.), *Türk Dış Politikası Cilt 1: 1919–1980* [*Turkish Foreign Policy Volume 1: 1919–1980*], İstanbul: İletişim, pp. 615–53.

Gürcanlı, Z. (2011) "Erdoğan Mısır Halkına Seslenecek" ["Erdoğan Will Address the Egyptial People"], *Hürriyet*, 1 February, www.hurriyet.com.tr/gundem/16904134.asp.

Gürün, K. (1983) *Dış İlişkiler ve Türk Dış Politikası (1939'dan Günümüze Kadar)* [*Foreign Relations and Turkish Foreign Policy (from 1939 to Date)*], Ankara: Ankara Üniversitesi Siyasal Bilgiler Fakültesi.

Haaretz. (2011) "Israel Hopes Mubarak Resignation Won't Affect Bilateral Peace Accord", 11 February, www.haaretz.com/1.5121315.

Hamilton, D. (2011) "Israel Shocked by Obama's 'Betrayal' of Mubarak", *Reuters*, 31 January, www.reuters.com/article/2011/01/31/us-egypt-israel-usa-idUSTRE70U53720110131.

Hürriyet. (2011a) "Mısır'daki Türkler Tahliye Edilmeyi Bekliyor" ["Turks in Egypt Waiting to Be Evacuated"], *Hürriyet*, 28 January, www.hurriyet.com.tr/dunya/16881158.asp.

———. (2011b) "Mısır'da 'düzenli geçiş hükümeti'ne destek" ["Support for a Transitional Government in Egypt"], *Hürriyet*, 31 January, www.hurriyet.com.tr/dunya/16894736.asp?gid=0&srid=0&oid=0&l=1.

———. (2011c) "Mısır'dan 1444 Türk tahliye edildi" [1444 Turks Evacuated from Egypt"], *Hürriyet*, 31 January, www.hurriyet.com.tr/misirdan-1444-turk-tahliye-edildi-16895538.

———. (2011d) "25 Türk okula sığındı" [25 Turks Took Refuge in a School"], *Hürriyet*, 30 January, www.hurriyet.com.tr/25-turk-okula-sigindi-16889154.

———. (2010) "Erdoğan yeni Cemal Abdül Nasır olamaz" ["Erdoğan Cannot Be the New Abdel Nasser"], *Hürriyet*, 23 June, www.hurriyet.com.tr/planet/15087811.asp.

Hürriyet Daily News. (2011) "Turkish PM Erdoğan Urges Mubarak to Heed Egyptian Outcry", *Hürriyet Daily News*, 1 February, www.hurriyetdailynews.com/default.aspx?pageid=438&n=turkey-calls-on-mubarak-to-heed-calls-for-change-2011-02-01.

Lander, M. (2011) "Obama Cautions Embattled Ally Against Violence", *New York Times*, 28 January, www.nytimes.com/2011/01/29/world/middleeast/29diplo.html.

Ministry of Foreign Affairs of Turkey. (2015) "Relations Between Turkey and Egypt", Ankara, Turkey, www.mfa.gov.tr/relations-between-turkey-egypt.en.mfa.

———. (2011) "Twitter Page of the Ministry of Foreign Affairs of Turkey", https://twitter.com/TC_Disisleri.

Pertusot, V. (2011) "Tiptoeing Around the Issue: Europe's Response to the Egyptian Uprising", *Carnegie Europe*, 27 May, https://carnegieeurope.eu/2011/05/27/tiptoeing-around-issue-europe-s-response-to-egyptian-uprising-pub-44230.

Pinfari, M. (2013) "The EU, Egypt and Morsi's Rise and Fall: 'Strategic Patience' and Its Discontents", *Mediterranean Politics* 18(3): 460–66.

Raddatz, M., and Wong, K. (2011) "Egypt, Yemen Protests Unnerve U.S. Officials", *ABC News*, 27 January, http://abcnews.go.com/WN/egypt-yemen-protests-spark-fears-us-officials/story?id=12780724.

Ravid, B. (2011) "Israel Urges Allies to Curb Criticism of Mubarak", *Haaretz*, 31 January, www.haaretz.com/1.5115335.

Reuters. (2011) "US Urges Restraint in Egypt, Says Government Stable", *Reuters*, 25 January, www.reuters.com/article/2011/01/25/ozatp-egypt-protest-clinton-idAFJOE70O0 KF20110125.

Sadiki, L. (2015) *Routledge Handbook of the Arab Spring: Rethinking Democratization*, New York: Routledge.

Tankersley, C. (2011) "Netanyahu: Egyptian Extremists Represent 'Tremendous Threat'", *CNN*, 31 January, http://edition.cnn.com/2011/WORLD/meast/01/31/egypt.protests. israel/.

UK Prime Minister's Office. (2011) "Joint UK-France-Germany Statement on Egypt", 10 Downing Street, London, UK, 29 January, www.gov.uk/government/news/ joint-uk-france-germany-statement-on-egypt.

Ülsever, C. (2011) "Hayal ile gerçek arasında: 'Biz bize yeteriz'" ["Between Reality and Imagination: 'We Are Self-Sufficient'"], *Hürriyet*, 16 January, www.hurriyet.com.tr/ yazarlar/16775529.asp.

Waterfield, B. (2011) "Baroness Ashton in Political Correctness Row Over Word 'Christian'", *The Telegraph*, 1 February, www.telegraph.co.uk/news/worldnews/europe/ eu/8296403/Baroness-Ashton-in-political-correctness-row-over-word-Christian.html.

Yenel, S. (2012) "Turkey and the New Middle East: Blueprint For Arab Transformations", Speech, Carnegie Europe, Brussels, Belgium, 26 January, http://carnegieendowment. org/files/26-01-2012_Turkey_and_the_New_Middle_East.pdf.

Yetkin, M. (2011) "Dış Politikada Sükûtu Hayal" ["Disappointment in Foreign Policy"], *Radikal*, 13 January, www.radikal.com.tr/yazarlar/murat_yetkin/ dis_politikada_suktu_hayal-1036303.

Zaman. (2009a) "Mısır'da Davutoğlu fırtınası esti" ["Davutoğlu Took Egypt by Storm"], *Zaman*, 4 September, www.zaman.com.tr/dunya_misirda-davutoglu-firtinasi-esti_888526.html.

———. (2009b) "Gül'den Mısır liderine 'vizeyi kaldıralım' teklifi" ["Gül's Proposal to the President of Egypt to Lift Visas"], *Zaman*, 16 December, www.zaman.com.tr/dunya_ gulden-misir-liderine-vizeyi-kaldiralim-teklifi_927835.html.

Zengin, G. (2013) *Kavga: Arap Baharı'nda Türk Dış Politikası* [*Conflict: Turkish Foreign Policy in the Arab Spring*], İstanbul: İnkılap.

Zeyrek, D. (2011) "Mısır kardeşliği: Obama-Erdoğan'dan işbirliği çağrısı" ["Egypt Solidarity: Call for Cooperation from Obama and Erdoğan"], *Radikal*, 31 January, www. radikal.com.tr/turkiye/misir_kardesligi_obama_erdogandan_isbirligi_cagrisi-1038488.

5 Turkey's foreign policy cooperation with the EU during the Libyan Civil War of 2011

Following the anti-government protests on 15 February 2011, hundreds of protesters clashed with police and government supporters in Libya's second largest city, Benghazi. Shortly thereafter, violence escalated and spread to other cities in Libya, triggering a civil war between forces loyal to Colonel Muammar Gaddafi and those seeking to oust his government. On 22 February, Gaddafi said he would fight "to his last drop of blood" to remain in power and denounced the anti-regime protesters as "rats" and "mercenaries" working for foreign agendas. On 26 February, the United Nations Security Council (UNSC) adopted Resolution 1970, condemning the violence against civilians and demanding an immediate end to the violence. On 17 March, the UNSC passed Resolution 1973, authorising a no-fly zone and "all necessary measures" to enforce it to protect civilians. Within days, NATO forces intervened. On 20 October, Gaddafi was killed and a regime change followed.

This chapter discusses the interests of the EU and Turkey in Libya and their responses to the crisis, and analyses Turkey's interaction with the EU regarding specific cooperative opportunities (COs) in order to assess why and to what degree there was cooperation (Table 5.1). The main question around potential cooperation for the EU and Turkey was how to react to the Gaddafi regime, including to its repression of protests and to the issue of whether to support the opposition. As will be discussed, the Turkish government faced questions of when to criticise the regime, what measures to take, and how to respond to the opposition movements.

Interests and reactions

A discussion of the approaches of Turkey and the EU in the face of the uprising is useful for the assessment of their cooperation. First, this section discusses the Turkish preferences and approach, focusing on the way in which the initial Turkish response was based on finding a balance between standing up for the Libyan people and protecting strategic interests in Libya through refraining from antagonising Colonel Gaddafi. In terms of policy choices, this meant that the Turkish government was not critical of the regime until criticism was not seen to be a costly action anymore. When the costs decreased after the evacuation of Turkish citizens, and after the international community was clearly against the Gaddafi

Table 5.1 Cooperative opportunities during the Libyan uprising

	Turkish government preference	Turkish government action	EU preference	Outcome in terms of cooperation
CO2: Initial Turkish reaction	Ensuring the safety of Turkish assets in Libya without damaging relations with Gaddafi too much	Avoidance of harsh criticism against the Gaddafi regime	Harsh criticism and sanctions against the Gaddafi regime	Information exchange despite divergence of views
CO3: Evacuation of citizens	Taking all necessary steps to ensure the evacuation of Turkish citizens, including asking Gaddafi for favours	Evacuation operation by sea	Evacuation operations by the EU and individual member states	Unilateral information. EU nationals evacuated by Turkey upon request by individual member states
CO4: Intervention in Libya	Initially strong opposition, then support for NATO intervention. A desire to be a part of the inevitable international action	Eventual support and participation in NATO intervention	Support for NATO allies	Turkish action influenced by international developments. Foreign policy dialogue at informational stage

regime, Turkish decision makers started to voice criticism (specifically after 1 February 2011). Then, this section moves on to identify the priorities as well the shortcomings of the EU policy, focusing on the EU preferences with regard to Libya, and finds that the EU prioritised its strategic interests, including energy resources. This analysis highlights the differences of views between the EU and Turkey and the implications for potential cooperation.

Turkish preferences

The Turkish government saw the Gaddafi regime as a strategic partner prior to the Arab Spring. The reaction of the Turkish government to the uprisings in the Arab world showed an "ethics versus self-interest dilemma" (Öniş, 2012: 46), which involved finding a delicate balance between supporting reform movements and protecting strategic interests. This dilemma can especially be seen in the reaction of the Turkish government to the crisis in Libya. The Turkish policy towards the region in the AKP era prior to the Arab Spring had two prominent dimensions: an economic dimension, with policy aimed at fostering transnational trade and economic interdependence; and a cultural dimension, based on cultural affinity and Muslim fraternity, with policy aimed at promoting closer political ties (ibid). Stronger ties with Libya were consistent with the idea of a "new" Turkish foreign policy. Libya was a former Ottoman province, a strategic ally in North Africa for Turkey to develop its newly formed policy in Africa, and an important trade partner in the Mediterranean.

In Turkey-Libya relations, since Libya gained independence, there was a long period of indifference until PM Turgut Özal visited Libya in an attempt to develop ties in the 1980s. Other attempts to form ties with Libya came from PM Tansu Çiller (1993–1996) and from PM Necmettin Erbakan (1996–1997), whose idea of building close relations with Islamic states led him to include Libya in his Africa tour. However, Gaddafi did not respond to Turkey's invitations for a reciprocal visit.

In the AKP era (after 2002), which also corresponds to the period in which Libya normalised its relations with the West and discontinued its nuclear program, relations were greatly improved, especially after PM Erdoğan's key visit to Tripoli in November 2009. During his visit, Turkey and Libya mutually lifted visa requirements and signed numerous agreements in various fields, including investment, agriculture, and transportation. The Turkish minister responsible for foreign trade at the time underlined that 85 per cent of the undertakings of Turkish construction and infrastructure companies in Africa (amounting to USD 21 billion) were in Libya (*Hürriyet*, 2009). Furthermore, the visit coincided with *Eid al-Adha*. When mentioning that lifting visas was an important step in developing closer economic ties, PM Erdoğan pointed out that "Turkey [had] lifted visas with Syria in *Eid al-Fitr* and with Libya in *Eid al-Adha*" (*Sabah*, 2009). This is an example of how religious references were used in bilateral relations to enhance political relations. The PM also stressed that Turkey saw Libya as a "vital partner" for the "Opening to Africa" policy of Turkey as well as for the Turkish counter-terrorism policy and mentioned that the "friendship and brotherhood between Libya and Turkey had a unique characteristic" (ibid.). This shows how the notion that Libya was a "brother" state to Turkey was being used in political discourse. Moreover, it was reported that, in his tent, Colonel Gaddafi told PM Erdoğan that he appreciated Turkish foreign policy, especially after PM Erdoğan had stormed out of a heated debate on the Gaza war with Israel's President Shimon Peres at the Davos forum on 29 January 2009 (ibid.).

Bilateral relations continued to improve rapidly in 2010 too. In November 2010, a few months before the start of the crisis in Libya, Colonel Gaddafi invited PM Erdoğan to the EU-African Union Summit in Tripoli as an "honorary guest". It was reported that PM Erdoğan was initially not in the group picture, but after Colonel Gaddafi's gesture of goodwill, he was included in the photo with other world leaders (Şenyüz, 2010). In his visit, Erdoğan was given the "Al-Gaddafi International Prize for Human Rights". During his speech, PM Erdoğan claimed that the Turkey-Libya partnership was "exemplary" and stressed that by mutually lifting visas between Libya and Turkey, they had "ended the hundred years of longing between nations" (Haberturk, 2010).

It is therefore possible to claim that the Turkish policy towards Libya in the AKP era prior to the onset of the crisis in February 2011 consisted of two fundamental aspects. First, there was an economic aspect based on mutual gains from building closer economic relations. Turkish companies, especially construction and infrastructure companies, played an important role in this area. Second, there was a cultural aspect that was used to maintain good political ties that complemented the improvement of economic relations. The cultural aspect was based on shared Ottoman history and Muslim culture. As Gaddafi spelled out in relation to the Davos incident, he appreciated that under the AKP, Turkish foreign policy favoured Muslim states over old allies, such as Israel. In other words, the cultural aspect worked as a glue – it aimed to maintain good political relations so that mutually beneficial economic interdependence could continue to develop. As a result of this rapprochement, thousands of Turks went to Libya to work and live, and these two fundamental aspects of Turkish policy were the main reasons why so many Turkish citizens were stranded when the crisis started, which will be discussed in depth later on.

It should be stressed here that the rapprochement was strategic in nature in line with the "zero problems with neighbours" policy of the AKP government. In other words, there was a general interest in Libya as a former Ottoman territory, and interests were not tied to the specific person of Gaddafi as much as they had been to Morsi and the Muslim Brotherhood in Egypt, which this book will discuss later. This means that support for Gaddafi might therefore have resulted from a desire to avoid uncertainty but had less of an ideological/cultural underpinning than was the case in Egypt.

The function of this section on interests is to assess whether cooperation was particularly costly. Similar to the EU, the Turkish government saw the Gaddafi regime as an important strategic partner and had vital interests at stake in maintaining a close relationship. Yet, in contrast to the EU, the Turkish government had fewer concerns about Gaddafi's human rights record. As will be discussed, PM Erdoğan even refused to talk about the fact that he had received the "Al-Gaddafi International Prize for Human Rights" when there was a public debate in Turkey about whether or not he should return the prize.

Essentially, the Turkish government had established a close relationship with the Gaddafi regime, presumably closer than the EU-Libya relationship, and had strong strategic and economic interests in Libya. Moreover, the relationship was one of the success stories of the new Turkish foreign policy, and the regime was seen as a supporter of the Turkish government in regional affairs. What ultimately made a difference was that it was difficult for the Turkish government to let go of its relationship with the Libyan regime without being certain that it was going to fall. A discussion of Turkish interests is especially helpful when seeking to understand the initial approach of the Turkish government in the face of unrest in Libya. The main question around potential cooperation for the EU and Turkey was how to respond to the Gaddafi regime. Specifically, because the strategic value of relations with Libya was high, the Turkish government paused before joining those, including the EU, who harshly criticised the Gaddafi regime and imposed sanctions.

When the crisis began, Turkish policy makers showed a certain degree of reluctance to criticise the Gaddafi regime, preferring to avoid any statements on the grounds that what was going on in Libya was a domestic issue. The Turkish government did not align itself with those who imposed sanctions, including the EU, which was the main policy divergence from the EU and will be discussed in detail later. Then, there was a change from reluctant involvement towards vocal criticism of Gaddafi, which was very similar to the initial reaction of the Turkish government to the uprising in Syria.

There were two prominent turning points that need to be mentioned in the Turkish reaction until alignment with the international community. As Efegil (2012) mentions, the Turkish government had more than one turning point, and these were due to changing circumstances. The first one was in the period from the start of the conflict until the end of February (15–28 February). In this period, Turkish policy makers were reluctant to engage in the conflict and avoided making statements against Gaddafi. They had a chance to impose sanctions and call for Gaddafi's resignation; however, they chose not to intervene in the "domestic affairs" of Libya, continued to talk to Gaddafi (Erdoğan stated on 24 February that he had talked to Gaddafi on the telephone three times since the crisis had started) and opposed discussing sanctions or intervention altogether (*Sabah*, 2011a). The first turning point was at the end of February when the Turkish government adopted a critical stance, advising Gaddafi on what to do, expressing concerns over the situation, and calling for an end to the violence. However, it was still reluctant regarding any possible military intervention, while, at that point, the issue was under discussion by actors in the international arena.

The second turning point was when Turkey changed its position on intervention and started supporting NATO involvement. As the European Commission (2011b: 107) highlighted in Turkey's Progress Report, "Turkey *eventually* agreed to support NATO's command of operations for the enforcement of UNSC Resolutions 1970 and 1973 on Libya" [emphasis added]. After participating in the NATO intervention, the Turkish government aligned itself with the international community until the end of the crisis. This was a dramatic change of policy because the Turkish PM had previously opposed any intervention in Libya and had accused states of discussing intervention of imperialism.

EU preferences

Over the course of the Libyan uprising, the EU received sharp criticism regarding its response to the crisis in Libya on the grounds that it was too slow, too weak, too divided, and essentially incoherent (see e.g., Koenig, 2011: 11–30; *The Economist*, 2011; McNamara, 2011). This was mainly due to divergent opinions among major EU members, such as Germany disagreeing with the UK and France over the critical issues of the no-fly zone and the recognition of insurgents (e.g., Germany decided to abstain from voting on UN Security Council Resolution 1973 authorising a no-fly zone). The EU's incapability to act in a timely and effectively manner, especially at a time when the US looked to its European partners to take the lead, led observers to mark the effective end of the Common Security and Defence Policy (CSDP), and of course the Common Foreign and Security Policy (CFSP), of which the CSDP formed a part (Menon, 2011: 76). An anonymous EU diplomat even declared that the "CFSP died in Libya – we just have to pick a sand dune under which we can bury it" (Atlantic Council, 2011). A lot has been written on why the EU did not live up to expectations and what that means for the EU's aspiration to be a global actor (Menon, 2011). The important point for this analysis is that there was not a clear or strong "EU position" but divergence across member states, which also had implications for the possibility of cooperation of Turkey with the EU.

Despite its internal problems, the EU managed to employ a wide range of crisis management tools in response to the situation, including diplomatic tools, humanitarian assistance, and restrictive measures against the Gaddafi family. For example, the first EU response came on 20 February: High Representative Catherine Ashton issued a statement saying that the Union was "extremely concerned by the events unfolding in Libya" (Ashton, 2011b) and urged the authorities to stop the violence. On 11 March, the European Council declared that the Gaddafi government had lost its legitimacy and recognised the National Transitional Council of Libya (NTC) as a transitional government, urging Gaddafi to step down (European Council, 2011). On 22 May, the European External Action Service (EEAS, 2011b) opened a liaison office in Benghazi in order to support the democratic transition.

What is important for the analysis here of cooperation between Turkey and the EU is the strategic importance of Libya for the EU so that we can have an idea of the EU interests at stake in the Libyan crisis. In other words, the EU needed Turkish cooperation much more than Turkey needed the EU's. Moreover, Libya was more important for the EU than Egypt since Libya was not only an ally of the EU in the region after the normalisation of relations but also a source for the EU's energy needs, on which this analysis will elaborate. Therefore, it is particularly important to examine EU-Libya relations prior to the uprising too.

It is possible to claim that the Libyan regime was an important ally for the EU in three main areas: energy, counter-terrorism, and fighting illegal migration. As a re-orientation of foreign policy after Libya had been subject to isolation and sanctions as a sponsor of terrorism, Colonel Gaddafi signed trade deals and friendship treaties with various European leaders throughout the 2000s and was able to present himself as a valuable partner in fighting terrorism and illegal migration. Particularly, Libya's decision to abort its nuclear program in 2003 boosted its relations with the EU. In 2005, the Council of Ministers initiated "dialogue and cooperation with Libya on migration issues" as a "priority work" and concluded with a decision to work on the EU-Libya Action Plan (The Council of the European Union, 2005). Libya was described as a "fundamental energy exporter to the EU", and the EU started to negotiate a Framework Agreement in November 2008 with the aim of including a Free Trade Agreement covering trade in goods dominated by gas and oil (European Commission, 2013). As one commentator highlighted, towards the end of the 2000s, Libya became "one of the most rated prospective partners in Mediterranean Africa – a key energy supplier, an indispensable migrant gate-keeper, a huge trading partner, an important ally in the global 'war on terrorism', and a good interlocutor for improving EU-Africa dialogue as well" (Gioanna, 2010: 2).

However, there was one problem. The country was still a dictatorship with a poor human rights record. Human Rights Watch (2008) welcomed the strengthening of EU-Libya relations but stipulated "not at the expense of human rights". Scholars criticised the EU on the grounds that the relationship did not put human rights and democracy at the forefront (see e.g., Zoubir, 2009), even though the promotion of human rights and democracy were two fundamental aims of the European Neighbourhood Policy (ENP), which covered Libya. Other commentators (e.g., Koenig, 2011; Zoubir, 2009) have criticised the EU on the grounds that it was merely trying to satisfy member states' energy and migration concerns. A particular example to point to the way in which the Gaddafi regime had become a strategic partner for the EU is Colonel Gaddafi's visit to Italy in 2009. He was given a red-carpet welcome in Italy (which is, along with Malta, affected the most by illegal migration coming into the EU from Africa), and the top item on the agenda was strengthening the partnership on the issue of tackling illegal migration.

To sum up, leaving aside the normative questions raised by having a close relationship with an authoritarian country, what could be claimed about the EU's strategic interests in Libya was that there were three fundamental aspects of the relationship that concerned Brussels particularly. First, Libya had energy resources that the EU needed. Second, having close relations with the Libyan regime provided an opportunity for the EU to address the issue of illegal migrants more effectively. And third, Libya was a strategic ally in the region who could boost the EU's capability regarding counter-terrorism and influence in regional matters.

Fundamentally, both Turkey and the EU saw Libya as a strategic partner and had an interest in the restoration of stability in Libya. However, when the crisis began, they did not react in a similar way, as the next section will discuss in detail. The way in which there were internal divisions in the EU particularly made cooperation difficult. In the next section, the Turkish behaviour regarding particular COs will be examined in depth and the interactions between the Turkish government and the EU will be analysed in order to assess why and to what extent there was cooperation. The empirical analysis in the next section will draw on the interests and reactions discussed in this section.

Initial Turkish reaction to the violence and Turkish decision to support the opposition in Libya on 1 March

After the crisis had started, there was a possibility for cooperation regarding how to react to the uprising, particularly how to respond to the Gaddafi regime. Despite the divergence of views between the Turkish government and the EU, there was continuous communication on the matter, which allowed a mutual understanding of each other's policy. Following a discussion of the nature of divergence and the motivations of Turkey's initial behaviour, the interactions between the EU and the Turkish government are examined to assess the extent to which there was cooperation.

At the start of the crisis in mid-February, there was a clear distinction in the way in which Turkey and the EU reacted. This distinction can be seen particularly with regard to the issue of sanctions against the Gaddafi regime. Turkey was extremely reluctant to take any action that would jeopardise its relations with the Gaddafi regime; whereas, the EU was determined to impose restrictive measures and cut its relations with the regime right away. Even though their reactions were different, there was a clear line of communication between the EU and the Turkish government, especially through informal ministerial dialogue, and this would suggest that both the EU and the Turkish government were keeping each other informed about their positions.

Specifically, following the violence, the EU harshly criticised the Libyan government, but the Turkish government refrained from using language that Turkish decision makers thought would upset Gaddafi. What constrained the Turkish government was the large number of Turkish citizens inside Libya and the possibility that they might be harmed if Turkey took sides against Gaddafi. So, the main driver of the initial Turkish behaviour, and essentially what led to the divergence from the EU on the matter, was the Turkish government's fear that it could be drawn into a serious crisis in the event that large numbers of Turkish citizens could become stranded, lost, or killed in the violence. Indeed, this concern was only a part of the story because holding back criticism was in line with the Turkish government's interests, and Turkish decision makers preferred to see the events as internal affairs of Libya. So, to a certain degree, the concern for Turkish citizens in Libya can also be regarded as a convenient and legitimate coverup in the domestic arena until it was clearer whether Gaddafi could retain power.

The Turkish government viewed the possibility that Turkish citizens might be harmed as an important security issue in two ways. First, it was a security issue because it had the potential to draw Turkey directly into the conflict. Second, the Turkish government was concerned that, if anything were to happen to Turkish citizens in Libya, it would put the government in an undesirable position in the domestic political arena; whereas, if they could repatriate Turkish nationals safely, they might take credit for successful crisis management. So, the issue of Turkish citizens could also be seen as a matter of political survival for decision makers.

Essentially, openly criticising the regime right away would have been costly. Stepping back and observing the situation was preferable, at least until there was no danger for Turkish citizens and it was clearer whether Gaddafi could hold power. Therefore, the safe evacuation of Turkish citizens was prioritised before any comments that could risk relations with Gaddafi were made.

Another contributing factor to Turkish behaviour was resistance from the "zero problems with neighbours" policy. Similar to the case of Syria, Turkish policy makers had developed close ties with the Gaddafi regime, consistent with their understanding of the "new" Turkish foreign policy, and they did not wish to turn against the regime unless absolutely necessary. They did not want to cut relations and let the strategic relationship that they had built go to waste, so to speak, right away. Moreover, the "zero problems with neighbours" policy had the ambition to make Turkey influential as a rising soft power in the region, and Turkish policy makers even believed they had the potential to play a mediating role in the uprisings, which was especially evident in the case of Syria. It was undesirable to openly criticise the regime and abandon this policy straight away, and it would have been costly to cut all ties with a strategic partner. Instead, staying disengaged while observing the international reaction in order to make a better judgement about how to respond to the crisis was a more convenient action. To put it simply, the large number of Turkish nationals in Libya was the main determinant of the Turkish behaviour, but it should also be pointed out that Turkish decision makers were not initially keen to criticise Gaddafi because they saw their new alliance with Gaddafi as a success story of their new foreign policy.

Moreover, in order to appear friendly to Gaddafi before the evacuation of Turkish citizens, Turkish officials strongly opposed the idea of foreign intervention and sanctions. Some of them even played the anti-Western card, dismissing intervention as an act of imperialism, and tried to appeal to the anti-imperialist sentiments of the Libyan authorities (e.g., the Turkish PM himself implied that the West was making plans to capture Libya's oil resources (Erdoğan, 2011a)).

The Turkish government adopted a more critical approach and imposed sanctions, although it had concerns over their consequences for the Turkish economy, when the evacuation operation was being finalised, which will be the main focus of the next section (Figure 5.1). Throughout the crisis, there were talks with the EU involving foreign policy matters and, as will be discussed in more detail shortly, they were up-to-date on each other's policy, which indicates that it is unlikely that the Turkish position caught the EU by surprise.

To elaborate, the primary Turkish concern was the fact that there was a mass of Turkish citizens in Libya (amounting to 25,000 people – more than the number many other states had). On the fifth day of the uprising (19 February), during his trip to India, when asked about the crisis in Libya, FM Davutoğlu stated that Turkish citizens were very "dense" in Libya, and Turkey was preparing to act to ensure their well-being, which made it clear that the evacuation of Turkish citizens was going to be the top priority of the Turkish government (*Hürriyet*, 2011a).

Another important point about Davutoğlu's statement in India was that he made it clear that he was in touch with the EU regarding the crisis. He specifically mentioned that during his visit, he had had a number of telephone conversations, one of which was with the EU High Representative, and he revealed that he was going to meet with her, upon her request, to discuss developments in Libya (ibid.). This is an important piece of information because it indicates that there was communication with the EU in the area of foreign policy and specifically on the matter of Libya during the period when the Turkish government was preparing its response. When asked to elaborate on foreign policy dialogue with Turkey, the

Monday	Tuesday	Wednesday	Thursday	Friday	Saturday	Sunday
14	15 Uprising starts in Libya	16	17	18	19 Turkey avoids criticism and starts evacuation	20
21 Erdoğan- Gaddafi telephone calls	22 EU discusses sanctions	23 EU introduces measures	24	25	26 UNSCR 1970/2011	27
28 Further EU sanctions	1 Evacuation completed, U-turn in Turkish policy	2	3	4	5	6

Figure 5.1 Timeline of events showing the U-turn in Turkish position in February 2011

Turkey advisor of the EU High Representative confirmed that the High Representative and Davutoğlu were frequently in touch in formal and informal settings to exchange views during the Libyan crisis (Interview EU04). Davutoğlu's statement indicates that there was at least information exchange when the Turkish government was formulating its policy.

On the fifth day of the uprising, the Ministry of Foreign Affairs of Turkey was alarmed by reports of Turkish construction sites being looted by opposition groups in Libya. The Turkish minister in charge of trade expressed his concerns about the looting, while the Ministry of Foreign Affairs declared that two planes were on their way to airlift Turkish citizens to safety (Aktan, 2011). The first plane landed in Istanbul on 20 February with 287 Turkish citizens who claimed they had "no safety" in Libya (*Hürriyet*, 2011b, 2011c). After this point, the government became increasingly concerned about how the violence would affect Turkish citizens. Moreover, after such a public statement, the government felt that it was imperative that they evacuate Turkish citizens first before proceeding with any openly critical action, such as imposing sanctions. According to a political officer at the EU Delegation in Ankara, this was not a position openly communicated to the EU (Interview EU02).

The reluctance of the Turkish government to be critical came at the expense of the government's image because it appeared to be protecting the Gaddafi regime. However, the government continued to refrain from using harsh language. Notably, on 21 February, the Turkish PM stated that he had no intention of giving back the "Al-Gaddafi International Prize for Human Rights" that he had received earlier in November 2010. He attracted wide criticism in Turkey, especially from the leader of the opposition, who criticised his silence (Cumhuriyet Halk Partisi, 2011). The main criticism, and the main question, was why Turkish decision makers were disengaged and avoiding open statements about Libya. The Prime Minister's office issued a statement saying that the prize was not going to be returned but, more importantly, the PM accused the opposition leader of being "irresponsible" for bringing up the prize and criticising the government (Işık and Tutcalı, 2011). His precise words once again show that the main reason why the government avoided criticising Gaddafi was the large number of Turkish citizens in Libya at the time. The PM stated:

> If you ask how many Turkish citizens live in Libya, he [the opposition leader] wouldn't know. He doesn't know about Turkish investments there. . . . But only to criticise the AKP, he can go so far as to undermine the security of [Turkish] citizens. . . . Today we have a minimum of 25 thousand citizens and over 200 businessmen there.
>
> (Euractiv, 2011a)

Whether or not to return the prize had symbolic value, and the questions around the prize also prompted a clearer response from the government from which to work out the Turkish position with regard to the Gaddafi regime. Clearly, the controversy showed once again that the avoidance of criticising Gaddafi was about the Turkish citizens and assets in Libya. Also, due to the controversy around the prize, it was clear that the Turkish government, as of 21 February (the seventh day of the uprising), had not been openly critical of the Libyan regime.

In fact, Turkish decision makers continued to make statements appearing friendly to Gaddafi. For instance, the FM stated (on 21 February, the seventh day of the crisis) that Turkey did not want a civil war in Libya, without a word directed at Gaddafi (Sabah, 2011b). The minister responsible for foreign trade emphasised that Turkey and Libya had a "close friendship" but at the same time underlined that Turkey's "primary expectation and request" from Libya was to ensure the safety of Turkish citizens in Libya (*Hürriyet*, 2011e). The minister also added that there was "no need for too much panic" because no harm had been done to Turkish citizens at that time. However, the Ministry of Foreign Affairs established a crisis centre for Turkish citizens as a precaution (*Hürriyet*, 2011c). At least until the evacuation was complete, the Gaddafi regime was not to be upset.

Again, on the seventh day of the crisis, there were voices in the Gaddafi government claiming that Turkish citizens were involved in groups who were planning the anti-Gaddafi demonstrations in order to serve foreign agendas. It was even reported by Libyan national news agencies that some Turkish citizens were being held under arrest because of their connections to "Zionist groups" (Lüle, 2011a). The Turkish government was alarmed again, not just because of these rumours but also because Turkish planes were unable to land. The Turkish PM made two telephone calls to Gaddafi on 21 February. It was reported that Gaddafi promised to help with the problems of Turkish citizens in Libya and that the following conversation took place between the two:

ERDOĞAN: What's going on with the turmoil?
GADDAFI: Nothing important. There are some opposition groups but the people support me.
ERDOĞAN: There is a problem in Benghazi. Our planes cannot land.
GADDAFI: Send your planes. There is no problem (Lüle, 2011a; *Sabah*, 2011c).

Meanwhile, the Turkish media focused on the silence of the Turkish government regarding the Gaddafi regime. A Turkish journalist who travelled with the Turkish FM on 21 February observed:

> Inevitably, we began to talk about Libya. Minister Davutoğlu deliberately avoids making a political statement but underlines only one thing: 'our utmost priority is the safety of our citizens'. . . . Despite all our efforts, we cannot make the Minister talk. The message of 'listen to the voices coming from streets' that both Erdoğan and Davutoğlu previously sent to the Mubarak regime somehow does not come from the government for Libya. . . . In Egypt, there were 2,000 Turkish citizens but the number is 25,000 in Libya. Turkey fears that its citizens will be targeted in the event that it sends a political message. To our questions about why Turkey is so silent, all we can get is the answer: 'the Arab world is not one, the situation in every country is different'. To sum up, for now, the government will remain silent for its citizens. The political attitude will only be shown after the evacuations are complete.
> (Gürcanlı, 2011)

A day later, on 22 February, the question of why Turkey was silent was also directed at the Turkish President, who made similar remarks to the FM and specifically underlined that Turkey's priority was to ensure the safety of its citizens in Libya while avoiding any criticism of Gaddafi (*Hürriyet*, 2011f).

There was no mention from the Turkish government of sanctions or intervention, while these were, at this point, being discussed between EU member states. For instance, on the EU side, on the same day (22 February, the eighth day of the crisis), there was a Council of Foreign Ministers meeting in Brussels, and the Council strongly "condemned the ongoing repression against demonstrators in Libya" (The Council of the European Union, 2011a: 2). It was reported that during the heated debate, the Finnish foreign minister clearly pushed the EU to impose sanctions against the Libyan regime (Phillips, 2011), which was well founded, especially after the UN Security Council had urged "the Government of Libya to meet its responsibility to protect its population" on 22 February (United Nations Security Council, 2011).

The Turkish government was still fully occupied with the evacuation of Turkish citizens, particularly because they were alarmed by the remarks of the Turkish consul general in Benghazi, who said that the lives of the remaining Turkish citizens were in danger and that there was an "urgent" need to speed up the evacuation (*Hürriyet*, 2011b). It was shortly thereafter reported on 22 February that approximately 4,000 Turkish citizens were stranded without enough food or water, having taken refuge in a hangar near Benghazi (Lüle, 2011b).

So, at this point in time, the priority for the Turkish government was the evacuation operation, and, as mentioned earlier, it was not so keen to criticise Gaddafi anyway because the Turkish decision makers preferred stability over regime change. It was still not clear whether Gaddafi could retain power, and it was less costly for the Turkish government to keep the line of communication open with him so that the Turkish PM could talk to him in case Turkish planes and ships needed the assistance of the Libyan government.

On 23 February (the ninth day of the crisis), welcoming the statement of the UNSC, the EU issued a statement condemning the "repression against peaceful demonstrators" and "brutal mass violations of human rights" and declared that it had decided to "suspend negotiations with Libya on the EU-Libya Framework Agreement" (Ashton, 2011a). The EU invited the Turkish government to join the EU statement and to introduce restrictive measures against the Libyan regime, but the Turkish government turned these down. The EU noted that it was "ready to take further measures" and called on the government of Libya to meet its responsibility to protect its population (ibid.). When the EU was making such critical statements against the Gaddafi regime, the Turkish government kept its silence.

It is important to clarify how the process regarding EU statements worked at this stage. The Turkish government was invited to join the EU statement; however, it refused to do so. A political officer at the EU Delegation in Ankara explained the interaction during that period: "The [EU] delegation was constantly in touch with the MFA and Turkish officials. We received instructions from our capital, Brussels, to explain our policy to Turkey and to try to get them on board" (Interview EU02). So, mainly through the delegation, the EU side explained its policy and, following the procedure, invited the Turkish government to declare its alignment with a statement that read: "We strongly condemn the violence and use of force against civilians and deplore the repression against peaceful demonstrators", stressing that "those responsible for the brutal aggression and violence against civilians will be held to account" (Ashton, 2011a).

However, the invitation to join the EU statement was a "take-it-or-leave-it" offer because the Turkish side could not comment on the decision since it was not officially a part of the decision-making mechanism. As the interviewee clarified, "Once the EU statement is approved, you accept it as it is or you don't accept it. There is no room for consultation or compromise" (Interview EU02). Also, through the delegation, EU officials were receiving information about the Turkish position (ibid.). Therefore, the nature of interaction involved information exchange, as both sides kept abreast of each other's views, but also an absence of much discussion.

Similarly, when the EU declared its sanctions, the Turkish side was still hesitant to be critical of the Gaddafi regime and refused to join the EU statements. On 28 February (the 14th day of the crisis), the EU adopted "a decision implementing the

UN Security Council Resolution on Libya of 26 February (UNSCR, 1970/2011)" and imposed "additional restrictive measures against those responsible for the violent crackdown on the civilian population" (The Council of the European Union, 2011b). Specifically, these measures included an arms embargo and targeted sanctions against the Gaddafi family and top officials. When the EU's decision was announced, the EU High Representative was in Geneva for the Human Rights Council meeting, and she met foreign ministers around the world, including the US Secretary of State Clinton, to discuss the situation in Libya, especially the issue of the no-fly zone (Quinn, 2011). The general consensus of the meeting was that "Gaddafi must go" (ibid.). The Turkish FM was also in the meeting, and it was indicated in his program that he had attended bilateral meetings with his counterparts, including the EU High Representative (*Hürriyet*, 2011d). In his speech at the Council meeting, the Turkish FM refrained from making critical statements about Gaddafi; instead, he said, "We cannot and should not dictate our own solutions to these countries. As in every democratic system, these countries must find their own solutions, based on their people's will" (Davutoğlu, 2011). He hinted at Turkey's reluctance to support any foreign intervention in Libya, which also meant that Turkey would not support a possible NATO action at that point in time. There was a bilateral meeting between the EU and the Turkish government in Geneva; so, there was information exchange. Yet, ultimately, the Turkish government again did not align itself with the restrictive measures imposed by the EU.

Instead of supporting or aligning with the EU, the Turkish PM openly opposed sanctions and intervention, pointing to the potential harm they could have for the Libyan people. He said:

> We are concerned in the name of the Libyan people that sanctions and intervention are being discussed regarding the events in Libya. . . . Peoples should not pay for the wrong doings of administrations . . . all sanctions and measures might have unacceptable consequences.
>
> (Erdoğan, 2011a)

His remarks indicate that there was a clear divergence between the EU and Turkish positions. However, it is also possible to say that Turkish and EU officials were meeting both in international and bilateral settings and exchanging information about each other's policy quite frequently.

While sanctions and intervention were being discussed in the international arena, the Turkish decision makers were aware that Gaddafi expected them to be on his side and to oppose such actions. As Gaddafi's chief of security at the time revealed after the uprising, Gaddafi resented the Turkish PM and felt "abandoned" by him (*Hürriyet Daily News*, 2011) when there was a U-turn in Turkish policy in favour of sanctions and intervention after the evacuation of Turkish citizens was over. The Turkish government was well aware that Gaddafi wanted and expected them to refuse support for talks on sanctions or intervention, and that is what they did at the time.

In fact, Turkish decision makers even appealed to the anti-Western sentiments in the Gaddafi government in order to make it absolutely clear that they did not support any action against the regime. Notably, the remarks of the Turkish PM on 28 February is the prime example of how the Turkish government opposed the idea of intervention:

> Should NATO intervene in Libya? Could there be such absurdity? What business does NATO have in Libya? . . . Look, we, as Turkey, are against this, such a thing cannot be discussed, cannot be thought.
>
> (Erdoğan, 2011a)

His statement also had an anti-imperialist flavour because he not only opposed intervention but also implicitly accused Western states of using intervention as a way to capture Libya's oil resources:

> Libya belongs to Libyans. . . . They should determine their own future. Nobody else. No one should make calculations about oil wells in those countries. That is the problem. If we are going to talk about fundamental freedoms in order to give advice, let's talk about that but let's not make calculations about the oil there.
>
> (ibid.)

The Turkish government at that point was still worried about the remaining Turkish citizens in Libya, and it could be claimed that one of the fundamental reasons why the Turkish PM vehemently opposed NATO intervention on that day, as also pointed out by a Turkish broadcaster (Zengin, 2013: 70), was because an intervention meant that the thousands of remaining Turkish citizens in Libya who were waiting to be evacuated would be under NATO bombardment. It would have been costly to have supported intervention at that time. So, the government preferred to appear as a friend to Gaddafi in order to make sure the evacuation was safely completed.

In terms of cooperation with the EU, it is possible to say that the way in which the Turkish PM spoke out so strongly about the intervention was not much of a surprise to the EU, because EU and Turkish officials were regularly in touch, sharing their policies with each other. The policies indeed clearly diverged. Having already imposed restrictive measures, EU states were discussing intervention to end the violence; whereas, the Turkish government not only strongly opposed the idea of imposing punitive measures but also appeared as a friend to the Gaddafi regime. However, it is important for the analysis presented here that the EU and the Turkish government were in touch and were able to keep each other informed. It indicates that there was at least "unilateral information". The Turkish government did not specifically seek the EU's feedback on its policy in the form of consultation or inform the EU about the stance it was going to take beforehand; however, the EU was briefed about the policies of the Turkish government, and the Turkish government was up-to-date about the EU's policy.

When the evacuation was complete on 1 March, there was a dramatic change in Turkish policy. The Turkish government took a critical stance and started considering measures against the Libyan regime. The finalisation of the evacuation was a major relief for the government, and, after that point, the costs of being critical of Gaddafi decreased. The Turkish PM clearly stated that the Turkish government had remained silent because they were afraid Gaddafi would hurt Turkish citizens in Libya, causing a political crisis in Turkey. He said:

> Some give advice to us asking why we don't say anything against Gaddafi. We are not running a tribe here. We manage Turkey with 74 million people. How would I be supposed to pay the price if one of my 30 thousand citizens there had gotten killed?
>
> (*Sabah*, 2011d)

It should also be pointed out that the concern for Turkish citizens might also have been, to some extent, a cover or a convenient excuse in the domestic arena to delay expressing criticism of Gaddafi. As mentioned before, the Turkish government preferred stability to regime change and thereby appeared close to Gaddafi until they were convinced that the regime was going to fall. So, although concern for Turkish citizens seems to have been a main driver, since the Turkish rhetoric dramatically changed as a result of the finalisation of evacuation, the words of the Turkish PM should not be taken at face value. It could also be claimed that around this time, it was more likely that an international intervention would take place, which meant that it was less likely that Gaddafi would be able to retain power.

On the day the evacuation was completed, it was reported that the Turkish PM called Gaddafi and Gaddafi's son. The content of the conversation was revealed to the public later on (20 March) by the Turkish PM. In response to a question, the Turkish PM claimed Gaddafi must leave and detailed his conversation:

> Gaddafi contradicts himself. He said, 'I don't lead Libya with an official duty'. What the one who does not lead Libya officially must have done was to hand over Libya to the ones who had an official duty to lead Libya. I told this to him and to his son. I said, 'This must be done'. I said, 'From now on, you must respect the will of the people and this must end immediately'. Unfortunately, we have come to this point. This conversation I had is dated 1 March. Unfortunately, we didn't succeed.
>
> (Erdoğan, 2011b)

So, on the day the evacuation was over, the Turkish PM started to make critical statements for the first time and even urged Gaddafi to step down to respect the will of the Libyan people. As there were no Turkish citizens left and the international response was hardening against the Libyan regime, there was little reason for him to appear to support Gaddafi. To put it another way, from this point onwards, the deterioration of the relationship with Gaddafi was not so much a concern.

A critical approach was adopted and sanctions were considered. Turkish officials had previously said that they opposed even the discussion of sanctions, pointing to the way in which Libyan people might suffer as a consequence. After 1 March, Turkish officials started to advocate sanctions, saying there was a need to introduce sanctions but to do so with special care so that Libyan people would not suffer. For instance, the spokesperson of the Ministry of Foreign Affairs of Turkey claimed that they wanted "a solution that would ensure the legitimate demands of the Libyan people" and urged international actors to use sanctions carefully so that they would not harm the population in Libya (Ministry of Foreign Affairs of Turkey, 2011). Therefore, the government, which had not made open comments before, officially declared that the demands of the protesters were "legitimate" and that Gaddafi should listen to them.

Also, the government started to base its criticism on the UNSC decision (Resolution 1970). It was mentioned that Turkey would support and implement the measures specified by the UNSC (Erdoğan, 2011c). When the UNSC decision was made, the Turkish PM opposed the decision, accusing states of making calculations about Libya's oil resources (Euractiv, 2011b). At that time, the Turkish government did not want to take sides against the Gaddafi regime and wanted to appear friendly to Gaddafi because of the presence of Turkish citizens in Libya. However, the costs of being critical of Gaddafi decreased after the evacuation was complete and it was clearer that Gaddafi was losing power, so the Turkish government eventually aligned with the broader international community.

The policy of the Turkish government was praised in Turkey because the evacuation operation was presented as a heroic act to save thousands of Turks who needed help in Libya. Commentators wrote that because of the "success" of Turkish foreign policy over the last decade, Erdoğan was able to talk to Gaddafi, unlike other world leaders, and carry out this exceptionally successful evacuation in a way that the whole world envied. For instance, a columnist in *Today's Zaman* praised the Turkish government, especially the PM, for being able to personally call Gaddafi to request help when there was an issue having to do with arranging flights that would take Turkish citizens from Libya (Yanatma, 2011). This again points to the way in which the government policy was based on prioritising strategy, mainly the evacuation, and it was not motivated by norms or identity.

The timing of the U-turn in Turkish policy signifies that the evacuation was one of the main factors causing divergence from the EU, which means that rationalism better explains the motivation of Turkish behaviour based on costs and benefits of action. However, this divergence does not necessarily explain the degree of cooperation since, as mentioned previously, cooperation can take place in the absence of convergence too.

In terms of the specific factors determining costs and benefits of cooperation with the EU, it can be claimed that the urgency of action, the fact that the evacuation was a security matter, and the differences of views between Turkey and the EU particularly increased the costs of cooperation. As a result, achieving a higher degree of cooperation, such as "co-decision" or "consultation", would have been highly costly. However, this does not mean that cooperation did not take place at all.

Based on the empirical evidence, it is possible to conclude that EU and Turkish officials were regularly in contact both before and after the public announcement of the Turkish position on 1 March that criticised Gaddafi for the first time. They exchanged information about their policies, both in formal contexts (e.g., delegation or working groups exchanging information) and in informal contexts (e.g., telephone conversations between the Turkish FM and the EU High Representative).

There is no conclusive evidence that the Turkish government contacted the EU to discuss any of its policies or to request any form of feedback, which would mean that "consultation" did not take place, although there were contacts between officials. In fact, there is evidence that the EU wanted to reach out to the Turkish side regarding Libya. This was the case when the EU High Representative telephoned the Turkish FM to talk about regional developments including Libya when he was in India on 19 February.

In addition, the EU invited the Turkish government to join its statements, but the Turkish government, due to the reasons discussed, turned it down. In this process, both the Turkish government was informed about the EU position and the EU was informed about the Turkish stance, mainly through the EU delegation in Ankara, which is again important for this analysis since it means that they were up-to-date on each other's stance.

As a conclusion, it could be claimed that there was at least "unilateral information" and presumably some consultation from time to time to the extent that the EU was able to provide its feedback on the Turkish position in conversations with the Turkish government. Overall, the interaction was closer to the "unilateral information" point than "consultation".

Turkish decision to initiate evacuation operation by sea on 20 February

The previous CO looked at the initial Turkish reaction leading to the Turkish decision to take a critical stance against the Gaddafi government. There was another opportunity for cooperation with regard to the evacuation of citizens from Libya. Specifically, potential cooperation had to do with the extent to which consultations with the EU took place in the planning and execution of the evacuation operation and its aftermath. The relationship during this CO corresponds to the "unilateral information" point because the flow of information was rather one way in the sense that the Turkish government informed the EU of its intentions and then proceeded with actions without much discussion or exchange of views.

Indeed, Turkey was not officially a part of the EU crisis management mechanisms since it was not a member. Yet, evacuation was not only an important issue for Turkey but also a key area in which the EU member states cooperated, as their citizens were also stranded in Libya. Therefore, there was a mutual concern about evacuating people from Libya, which provided a shared context in which coordination could have taken place.

What happened was that the Turkish government immediately began its evacuation before the EU could even decide on an action. Unilateral action was preferable for the Turkish government because, due to the large number of Turkish citizens in Libya and the rapid escalation of violence, they were working against time to remove people from the conflict zone.

Cooperation took place on a bilateral basis with individual EU states in the sense that the Turkish government helped the evacuation of a number of EU citizens upon requests from individual member states. There is no evidence that the Turkish government specifically offered help to EU member states, but it helped those requesting help, which was particularly welcomed by the EU (Interview EU06). It was reported that Germany, France, the UK, Italy, and Sweden were among the EU member states who formally requested help from the Turkish government (*Zaman*, 2011). For example, the Bulgarian PM publicly stated that the evacuation of Bulgarian citizens from Benghazi was only possible by sea, and, for that, he requested Turkey's help (ibid.). In this case, the safe evacuation of Bulgarian citizens was achieved via bilateral coordination in the sense that the Bulgarian and Turkish governments jointly made sure Bulgarians were safely transferred to Bulgaria.

The Turkish government informed the EU about its position, and the EU was kept up-to-date about Turkish actions. A counsellor at the EU Delegation in Ankara noted that they were thankful to the Turkish government for helping EU nationals (Interview EU02). Similarly, the Turkey advisor of the High Representative stated that the Turkish response in terms of the evacuation was "impressive" and claimed that the Turkish government was able to mobilise resources in a way that was actually harder for some member states because the Turkish government owned airlines and civil vessels and was able to mobilise them quickly, whereas some member states' airlines or civil vessels did not have any government connections at all (Interview EU04). By 26 February, the number of foreigners, including EU citizens, evacuated by Turkey was 579, on top of some 14,000 Turkish nationals (*Milliyet*, 2011).

It should be noted that the Turkish government helped foreigners on request from more than 40 states, and these states happened to include some EU member states (*Milliyet*, 2011). So, it was done on a bilateral basis. It could be possible to say that, to some degree, there was coordination with individual states that the Turkish government helped since there needed to be some kind of agreement and understanding about the logistics of the operation, for example, with regard to how to arrange the return of foreigners after they had arrived in Turkey. Nevertheless, the Turkish government did not offer help to the EU as a body, and it acted without having conducted any discussion with the EU (Interviews EU02 and EU05). Therefore, "unilateral information" took place instead of "consultation" or "coordination".

Foreigners evacuated by Turkey included citizens of EU member states, but it is hardly possible to say that the Turkish government adjusted its behaviour to accommodate requests from EU member states. The evacuation operation was already taking place specifically for Turkish citizens, and after requests for help, foreigners were also taken aboard. There is no evidence that the Turkish government adjusted itself to accommodate the preferences of EU member states, or put much effort into coordinating evacuation operations with EU member states, or carried out its operation in any other way than the way it had planned.

It should be pointed out that there was no formal mechanism through which the Turkish government and the EU could talk on crisis management issues. Turkey, at that time, did not participate in the EU's civil protection and crisis response mechanisms, namely the EU Emergency Response Coordination Centre (at the time of the crisis in Libya it was called "Monitoring Information Centre", MIC) located in the Commission's DG for humanitarian aid and crisis response (DG ECHO), even though other non-EU states, such as Iceland, Norway, the Former Yugoslav Republic of Macedonia (FYROM), and Lichtenstein, participated.

According to the Head of the International Cooperation Department at DG ECHO, the issue of evacuation was more in the domain of member states rather than the EU, and the EU assistance in the area of consular affairs and evacuation of EU citizens was only of a supporting character, taking place only when requested by member states (Interview EU08). The interviewee also explained that "in the case of Libya, EU member states were conducting their own evacuation activities, similar to what Turkey was doing for its citizens, and the MIC was using member states' expertise and experience" (ibid.). In other words, the EU's role was to assist member states carrying out evacuation operations, some of which had requested Turkey's help, and the EU assistance to member states was coordinated through MIC in DG ECHO.

If Turkey had participated in the EU civil protection mechanism, it would have been formally involved in the exchange of information and the coordinated emergency response. However, the Turkish government refrained from participating in the mechanism and relied solely on its own crisis management apparatus, namely AFAD. According to a DG ECHO representative in Ankara, the primary concerns on the Turkish side were that they were not sure if it would really benefit them and, most importantly, the Turkish government was not comfortable having no voting rights in the mechanism (Interview EU09). Basically, according to the interviewee, the EU had requested for years that Turkey join, but the Turkish response had been, "we don't want to be a part of any new organisation or coordination mechanism geared by Europeans if we don't have equal rights" (ibid.). For this reason, during the crisis in Libya, and particularly during the evacuation operation, there was no contact between the Turkish emergency management authority and the MIC located in the European Commission (Interviews EU03, EU05, EU08, and EU09). To put it another way, the Turkish government chose not to participate in an institutional platform in which it could have consultations with the EU prior to action.

The Turkish attitude to participating in the civil protection mechanism needs to be underlined here. Had norms of cooperation or a coordination reflex come into play, we would have seen an inclination towards achieving coordination. After all, as mentioned before, on numerous occasions the Turkish government voiced a desire for closer cooperation with the EU involving more institutionalisation, and pointed to the Cyprus problem as an obstacle to cooperation. However, here in this example, the Turkish government turned down participating in a platform that would have involved consultation with the EU, claiming that it would be costly to be involved when they did not have voting rights.

It should also be noted that the Turkish government changed its mind and decided to participate as of May 2015. According to an interviewee working for DG ECHO, the new commissioner, who had a good relationship with Turkish officials, was able to reassure the Turkish government that voting rights were of little importance, and the Turkish government agreed to participate after seeing that Norway had participated without having had any problems without voting rights (Interview EU09). This does make a difference to cooperation. It means that presumably more "consultation" has taken place since May 2015, and it is a move towards having more cooperation in terms of crisis management. However, it also shows that the Turkish approach to participating in the mechanism was not based on norms of appropriate behaviour and such, but on the costs and benefits of participation. Any implication that this has for the future of cooperation is another question. The key issue here is that at the time of this CO, the Turkish concern was that participating would be a costly action, which would indicate that rationalism better explains the absence of "consultation" at that time.

Another important point about this CO is that presumably the Turkish decision to use the sea route for evacuation set an example for the EU to follow. Figure 5.2 shows the timeline of events, showing the evacuation operations of Turkey and the EU. Immediately after Turkish citizens were at risk, the Turkish response was to send planes for evacuation on 19 February, but, due to the escalation of violence, the planes were unable to land and Turkish decision makers needed to find alternative ways to get people out of Libya, which could have been a reason for cooperation with EU member states, to be cost efficient. The problem with the planes was also why the Turkish PM made a personal telephone call to Gaddafi on 21 February, as mentioned earlier in this chapter. Although Gaddafi responded positively to helping Turkish planes, Turkish decision makers thought sending planes was not the best strategy anymore. After a crisis meeting in the Ministry of

Monday	Tuesday	Wednesday	Thursday	Friday	Saturday	Sunday
14	15 **Uprising starts in Libya**	16	17	18	19 Turkey starts evacuation	20
21 Erdoğan-Gaddafi telephone calls. Turkish fleet set sail	22	23 MIC started working on evacuation, thinking about sea route	24	25	26	27

Figure 5.2 Timeline of events for the evacuation operations of Turkey and the EU, March 2011

Foreign Affairs in Ankara, it was decided to send ships accompanied by a frigate (NTV, 2011). So, by 21 February, the Turkish government had decided to go about the operation using the sea route, and the fleet set sail.

EU member states also individually worked on evacuating their citizens. For instance, France, Germany, and Italy sent charter planes, whereas the UK sent ships and frigates, as Turkey had done, for evacuation (Donadio and Arsu, 2011). Meanwhile, the EU was preparing an action plan for the evacuation of EU citizens. On 23 February, the EU commissioner for aid and crisis response, stated, "Thousands of EU citizens are struggling to evacuate from Libya under extremely difficult circumstances. It is our duty to live up to this challenge of facilitating the evacuations" (Pop, 2011), and on the same day the Commission's crisis response centre (MIC) started working to facilitate the evacuation of EU citizens. The EU stated that it "was preparing a plan for evacuation by sea in the event that evacuation by air becomes impossible" (EEAS, 2011a).

The timing and nature of the EU's evacuation operation are important here. The EU declared it would facilitate the evacuation through MIC on 23 February (two days after the Turkish fleet had set sail), but how exactly it planned to carry out the operation was not determined for sure; it was only mentioned that the MIC was working on a plan that involved "evacuation by sea" (*Le Parisien*, 2011; European Commission, 2011a). The EU's coordinating spokesperson for Libya stated that the EU was "identifying additional evacuation means in particular by sea, in the next hours and days" (Bailly, 2011). So, the point here is that the EU was considering an operation by sea at a time when the Turkish government had already sent ships after deciding that the air route was not preferable.

The spokesperson also mentioned that the High Representative was going to have a "very important meeting with several Commissioners, but most importantly key Member States and third countries", which included Turkey (ibid.). Therefore, when the evacuation reached the top of the EU agenda, the High Representative spoke with the Turkish FM, who certainly had an opinion about how to proceed with any evacuation based on Turkey's own experience over the preceding days. Therefore, arguably, Turkey's experience might have helped the EU to consider evacuation by sea because Turkey had already experienced problems with the air route at the time. So, the point here is that it is more likely that the EU listened to the Turkish experience of evacuation in this specific CO rather than the other way around, especially considering the timing and subject of the meetings between the Turkish and EU officials.

Overall, with regard to this CO, it is possible to claim that the nature of interaction corresponded more with the "unilateral information" point because the EU was only informed about Turkish actions and no "consultation" took place. Although the Turkish government agreed to take some foreigners, which included foreigners from EU member states, the EU itself was not involved and there was no specific adjustment of Turkish behaviour for the evacuation of foreigners from EU member states.

The Turkish response could have constituted an example for the EU when it was working on an action plan, particularly involving evacuation by sea. Considering the formation of Turkish preferences with regard to evacuation and the general attitude of the Turkish government regarding participation in the civil protection mechanism, it is possible to claim that rationalism better explains the Turkish behaviour and the absence of "consultation" in this specific instance. Specifically, urgency of action and the fact that the issue of evacuation was a major security issue for the Turkish government particularly increased the costs of cooperation with the EU during the planning and execution of the evacuation operation.

Turkey's decision to support and participate in the NATO intervention, "Operation Unified Protector"

There was a U-turn in the Turkish policy not only on the subject of supporting the opposition and imposing sanctions but also with regard to supporting NATO intervention in Libya. The Turkish government initially opposed foreign intervention and even accused states of following imperialist agendas and going after the oil resources of the country. This opposition to NATO intervention should be seen as a part of the general Turkish reluctance to criticise Gaddafi before the U-turn on 1 March.

Before March, the Turkish PM made it clear that Turkey would not be a part of NATO intervention and harshly criticised those who discussed the possibility of intervention. Specifically, on 28 February, he said, "Should NATO intervene in Libya? Could there be such absurdity? What business does NATO have in Libya?" (Erdoğan, 2011a). After 1 March, and after the Turkish government changed its general attitude towards Gaddafi, the Turkish government dropped its strong opposition towards an intervention and gradually started to see an intervention as a necessary measure to end the conflict. Notably, on 21 March, it was clear that the Turkish leadership had changed its mind about the intervention – the Turkish PM claimed, "NATO should go into Libya to 'determine' and to 'register' Libya for the Libyans!" (Erdoğan, 2011c).

It is possible to argue that a number of factors came into play in the change of policy. The general change in the Turkish attitude following the end of the evacuation, increasing international pressure against the Gaddafi regime, and the inevitability of international intervention were all influential factors that led the Turkish leadership to decide to support the NATO intervention. This analysis will discuss each factor, but the overall view here is that the change in policy was based on a strategic adjustment to avoid costly actions that could have resulted in Turkey being marginalised when the intervention took place.

This analysis will also discuss interactions with the EU. This CO is another example of an instance in which cooperation was slightly more than the "unilateral information" level. Primarily through diplomatic channels, the Turkish government informed the EU about its actions and positions, and it is possible to say that there was information exchange in the time period until the Turkish government decided to contribute to the intervention. However, no discussion took place about what course of action to follow, and the Turkish government never asked the EU for its views.

In addition, this CO is another example of an instance when it was clear that the EU needed Turkish cooperation more. The EU wished to play a leading role in the intervention, and Turkish consent was essential for them to be able to use the NATO command structure. Being aware of their strategic importance, Turkish decision makers frequently underlined that they could make EU foreign policy more effective, which again indicates that Turkish decision makers strategically used their position in a way that helped them to demonstrate to the EU that they were valuable partners. There are three points that need to be emphasised.

First, the general change in Turkish attitude was important because, as discussed before, the costs of adopting a critical stance against Gaddafi decreased after the evacuation was over. Criticising the regime and supporting democratic change, on the other hand, had more benefits because, by the time the evacuation was over, international pressure against the regime had mounted and it was risky to continue supporting Gaddafi. Here, general Turkish interests in Libya became more important because Turkish decision makers did not want to appear to support an oppressive leader, especially after it seemed less likely that Gaddafi would retain power.

Second, the international pressure against the regime was increasing, which meant that Turkey could be marginalised if it continued its support for Gaddafi. After the UNSC agreed on UNSCR 1973 (2011) on 17 March authorising all necessary measures to protect civilians in Libya, Turkish decision makers believed it was less costly to align with the international community.

It should be noted that the US position was also influential, as had been the case in Egypt (Chapter 4). The US had been an important ally for the Turkish government, and the fact that it supported intervention particularly increased the likelihood of an international military action taking place against the Libyan regime. However, the US deliberately remained low key, and US President Obama encouraged European allies to take the lead without depending solely on US military capabilities (Hachigian and Shorr, 2013: 80). According to analysts Hachigian and Shorr (2013), this was an example of the Obama administration pursuing a strategy that they named the "responsibility doctrine", which was based on prodding other influential actors to stand up for international peace so that the responsibilities and burdens for operations, such as the one against the Libyan regime, could be spread. So, the EU had an opportunity to lead an international offensive, which meant that they needed Turkish cooperation even more, particularly to rely on the NATO command structure.

Third, and most importantly, the Turkish leadership realised that the intervention was going to take place anyway regardless of their opinion. The inevitability of intervention motivated them to be part of it so that they could play a role in the restructuring of Libya. This last point needs more unpacking.

The Turkish government, because of its opposition to NATO intervention, initially blocked NATO involvement in the conflict. After the international pressure increased, and especially after the UNSC 1970 (2011), it was likely that an intervention was going to take place. As a result of the Paris summit, to which the Turkish government had not been invited because of its attitude towards intervention, the international coalition led by the US intervened on 19 March ("Operation Odyssey Dawn"). The coalition could not use the NATO command structure, although it would have been more convenient for all parties involved, because of Turkey. When the intervention took place, Turkish decision makers realised there was no use blocking NATO because an intervention was taking place anyway (Figure 5.3). A few days later, on 24 March, the Western allies agreed with the Turkish government to put the offensive – consisting of a no-fly zone, an arms embargo, and air strikes – under a NATO command umbrella, naming it "Operation Unified Protector" (Traynor and Watt, 2011; Ames, 2011). On the same day, the Turkish Parliament approved NATO involvement in a closed session and agreed to send Turkish troops (TBMM, 2011). As the main reason, it was declared that it was in the "national interest" of Turkey, as a country that was "interested in Libya's future", to participate in the intervention (ibid). Not opposing NATO intervention and allowing the use of its command structure do not necessarily have to involve active support. However, it was clear that an intervention was going to take place anyway, and Turkish decision makers contended that it was more beneficial for them to be more than a spectator and to receive the chance to play a role in the regime change in Libya through actively participating in the intervention (e.g., Turkey sent warships to contribute).

Monday	Tuesday	Wednesday	Thursday	Friday	Saturday	Sunday
28 Erdoğan: "What business does NATO have in Libya?"	**1**	**2**	**3**	**4**	**5**	**6**
7	**8**	**9**	**10**	**11**	**12**	**13**
14	**15**	**16**	**17** UNSCR 1973/2011	**18**	**19** Operation Odyssey Dawn	**20**
21 Erdoğan: "NATO should go into Libya"	**22**	**23**	**24** **Operation Unified Protector** Turkey decides to send troops	**25**	*26*	

Figure 5.3 Timeline for the change in Turkish position regarding military intervention, February–March 2011

There was such a radical and a rapid change in the Turkish position that Turkish decision makers felt the need to justify their actions, at which point they used the notion of Responsibility to Protect (R2P) and that Turkey had a moral duty to support intervention. For example, the Turkish President and FM stated that Turkey would provide "all necessary support" for the international community because the international action was "legitimate" (İhlas Haber Ajansı, 2011). The Turkish President said, "Now, we are talking about 'international legitimacy' [referring the UNSCR, 1973 (2011)]. We believe that it is 'right' for us to act within this framework" (ibid.). However, the Turkish support for intervention was not about whether it was "right" or not; it was about the realisation that support for the intervention was more beneficial since it was inevitably going to take place. The emphasis on the "moral" aspect of intervention was merely a convenient cover to justify the inconsistency of Turkish positions on the matter.

The EU was informed throughout about the Turkish position, both before and after the change in Turkish stance, mainly through the EU delegation in Ankara, who were also able to communicate the EU position (Interviews EU02, EU05, and EU06). However, again, this was based on information exchange and finding out about each other's position only, and no discussion or consultation took place, which indicates that cooperation did not reach the "consultation" level but did surpass the "unilateral information" level.

It should be pointed out that the EU as a body struggled to find a unified voice due to internal divisions, which made it even harder for Turkey to cooperate with the EU. Specifically, there were internal disagreements about whether or not to establish a no-fly zone, and, most notably, Germany abstained in the UNCSC on the matter [UNSCR, 1973 (2011)]. However, still, the foreign policy dialogue between the Turkish government and the EU continued. Particularly, the informal dialogue between the Turkish FM and the EU High Representative continued, which once again indicates that the Turkish government valued its foreign policy relationship with the EU (Interview EU02).

In addition, the Turkish government became much more involved in discussions in NATO after deciding that the NATO command structure could be used for intervention. This meant that the Turkish government held consultations with its NATO allies, which included EU members, such as the UK and France. So, it can be claimed that the Turkish government achieved more cooperation/consultation with individual EU members within the framework of NATO rather than with the EU itself as a body.

It should also be pointed out that during the crisis in Libya, the Turkish government used the opportunity to make the point that the EU should consider Turkey to be a valuable asset to EU foreign policy. EU member states, especially France, wanted to play a leading role in the resolution of the Libyan crisis, and Turkish consent was essential for the use of the NATO command structure, as mentioned earlier. Turkish opposition to NATO action not only meant that the Turkish government would veto any action but also that they would block potential EU-NATO cooperation, as in the case of Afghanistan. During the crisis, the Turkish PM from time to time touched upon the problems of Turkey's accession process in a resentful manner and always underlined that the EU needed Turkey to be effective in the region.

For instance, while talking about the Libyan crisis, the Turkish PM was upset with the EU due to the issue of visa liberalisation, and he stated, "If they [EU] don't want us, they should say, 'we don't want Turkey'. Then, we would say OK. Let's not tire each other and take each other's time; let's not fool each other" (Erdoğan, 2011a). Considering that EU states wanted to play a leading role in the solution of the crisis, he also used the opportunity to point out that Turkey's importance to the EU had become "clearer" with the Libyan crisis and said, "The EU has an opportunity to make use of Turkey's experience in order to establish healthy relations with the regions" (ibid.). So, again, there was an emphasis that Turkey could make the EU more effective, which highlights the way in which the Turkish attitude to a foreign policy relationship with the EU was based on costs and benefits. Whenever the Turkish government had the chance, it stressed the benefits of Turkish accession.

Conclusion

This chapter has focused on three key COs in which the Turkish government took the initiative to act and had a chance to cooperate with the EU during the Libyan uprising. It is possible to claim that Turkey's cooperation with the EU slightly varied across the cases but did not go far beyond the "unilateral information" point. There was a difference in the way in which EU and Turkish officials reacted to the crisis, especially at the very beginning. However, despite the differences of views, there was a continuous exchange of information between EU and Turkish officials regarding the developments. These exchanges allowed the two sides to develop a better understanding of each other's positions.

One of the main factors influencing Turkey's initial reaction was the evacuation of its citizens. Turkish decision makers did not criticise the Libyan regime at first because it would have been a highly costly action, but then they changed their stance when the costs of criticising the regime decreased, after the evacuation had been completed. It could also be claimed that concern for citizens was a convenient cover for supporting Gaddafi. The Turkish government preferred stability to regime change and thereby appeared close to Gaddafi until they were convinced that the regime was going to fall. So, by waiting, the Turkish government bought time to carry out a smooth evacuation operation as well as to see whether Gaddafi would be able to retain power.

The EU and Turkish decision makers met both in bilateral and international settings and had a chance to talk about developments in Libya. Specifically, the EU HR and the Turkish FM kept in touch informally, which indicates that the EU HR also had a chance to communicate the EU position to the Turkish government. Moreover, the EU explained its position and invited Turkey to align itself, which was turned down by the Turkish government at the time because it was still showing support for Gaddafi. Considering that the EU presumably also had a chance to communicate its position in bilateral and international settings, the relationship may have surpassed the "unilateral information" point, since there was exchange of information from both sides. However, it is still not possible to say that "consultation" took place, since there is no evidence that the EU provided feedback on the Turkish position before or after the announcement of the Turkish position or that the Turkish government sought the EU's opinion. In fact, it is possible to say that the EU sought the Turkish view on the crisis and requested information on the Turkish position. Considering their interaction, it could also be claimed that they were up-to-date on each other's policy, which means it is highly unlikely that Turkish policies, with regard to its reaction in Libya, caught the EU by surprise.

As for the specific factors determining costs and benefits of cooperation with the EU, it could be claimed that the costs of cooperation with the EU were high particularly because the Turkish government believed there was a risk of upsetting the Gaddafi regime, which could then have jeopardised the evacuation of Turkish citizens. There were also economic and strategic reasons for avoiding being immediately critical of the regime since the Turkish government saw Gaddafi as a major partner in the region. Moreover, in the immediate aftermath of the crisis, there was no time to attain a higher degree of cooperation with the EU, as the evacuation necessitated an urgent action, which was the main focus of the second CO addressed in this chapter.

Potential cooperation regarding evacuation was especially a good case to test whether alliance norms specific to Turkey and the EU emerged in a way that encouraged coordination. However, the findings suggest that Turkish behaviour with regard to cooperation with the EU was based on costs and benefits. Specifically, the costs of cooperation were high because the government needed to take an urgent action and avoided any discussion that could delay action. It is possible to claim that during this CO, there was "unilateral information" because the flow of information was rather one way in the sense that the Turkish government informed the EU of its intentions and then proceeded with an action without much discussion or exchange of views.

The general change in the Turkish attitude following the end of evacuation, increasing international pressure against the Gaddafi regime, and the inevitability of international intervention were influential factors that led the Turkish leadership to decide to support a military intervention and NATO involvement. The Turkish reaction to international intervention was another example of a CO in which there was more than "unilateral information" since there was information exchange with the EU but no "consultation" or "coordination". As for the specific explanatory factors informing the calculation of costs and benefits, the costs of cooperation were high, particularly because it was a hard security issue and the Turkish government saw the EU as an incapable actor. Moreover, there were internal divisions inside the EU, which made cooperation even more difficult. For these reasons, the Turkish government prioritised a higher level of cooperation with actors whom it believed were capable of achieving change, such as NATO allies. Therefore, it can be claimed that the Turkish government mainly coordinated with EU states in NATO, whereas the EU itself was not so much in the picture.

Across the COs, the main difference between them is that there was more cooperation during the first and third COs. The first CO concerned the Turkish decision to criticise Gaddafi and support the opposition in Libya in favour of a democratic regime change. Turkish and EU officials were able to meet in international and bilateral meetings that facilitated the information exchange. Also, the way in which the Turkish government avoided risking its relations with the Gaddafi regime and its prolonged support for the opposition movement provided more time for cooperation to take place before the U-turn in Turkish policy on 1 March. Information exchange with the EU was not overly costly because it meant that the Turkish government had a chance to touch base with the international community, especially after the U-turn in Turkish policy. Similarly, for the third CO, the delayed support for intervention allowed time for information exchange, which was not so costly.

In the second CO, "unilateral information" took place mainly because of the necessity to act urgently. Cooperation to a degree higher than "unilateral information" would have been costly because the Turkish government felt like it would lose time if it did not act immediately or discuss its intended actions with the EU. In this case, the urgency of action as an explanatory factor is important since it increases the costs of cooperation.

Overall, analysis of Turkish behaviour suggests that it was mainly influenced by the costs and benefits of action. Turkish decision makers sought to minimise the costs of their actions with regard to the developments of the crisis as well as with regard to their attitude towards cooperation with the EU. Evidence also suggests that Turkish decision makers did not see the EU as a capable actor in the crisis. The crisis presents an example in which the EU had more to gain from cooperation with Turkey rather than the other way around. Despite all, there was at least "unilateral information", which means that the EU was consistently informed of Turkish actions. In other words, it is highly unlikely that Turkish actions caught the EU by surprise.

References

Aktan, S. (2011) "Libya'da Türk Firmaları Yağmalanıyor" ["Turkish Businesses Are Being Looted in Libya"], *İhlas Haber Ajansı*, 19 February, www.iha.com.tr/haber-libyada-turk-firmalari-yagmalaniyor-160976.

Ames, P. (2011) "Nato to Take Charge of No-Fly Zone; but US Role Is Unclear", *Independent*, 25 March, www.independent.co.uk/news/world/politics/nato-to-take-charge-of-no-fly-zone-ndash-but-us-role-is-unclear-2252533.html.

Ashton, C. (2011a) "Declaration by the High Representative Catherine Ashton on Behalf of the European Union on Libya", Brussels, Belgium, 23 February, http://europa.eu/rapid/press-release_PESC-11-36_en.htm.

———. (2011b) "Declaration by the High Representative, Catherine Ashton, on Behalf of the European Union on Events in Libya", Brussels, Belgium, 20 February, http://europa.eu/rapid/press-release_PESC-11-33_en.htm?locale=en.

Atlantic Council. (2011) "Diplomats Mourn 'Death' of EU Defence Policy Over Libya", *Atlantic Council*, 24 March, www.atlanticcouncil.org/blogs/natosource/diplomats-mourn-death-of-eu-defence-policy-over-libya.

Bailly, O. (2011) "Extracts from the EC Midday Press Briefing by Olivier Bailly, Head of Unit 1 'Growth and Jobs', Coordinating Spokesperson, on Libya", European

Commission, Brussels, Belgium, 23 February, http://ec.europa.eu/avservices/video/shotlist.cfm?ref=75273.

The Council of the European Union. (2011a) "3069th Council Meeting", The Council of the European Union, 21 February, www.consilium.europa.eu/uedocs/cms_data/docs/pressdata/EN/foraff/119435.pdf.

———. (2011b) "Libya: EU Imposes Arms Embargo and Targeted Sanctions", Brussels, Belgium, 28 February, http://europa.eu/rapid/press-release_PRES-11-41_en.htm?locale=en.

———. (2005) "2664th Council Meeting", The Council of the European Union, Luxembourg, 2–3 June, http://europa.eu/rapid/press-release_PRES-05-114_en.htm?locale=en.

Cumhuriyet Halk Partisi. (2011) "Genel Başkan Kılıçdaroğlu: İnsanların Açlıktan Öldüğü Bir Türkiye'yi Biz İçimize Sindiremiyoruz'" ["Chairman Kılıçdaroğlu: 'We Cannot Accept a Turkey Where People Are Starving to Death'"], 21 February, http://arsiv.chp.org.tr/?p=12509.

Davutoğlu, A. (2011) "Statement by HE Ahmet Davutoğlu Minister of Foreign Affairs of the Republic of Turkey, High Level Segment of the Human Rights Council XVIth Session", Geneva, Switzerland, 28 February.

Donadio, R., and Arsu, Ş. (2011) "Governments Try to Remove Citizens From Libya", *The New York Times*, 22 February, www.nytimes.com/2011/02/23/world/africa/23evacuate.html?_r=0.

The Economist. (2011) "EU Foreign Policy and Libya: Low Ambition for the High Representative", *The Economist*, 23 May, www.economist.com/blogs/charlemagne/2011/05/eu_foreign_policy_and_libya.

EEAS. (2011a) "Developments in Libya: An Overview of the EU's Response", European External Action Service, Brussels, Belgium, 10 March, www.eeas.europa.eu/top_stories/2011/040311_en.htm.

———. (2011b) "EU High Representative Catherine Ashton Opens European Union Office in Benghazi", Brussels, Belgium, 22 May, http://eeas.europa.eu/top_stories/2011/220511_en.htm.

Efegil, E. (2012) "Dış Politika'da Rasyonalite Sorunsalı: Libya Krizi Sırasında Türk Dış Politikasının Rasyonalitesi" ["The Rationality Problematique in Foreign Policy: The Rationality of Turkish Foreign Policy During the Libyan Crisis"], in Efegil, E. and Erol, M.S. (eds.), *Dış Politika Analizinde Teorik Yaklaşımlar: Türk Dış Politikası Örneği* [*Theoretical Approaches in Foreign Policy Analysis: The Example of Turkish Foreign Policy*], Ankara: Barış, pp. 1–20.

Erdoğan, R.T. (2011a) "Speech at Turkish-German Economic Congress", CeBIT Convention Center, Hannover, Germany, 28 February.

———. (2011b) "Speech at Jeddah Economic Forum", Jeddah, Saudi Arabia, 20 March.

———. (2011c) "Speech at Ummul Kura University", Mecca, Saudi Arabia, 21 March.

Euractiv. (2011a) "Erdoğan: 'Kılıçdaroğlu, Libya'yı haritada gösteremez'" ["Erdoğan: 'Kılıçdaroğlu Cannot Point to Libya on a Map'"], *Euractiv*, 23 February, www.euractiv.com.tr/politika-000110/article/erdogan-kilicdaroglu-libyayi-haritada-gosteremez-015920.

———. (2011b) "BM Kaddafi'ye yaptırımı kabul etti. Obama 'Hemen gitmeli!' dedi. Erdoğan yaptırıma karşı!" ["UN Approved Sanctions Against Gaddafi. Obama Said 'He Must Immediately Step Aside'. Erdoğan Against Sanctions"], *Euractiv*, 28 February, www.euractiv.com.tr/politika-000110/article/bm-kaddafi-rejimine-kar-yaptrmlar-kabul-etti-obama-kaddafi-gitmeli-dedi-016047.

European Commission. (2013) "Trade Relations: Libya", http://ec.europa.eu/trade/policy/countries-and-regions/countries/libya/.

————. (2011a) "The European Commission Facilitates Support to Evacuate Europeans from Libya", European Commission, Brussels, Belgium, 23 February, http://europa.eu/rapid/press-release_IP-11-222_en.htm?locale=en.

————. (2011b) *Turkey 2011 Progress Report*, Brussels, Belgium: European Commission.

European Council. (2011) "Extraordinary European Council, 11 March 2011 Declaration", 11 March, www.consilium.europa.eu/uedocs/cms_data/docs/pressdata/en/ec/119780.pdf.

Gioanna, M.D. (2010) "The European Union and Libya: Strange Bedfellows?" Conference Paper, Université catholique de Louvain, Belgium, www.uclouvain.be/cps/ucl/doc/spri/documents/communication_della_Giovanna.pdf.

Gürcanlı, Z. (2011) "Bakan Libya konusunda ilk kez konuştu: Önceliğimiz can güvenliği" ["The Minister Spoke on Libya for the First Time: Our Priority Is Safety"], *Hürriyet*, 21 February, www.hurriyet.com.tr/bakan-libya-konusunda-ilk-kez-konustu-onceligimiz-can-guvenligi-17078555.

Haberturk. (2010) "Erdoğan'a Kaddafi İnsan Hakları Ödülü Verildi" ["Erdoğan Awarded Gaddafi Human Rights Prize"], *Haberturk*, 29 November, www.haberturk.com/gundem/haber/576201-erdogana-kaddafi-insan-haklari-odulu-verildi.

Hachigian, N., and Shorr, D. (2013) "The Responsibility Doctrine", *The Washington Quarterly* 36(1): 73–91.

Human Rights Watch. (2008) "EU-Libya Relations: Human Rights Conditions Required", *Human Rights Watch*, 3 January, www.hrw.org/news/2008/01/03/eu-libya-relations.

Hürriyet. (2011a) "Türkiye, Libya'daki Türk vatandaşları için harekete geçti" ["Turkey Takes Action for Turkish Citizens in Libya"], *Hürriyet*, 19 February, www.hurriyet.com.tr/dunya/turkiye-libyadaki-turk-vatandaslari-icin-harekete-gecti-17065436.

————. (2011b) "Libya'dan gelen Türkler: Can güvenliği yok her yer yağmalanıyor" ["Turks Came from Libya: No Safety, Looting Everywhere"], *Hürriyet*, 20 February, www.hurriyet.com.tr/libyadan-gelen-turkler-can-guvenligi-yok-her-yer-yagmalaniyor-17071087.

————. (2011c) "Libya'daki Türkleri onlar kurtaracak" ["They Will Save the Turks in Libya"], *Hürriyet*, 21 February, www.hurriyet.com.tr/libyadaki-turkleri-onlar-kurtaracak-17080579.

————. (2011d) "Davutoğlu CERN'i ziyaret etti" ["Davutoğlu Visited CERN"], *Hürriyet*, 28 February, www.hurriyet.com.tr/davutoglu-cerni-ziyaret-etti-17148510.

————. (2011e) "Aşırı panik yapmanın anlamı yok" ["No Reason to Panic"], *Hürriyet*, 21 February, www.hurriyet.com.tr/asiri-panik-yapmanin-anlami-yok-17080237.

————. (2011f) "Gül: Libya'da ölen Türk yok" ["No Turks Killed in Libya"], *Hürriyet*, 22 February, www.hurriyet.com.tr/gul-libyada-olen-turk-yok-17090623.

————. (2009) "5 yılda 10 milyar dolarlık iş aldık, Libya vizeyi de kaldırdı" ["We Got Business Worth Ten Billion Dollars in Five Years, Libya Lifted Visas"], *Hürriyet*, 25 November, www.hurriyet.com.tr/5-yilda-10-milyar-dolarlik-is-aldik-libya-vizeyi-de-kaldirdi-13034893.

Hürriyet Daily News. (2011) "Erdoğan Abandoned Gadhafi: Former Aide", 4 November, www.hurriyetdailynews.com/erdogan-abandoned-gadhafi-former-aide.aspx?pageID=238&nID=7184&NewsCatID=338.

İhlas Haber Ajansı. (2011) "BM'nin Kararı Meşru" ["The UN's Decision Is Legitimate"], *İhlas Haber Ajansı*, 18 March, www.iha.com.tr/haber-gul-bmnin-karari-mesru-165248/.

Işık, E., and Tutcalı, M. (2011) "Kılıçdaroğlu Libya'yı Haritada Gösteremez" ["Kılıçdaroğlu Cannot Point to Libya on a Map"], *İhlas Haber Ajansı*, 22 February, www.iha.com.tr/haber-kilicdardoglu-libyayi-haritada-gosteremez-161335.

Koenig, N. (2011) "The EU and the Libyan Crisis: In Quest of Coherence?" *The International Spectator: Italian Journal of International Affairs* 46(4): 11–30.

Le Parisien. (2011) "Libye: Seule la région de Tripoli resterait aux mains de Kadhafi" ["Only the Tripoli Region Remains to in the Hands of Gaddafi"], *Le Parisien*, 23 February,   www.leparisien.fr/crise-egypte/libye-seule-la-region-de-tripoli-resterait-aux-mains-de-kadhafi-23-02-2011-1328040.php.

Lüle, Z. (2011a) "Kim Bu Türkler?" ["Who Are These Turks?"] *Hürriyet*, 21 February, www.hurriyet.com.tr/kim-bu-turkler-17077491.

———. (2011b) "4 bin Türk aç-susuz mahsur" ["4000 Turks Stranded Without Water and Food"], *Hürriyet*, 22 February, www.hurriyet.com.tr/4-bin-turk-ac-susuz-mahsur-17086302.

McNamara, S. (2011) "The Crisis in Libya Exposes a Litany of Failed EU Policies Heritage", *Heritage*, 3 March, www.heritage.org/research/reports/2011/03/the-crisis-in-libya-exposes-a-litany-of-failed-eu-policies.

Menon, A. (2011) "European Defense Policy From Lisbon to Libya", *Survival* 53(3): 75–90.

Milliyet. (2011) "Davutoğlu: Libya'dan 579'u yabancı 14 bin 776 kişi tahliye edildi" ["Davutoğlu: 14 Thousand 776 People, Including 579 Foreigners, Evacuated"], *Milliyet*, 26 February, www.milliyet.com.tr/davutoglu-libya-dan-579-u-yabanci-14-bin-776-kisi-tahliye-edildi/siyaset/siyasetdetay/26.02.2011/1357447/default.htm.

Ministry of Foreign Affairs of Turkey. (2011) "Dışişleri Bakanlığı Sözcüsü'nün Bir Soruya Cevabı" ["Answer of the Ministry of Foreign Affairs Spokesperson to a Question] [Press Release SC: 9"], Ministry of Foreign Affairs of Turkey, Ankara, 3 March, www.mfa.gov.tr/sc_-9_-03-mart-2011_-disisleri-bakanligi-sozcusu_nun-bir-soruya-cevabi.tr.mfa.

NTV. (2011) "2 feribot 1 fırkateyn Libya'ya gidiyor" ["Two Ferries and a Frigate Are Going to Libya"], *NTV*, 21 February, www.ntv.com.tr/turkiye/2-feribot-1-firkateyn-libyaya-gidiyor,vtbwNhEppUSFAMMFoIXC4w.

Öniş, Z. (2012) "Turkey and the Arab Spring: Between Ethics and Self-Interest", *Insight Turkey* 14(3): 45–63.

Phillips, L. (2011) "EU Denounces Libya's Brutal Suppression of Protests", *The Guardian*, 21 February, www.theguardian.com/world/2011/feb/21/eu-libya.

Pop, V. (2011) "EU Wary of Imposing Sanctions on Libyan Dictator", *EUObserver*, 24 February, https://euobserver.com/news/31860.

Quinn, A. (2011) "Clinton Says Gaddafi Must Go", *Reuters*, 28 February, www.reuters.com/article/us-libya-usa-clinton-idUSTRE71Q1JA20110228.

Sabah. (2011a) "Başbakan ATV'de Cevapladı" ["Prime Minister Answered on ATV"], *Sabah*, 24 February, www.sabah.com.tr/gundem/2011/02/24/basbakan_gundemi_yorumluyor.

———. (2011b) "İç savaş çıksın istemiyoruz" ["We Don't Want a Civil War"], *Sabah*, 21 February, www.sabah.com.tr/gundem/2011/02/21/ic_savas_ciksin_istemiyoruz.

———. (2011c) "Erdoğan Kaddafi ile görüştü" ["Erdoğan Talked to Gaddafi"], *Sabah*, 21 February, www.sabah.com.tr/gundem/2011/02/21/erdogan_kaddafi_ile_gorustu.

———. (2011d) "Nato'nun Ne İşi Var Libya'da" ["What Business Does NATO Have in Libya?"] *Sabah*, 28 February, www.sabah.com.tr/gundem/2011/02/28/natonun_ne_isi_var_libyada.

———. (2009) "Libya'ya Tarihi Ziyaret" ["Historic Visit to Libya"], *Sabah*, 24 November, www.sabah.com.tr/Siyaset/2009/11/24/erdoganel_mahmudi_gorusmesi_basladi.

Şenyüz, S. (2010) "Türkiye'nin AB Üyeliği Örselenmemeli", *Hürriyet*, 30 November, www.hurriyet.com.tr/turkiye-nin-ab-uyeligi-orselenmemeli-16409029.

TBMM (2011) "Türkiye Büyük Millet Meclisi Basın Açıklamaları" [Turkish Parliament Press Releases], *TBMM Meclis Haber*, 24 March, https://www.tbmm.gov.tr/develop/owa/haber_portal.aciklama?p1=108075

Traynor, I., and Watt, N. (2011) "Libya: Nato to Control No-Fly Zone After France Gives Way to Turkey", *The Guardian*, 25 March, www.theguardian.com/world/2011/mar/24/france-turkey-nato-libya.

United Nations Security Council. (2011) "Security Council Press Statement on Libya, SC/10180-AFR/2120", New York, 22 February, www.un.org/press/en/2011/sc10180.doc.htm.

Yanatma, S. (2011) "Turkey Demonstrates Successful Evacuation Operations in Libya", *Today's Zaman*, 27 February, www.todayszaman.com/news-236774-turkey-demonstrates-successful-evacuation-operations-in-libya.html.

Zaman. (2011) "72 saatte 5 bin kişi tahliye edildi" ["Five Thousand People Evacuated in 72 Hours"], *Zaman*, 24 February, www.zaman.com.tr/dunya_72-saatte-5-bin-kisi-tahliye-edildi_1098180.html.

Zengin, G. (2013) *Kavga: Arap Baharı'nda Türk Dış Politikası [Conflict: Turkish Foreign Policy in the Arab Spring]*, İstanbul: İnkılap.

Zoubir, Y.H. (2009) "Libya and Europe: Economic Realism at the Rescue of the Qaddafi Authoritarian Regime", *Journal of Contemporary European Studies* 17(3): 401–15.

6 Turkey's foreign policy cooperation with the EU during the Syrian uprising

The uprising in Syria presents another case study for investigating potential cooperation between Turkey and the EU. This chapter discusses the interests of both actors in Syria and their approaches to the crisis, clarifies the question around potential cooperation, and analyses Turkey's interaction with the EU with regard to specific cooperative opportunities (COs) in order to assess why and to what degree there was cooperation.

The Syrian uprising started in early 2011 and transformed into a complex civil war. Since the aim of this study is to analyse how Turkey reacted to the uprising, the focus will be on the initial civil uprising phase and its immediate aftermath. As in the previous chapters, the analysis is broken down into individual COs. These cases in their own right can provide an understanding of the Turkish attitude and decision-making process vis-à-vis the turmoil. Table 6.1 summarises the COs that will be examined, as well as the outcomes in terms of cooperation with the EU.

The analysis presented here focuses on the extent to which the EU was consulted or informed both before and after the formulation of Turkish stances or actions. The main question around potential cooperation for Turkey and the EU was how to react to the Assad regime. This included the issue of when to criticise the Assad regime, which was an issue especially in the immediate aftermath of the clashes. Based on an empirical investigation, this analysis then discusses what the Turkish reaction meant for potential foreign policy cooperation with the EU.

Interests and reactions

A discussion of Syria's strategic importance to the Turkish government is necessary because the immediate Turkish response to the uprising was based on a policy of finding a balance between supporting democratic change and protecting strategic interests in Syria through refraining from antagonising President Assad. Before proceeding with analyses of COs, this subsection addresses the question of what these interests were to establish an understanding of the motivation of the Turkish government when the uprising started. It then moves on to outline the main EU preferences and reaction to the crisis in order to establish an understanding of how the Turkish and EU approaches differed in Syria.

Table 6.1 Cooperative opportunities during the Syrian uprising

	Turkish government preference	Turkish government action	EU preference	Outcome in terms of cooperation
CO5: Initial Turkish reaction and decision to impose economic sanctions	Solution through dialogue with Assad, then coordination with the Arab League	Reluctance to criticise and 'three-stage response'. Delayed criticism and late sanctions	Strong condemnation of human rights violations, sanctions, calls for Assad to resign	Information exchange both before and after the public announcement of Turkish positions
CO6: Decision to participate in the Friends of Syria Group (FSG) following the veto of UNSC resolution on 4 February 2012	Seeking international support, with the desire to be recognised as a key actor in the region	Cooperation with individual EU member states and Arab states. Hosting the opposition and the FSG	Support for FSG. The EU requests Turkish cooperation, especially on matters to do with the Syrian opposition	More than unilateral information but no substantial consultation. Information exchange on the crisis both before and after the Turkish participation in FSG
CO7: Turkish reaction to the record refugee influx on 6–8 April 2012	International engagement regarding the refugee crisis, possibly a buffer zone	Urging UN and NATO allies to request an intervention to tackle the refugee problem	Support for Turkish efforts to host refugees. Increasingly needed Turkish cooperation	More than unilateral information but no substantial cooperation
CO8: Turkish reactions to the Syrian downing of Turkish plane on 22 June 2012 and Akçakale shelling on 3 October 2012	Gaining international support/ expressions of solidarity for Turkish military retaliation	Consultation with NATO allies, change of the rules of engagement, Turkish military retaliation	Expression of support for Turkey and preference against the escalation of conflict	Unilateral information. The Turkish government briefed the EU about its actions and requested the EU to express solidarity. No opportunity given to the EU to comment.

Turkish interests and reaction

Prior to the uprising, and even before he became a policy maker, Davutoğlu (2001: 119) argued that Turkey needed to use its geostrategic and "geocultural" potential to build economic interdependence in the region that would subsequently enable Turkey to expand its area of influence, which was the fundamental basis of his idea of "zero problems with neighbours". Improving relations with neighbours was the building block of the Turkish strategy, aiming to make Turkey a "soft power" and, to achieve this aim, transnational trade was encouraged while at the same time culture was used to maintain good relations.

Syria is a good example for this policy. Historically tense relations improved significantly in the first years of the AKP era. In fact, prior to the onset of the turmoil, the relationship with Syria was seen by the AKP elites as the epitome of Davutoğlu's "zero problems with neighbours" policy because relations were rapidly improving. To illustrate, in 1998, Turkey almost waged war with Syria over the crisis involving the extradition of the PKK leader (Hale, 2013: 233); in 2008, Turkish and Syrian leaders vacationed together with their families in Turkey's southern resort town of Bodrum (İHA, 2008). A prominent example of how political and economic relations improved in the AKP era is the High Level Strategic Cooperation Council, which was established in 2009 for cooperation in various areas, such as security, commerce, culture, and education, and was regarded as a "milestone in Turkish-Syrian relations" (Ministry of Foreign Affairs of Turkey, 2012a, 2012b). Many agreements were signed, including a visa exemption agreement that would allow Syrian and Turkish citizens to travel freely and an agreement to abolish taxes imposed on lorries carrying goods between Syria and Turkey in order to strengthen economic ties (CNN Türk, 2009).

The Syrian state became not only an economic partner but also a military and political ally. Military cooperation with Syria was important for Turkey's border security because Syria was a key actor that could help Turkey in the armed conflict against the PKK. Accordingly, in December 2010, Turkish and Syrian governments signed an agreement expanding the 1998 Adana Protocol which concerned cooperation against the PKK (TBMM, 2011). The Syrian government was also a political ally of the Turkish government in regional politics and most notably joined Turkey's criticism of Israel (see e.g., Eligür, 2012: 442–45). As Turkish-Israeli tensions rose in 2009 over the situation in Gaza, the Turkish government focused on strengthening its relations with Syria – an ally of Iran and Hamas. For example, in order to "boost friendship", as Turkish officials stated, Turkey and Syria held a joint military exercise, which Israeli Defense Minister Ehud Barak referred to as a "disturbing development" (*Today's Zaman*, 2009; Keinon, 2009). When Turkey excluded Israel from an Anatolian Eagle military exercise in 2009, which had been planned to include NATO members, the Syrian foreign minister supported Ankara, saying: "We extremely welcome [this] decision. This decision is based on Turkey's approach towards Israel and reflects the way Turkey regards the Israeli attack in Gaza" (quoted in Elci, 2009). Essentially, Syria was important not only because there were economic reasons for restoring and strengthening the relationship but also because it was seen by the Turkish government as a political and military ally in the region, which was why Turkish decision makers often underlined that there was "full cooperation between Turkey and Syria in regional matters" (Davutoğlu, 2010).

Moreover, there was a cultural dimension to the relationship in the notion that Syria was a "brother" for Turkey. The cultural aspect was intended to be used as a glue that would unite both countries in a spirit of solidarity based on shared experiences. In the discourses of Turkish elites, there was often the idea that Turkey and Syria were more than neighbours. For instance, addressing a group of business persons in Damascus, Turkish President Gül (2009) stated, "Syrian and Turkish people are much closer to each other than neighbours". When referring to his counterpart in a joint press conference in 2010, Foreign Minister Davutoğlu (2010) used the word "my brother".

This discourse of cultural affinity applied to President Assad too. For example, emphasising his personal friendship with the Syrian President, while talking about how the AKP government had improved relations with Syria, Prime Minister Erdoğan (2010) referred to the Syrian President as "my brother Assad". This changed later on, when the Turkish and Syrian governments became hostile toward each other – even the Turkish pronunciation of the name of the Syrian President changed after the Turkish government started to encourage the Arabic (and original) pronunciation of the name (*Esed*) over its Turkish equivalent that had been used for him and his father (*Esad*), in an attempt to alienate the Syrian President in the perception of the Turkish public. This became a public debate in Turkey, demonstrating the changing attitude of the Turkish government towards the Syrian regime, which will be discussed in depth later. For instance, a Turkish columnist asked:

> This is what 'image' is. . . . It matters how something is presented. . . . Have you ever thought why 'Esad' of 40 years suddenly became 'Esed'? Wasn't he 'Esad' when he was the brother and the buddy of our prime minister? One morning we woke up and he became 'Esed' in all the partisan media along with the TRT and the Anadolu Agency [state-run media] . . . Because before he was one of us, we even called him 'Esad' like in Turkish. . . . Things changed and suddenly 'Esad' turned into 'Esed'.
>
> (Özdil, 2012)

The costs of cooperation may vary across COs, which is why this analysis will examine each CO individually, but it is possible to provide a general assessment of whether cooperation was particularly costly in the case of Syria. The costs of cooperation with the EU increased to the extent that cooperation constrained the Turkish government from acting effectively in response to the crisis. When the Turkish government preferred unilateral action, cooperation, to the extent that it constrained unilateral action, became more difficult to achieve. However, cooperation could have been beneficial. For instance, especially after the crisis in Syria, Turkey's strategic value to EU foreign policy increased, giving an opportunity to the Turkish government to demonstrate to the EU that Turkey was an important ally and partner. Cooperation could also have issue-specific benefits, which will be discussed in detail. For example, in the case of refugees, achieving "coordination" with the EU could have potentially helped the Turkish government to tackle the refugee crisis more effectively if it had accepted the EU assistance before the issue grew uncontrollable. Both general and issue-specific costs and benefits will be taken into account here when assessing the degree of cooperation in each CO.

EU preferences and reaction

In addition to the Turkish position, it is important to clarify the EU's preferences with regard to Syria too because cooperation in the form of consultation ideally involves the EU's feedback on Turkish policy, which would have been based on the EU's preferences in Syria. If the EU had had fundamentally different preferences, this could also have been a cost and impeded cooperation in the sense of co-decision and consultation, but this would not necessarily have indicated a total absence of cooperation. Therefore, it is useful to establish an understanding of the EU's perspective on Syria.

According to the European External Action Service (2015a), prior to the crisis, the EU had "sought to develop a closer relationship with Syria, which would have provided for political dialogue, mutually beneficial trade and investment relations, and cooperation on economic, social and democratic reform". The EU–Syria Association Agreement, which was concluded in 2004 but not yet signed, laid out the bilateral relationship as having an emphasis on trade, cooperation in a number of fields including agriculture and environmental protection, and Political Dialogue on bilateral and regional issues of mutual interest (European External Action Service, 2015b). The draft agreement was frozen after the crisis started in 2011, but it highlights that the EU saw Syria as a partner in the region and sought to develop a closer and mutually beneficial relationship. EU policy and preferences during the initial phase of the uprising were based on strong condemnation of Assad, freezing relations, and establishing a policy of targeted restrictive measures.

The key differences between EU and Turkish preferences can be identified as the EU's greater concern for human rights abuses and greater aversion to being drawn into military intervention, since Syria was less of a direct security threat to the EU than to Turkey. These differences will be taken into consideration when discussing the main issue around potential cooperation, which was for both actors how to react to the Assad regime and opposition movement.

The EU made its stance clear from the beginning by imposing restrictive measures right away, as this analysis will discuss. It should be noted that, although there were different voices between EU members states from time to time, the EU approach was much less divided compared to the case of Libya. Most notably, there was a disagreement about amending the arms embargo before it expired in 2013. The UK, with the backing of France, Italy, and Cyprus, argued that the ban on arming the rebels should be amended because it would send a strong signal to

President Assad that the military balance was shifting. Other EU member states led by Austria pointed to the risks of the arms ending up in the hands of extremists (McDonald-Gibson, 2013). However, during the uprising phase of the crisis, taking into consideration the initial response of the EU, it is possible to claim that there was no radical divergence between EU member states in broad terms, especially compared to the EU response in Libya.

Initial Turkish reaction and the decision to impose economic sanctions

The first CO concerns the way in which the Turkish government reacted to the uprisings starting on 15 March 2011 and the degree to which there was cooperation on the issue of whether or not to use sanctions against the Assad regime. The key question for cooperation for both actors was what side to take, and in what form in terms of policy choices (only verbal criticism or sanctions). This section will focus on whether there was any consultation with the EU in view of these preferences with regard to the key question the CO raises. Specifically, this means that this analysis will focus on the extent to which there was communication and an exchange of views with the EU when the Turkish government decided to impose sanctions.

Before proceeding, the "three-stage strategy" (Davutoğlu, 2012b) of the Turkish government needs to be examined. At the centre of Turkey's response to the Syrian uprising was what Öniş (2012: 46) called an "ethics versus self-interest dilemma", that is, "[h]ow to find the delicate balance between supporting reforms and protecting strategic interests?" (see also *The Economist*, 2012). Figure 6.1 summarises the "three-stage strategy" that (Davutoğlu, 2012b) argued he (and the Turkish government) had followed. According to him, first, they tried "bilateral engagement – Turkey approaching the Assad regime and trying to work with them to support the reform process" (Davutoğlu, 2012b). Towards the end of this stage, on 20 June 2011, the Turkish government gave Assad a week to implement reforms, which Assad refused to do (*Hürriyet*, 2011b). Second, they pursed a "regional initiative with the Arab League . . . to find a solution without foreign intervention to our region" (Davutoğlu, 2012b). The Turkish government got together with the heads of Arab states to discuss the crisis in various meetings (Ergan and Özkaya, 2011). Third, after these did not yield a result, the Turkish government went to the UNSC with the Arab League to make it "an international issue" (Davutoğlu, 2012b; *Hürriyet*, 2011a).

As Öniş (2012) has pointed out, the Turkish government was cautious about supporting the opposition movement in the first two stages, but then it became vocally critical of the Assad regime. He has also suggested that there was a fourth phase in which the Turkish government returned to a cautious state by considering the uncertainty regarding how the events would unfold, with a particular focus on the potential economic costs that could be incurred as a result of policy action (ibid.). The three-stage strategy indicates that in the immediate aftermath of the crisis, the Turkish government was reluctant to appear vocally critical or give

Bilateral Engagement

The Turkish government tries to persuade the Assad government to make reforms and talks to Assad directly.

Regional Initiative

The Turkish government seeks the Arab League support to persuade Assad to make reforms and meets the leaders and ministers of Arab states in various meetings to discuss the crisis.

Making it International

The Turkish government and the members of the Arab League urge the UNSC for action after Assad refuses to comply.

Figure 6.1 Davutoğlu's three-stage strategy

support to the opposition in Syria. A cost-benefit calculation was involved, and the Turkish position was adjusted based on how Assad responded to calls for reform. When the Turkish decision makers realised that the bilateral engagement with the Syrian regime in which they sought to "work with" the regime to "support the reform process" (Davutoğlu, 2012b) was not yielding any results, they had to change their course of action. They were reluctant to do so because the improvement in relations with Syria was regarded as a success story of the "zero problems with neighbours" policy that Davutoğlu advocated; however, when Assad did not respond to calls for reform and continued to use violence, the costs of not being critical of the regime dramatically increased (Interview TR07).

As the costs of not criticising the Syrian regime increased due to continued violence, it became difficult to keep pursuing the "zero problems with neighbours" policy with regard to Syria and to appear to support a violent regime at a time of democratic upheaval. In fact, this was precisely why some analysts, such as Ülgen (2011a, 2011b) and Balcı (2012), declared that the policy was "dead". A Turkish columnist contended, "If there had not been an uprising in Syria and if the Assad regime had not used violence, it seems that the close relationship [between Turkish and Syrian governments] would have continued" (Kohen, 2012). It is a fair assessment that the wave of uprisings completely changed the nature of Turkey-Syria relations. The three-stage strategy essentially reflects the dilemma Turkish decision makers faced, which concerned seeking to maintain a mutually beneficial relationship with Syria that had been secured through good relations with President Assad over the years, while at the same time supporting democratic movements in the country and in the region overall.

The Turkish government and the EU had different initial reactions. Following the crackdown against anti-government protesters in Syria, the EU strongly condemned the widespread human rights violations, introduced a set of restrictive measures starting in May 2011 (see e.g., The Council of the European Union, 2011), and called on Assad to step aside (European External Action Service, 2011). Instead of taking a harsh stance, the Turkish government approached the Assad government to encourage reforms. There were several main reasons for this bilateral approach. The Turkish government had developed close ties with Syria over the previous decade under the AKP government, and the relationship had brought economic and security-related benefits. So, the strategic value of relations was high. Also, as Davutoğlu stated, Syria was a "success story" for the "zero problems with neighbours" policy because the improvement of relations with this policy had brought many benefits (quoted in Shadid, 2011). Therefore, the Turkish government was reluctant to abandon the policy before seeing whether it could persuade the Assad regime to implement reforms. Moreover, an approach based on bilateral engagement was seen as an opportunity to test the effectiveness of the "new" Turkish foreign policy, which aspired to make Turkey a soft power in the region. Furthermore, it was seen by members of the AKP elite, such as Erdoğan, who had developed a personal friendship with Assad over the past decade, that Turkey might succeed in talking Assad into making reforms (ibid.). In fact, Erdoğan himself made numerous telephone calls to Assad in May and June 2011, giving him advice about necessary reforms (*Hürriyet*, 2011c, 2011d).

The reactions of the Turkish government and the EU were also different in the sense that a friendly relationship between the Turkish and Syrian leaders continued while the Turkish government was figuring out if the "bilateral engagement" would work. For instance, the Turkish PM even received congratulatory telephone calls from the Syrian President in June 2011 for his re-election (*Hürriyet*, 2011d). There were signs at that time that the Turkish attitude was eventually going to toughen. For example, Erdoğan claimed in an interview, "We cannot remain silent to developments in Syria anymore, good relations [with Syria] will not last forever" (*Hürriyet*, 2011e). For Davutoğlu, the reason why the Turkish government preferred "working with" the Assad government and bilateral engagement was because they were positive they would be able to talk Assad into making reforms (*Hürriyet*, 2011g). As of 16 June, Davutoğlu was still referring to the "determination of Assad to implement reforms", saying that his determination needed to be taken into account (ibid.). The initial reluctance of the Turkish government to take a harsh stance against the Assad regime not only shows the significance of relations with the regime, but also it is a clear indicator that the EU and the Turkish government had divergent approaches about how to deal with the crisis.

A prominent example of the difference between the policies of Turkey and the EU concerns the resignation of Assad. On 18 August 2011, EU High

Representative Ashton (2011a) stated that it was a "necessity" for Assad to step aside and that there had been a "complete loss" of his "legitimacy" in the eyes of the Syrian people. A day after this statement, it was reported that the Turkish government claimed it was too early to make such a call (*Hürriyet*, 2011f). This clear divergence was mentioned in the Turkey 2011 Progress Report published later in October 2011: "Turkey did not align itself with EU restrictive measures with regard to Syria" (European Commission, 2011: 107).

The subject of Assad's resignation as well as restrictive measures against the regime could be areas in which potential cooperation could have taken place between the Turkish government and the EU. However, when examining how the Turkish government pursued its policy of bilateral engagement and interactions with the EU at the time, there is no conclusive evidence showing that it acted in coordination with the EU through discussing the policies it would pursue. "Co-decision" with the EU would have been costly because of policy divergence away from the EU and the way in which the Turkish government had more strategic interests at stake in maintaining its relationship with the Assad regime than with the EU.

Cooperation does not necessarily lead to alignment, and alignment does not necessarily mean cooperation. Although the EU and the Turkish government diverged, there was still cooperation that was a step further than "unilateral information" but that did not reach "consultation". The main reason for this was the contact between Turkish and EU officials. They were in touch, including at the highest levels, which indicates that there was information exchange both before and after the Turkish government decided to ask Assad to step aside and impose sanctions (Interviews TR05, TR07, EU02, EU03, EU04, EU05, EU06). Syria was on the agenda when Turkish and EU officials met, which is a clear indicator that the Turkish side valued its foreign policy relationship with the EU, as it was willing to discuss such matters.

A key issue with regard to "unilateral information" is whether the EU was warned before the Turkish government took a position that was at odds with the preferences of the EU. There is no conclusive evidence that the Turkish government informed the EU in advance that it was going to take a divergent position. This could have happened possibly when the EU declared that Assad needed to go on 18 August 2011, after which the Turkish government publicly stated it was too early to insist on his resignation, as pointed out earlier. As a general rule, when the EU issues a statement, Turkey, along with other candidate states, is asked to join the statement and the EU Delegation in Ankara liaises with the Ministry of Foreign Affairs to ascertain the Turkish position (Interview EU02, EU06). Therefore, even if the Turkish government takes a divergent position, or is about to take a divergent position, the EU has a chance to learn of this. So, it is unlikely that the Turkish responses caught the EU by surprise since they would have been informed, or at least had some idea, about the Turkish stance. However, in this CO, the Turkish government did not initiate contact to inform the EU of its intended actions. This was an important aspect of information exchange during this CO. There have been times when the Turkish government reached out to the

EU to inform, as when the Turkish plane was shot down, which will be discussed later in this chapter.

As mentioned, Turkish and EU officials met bilaterally and in international forums, and there was both formal and informal dialogue involving information exchange, which would indicate a certain degree of "consultation" taking place. The main point is not so much only whether they meet but also whether they discuss issues of mutual concern. And they generally do. Good evidence for this might be the informal meeting of the EU Foreign Affairs Ministers (Gymnich) on 2–3 September 2011, to which Davutoğlu was invited. According to a ministerial statement by UK FM Hague, a discussion on Syria took place in the presence of Davutoğlu, and the primary focus was on sanctions against the Assad regime (Hague, 2011). At the outcome of the meeting, the EU tightened economic pressure on the regime by imposing an oil embargo (Oweiss, 2011), whereas the Turkish government had not yet decided to impose sanctions. Since there was discussion of the issue, "consultation" was involved in the sense of hearing the other side's preferences with regard to action, even if their preferences were not then taken into account. Nevertheless, an important distinction that should be made here is that there is no evidence that the Turkish government specifically reached out to the EU for consultation. It did not request the EU's opinion or feedback on Turkish policy.

Although the EU's opinion was not sought, the Turkish government agreed to participate in such meetings with the EU, which could mean that the Turkish government regarded participation as a means to influence the EU attitude towards the regime. The Turkish government had such a motivation because initially it did not want the Assad regime to lose power in Syria. As in the case of Libya, the Turkish government had prioritised stability, which meant that it would support the regime until the situation became clearer. Also, essentially, the Turkish government felt that the EU should listen to what the Turkish government had to say because of the Turkish self-perception that Turkey was becoming a regional leader. The Turkish government also believed that the EU needed to realise the strategic importance of Turkey in the region, and participation in such meetings provided an opportunity for the Turkish government to demonstrate to the EU that it was an important asset. For this reason, when FM Davutoğlu participated in the Gymnich meetings, the EU leaders felt he was talking way too much, which was, according to an EU diplomat, the reason why he was not invited anymore (Interview EU06). According to another interviewed EU diplomat, FM Davutoğlu spoke as if he were a lecturer, telling the EU ministers the right way to act, and implying that Turkey knew the Middle East best, and that there was a "fatigue" of hearing Davutoğlu speak (Interview EU02). This is not specific to Syria, and it applies to other cases, but the lecturing tone was heard mostly on how to deal with the Syrian crisis (Interview EU02).

In November 2011, in response to a question at the European Parliament, HR Ashton (2011b) stated, "the EU and Turkey are in close and regular contact on this issue [the crisis in Syria], including at the highest levels". Evidence suggests a key motivation for such regular contacts could be the Turkish desire to demonstrate to the EU that it was a vital actor and influence EU policy in accordance with Turkish preferences to the best of its capacity. For this reason, the interaction does not qualify as substantial "consultation" although it is a step further than "unilateral information" since the EU was able to express its views on the crisis in bilateral and international meetings.

As for whether the EU attempted to persuade the Turkish government to align itself with the EU position, in fact, Turkey, along with other candidate countries, was invited to align itself. A political counsellor at the EU Delegation in Ankara explained:

> There is a constant channel of communication. We get instructions from Brussels to explain our policy to get Turkey on board. When we do sanctions we normally explain our position to our partners usually through the delegation here at the MFA or the dialogue covering the area. Turkey was a bit cautious on the sanction policy. We invited Turkey to try to follow them in the case of Syria. Sometimes Turkey follows and sometimes they don't, it's based on their assessment and all we can do is to try to explain our policy.
> (Interview EU06)

So, the EU did want Turkish support on this specific instance, but the nature of interaction did not involve active and collective pressure from the EU on the Turkish government to align itself and take measures against the Assad government. As the EU diplomat mentioned, the EU's attempt was more of a procedural course of action – all candidates were usually invited to align, and so was Turkey (Interview EU06). What is crucial here, however, is that the EU, valuing Turkish support on the matter, engaged in much information exchange with the Turkish government even though they held different views. According to the interviewee, the information exchange helped them to better understand each other's policy (Interview EU06).

The Turkish government decided to impose economic sanctions on 30 November (BBC, 2011). An examination of Turkish motivation indicates that contacts with the EU were not influential in any way and that the main reason for the timing of the Turkish decision was the declaration of the Arab League to impose sanctions. The Turkish decision makers even made it clear that the nature of sanctions was in line with the ones imposed by the Arab League.

To elaborate, the Turkish government waited to see the Arab League decision on sanctions and then imposed sanctions just a few days later. It is important to revisit Davutoğlu's three-stage strategy in order to make an assessment. By the time the Turkish government was in "bilateral engagement", economic and political sanctions had already been imposed on the Assad regime by major powers such as the US and EU members. When "bilateral engagement" failed, the Turkish government pursued what Davutoğlu framed as a "regional initiative with the Arab League". So, Davutoğlu himself revealed that they were coordinating with the Arab League regarding a response to the crisis. The rationale for prioritising working together with the Arab League was that they did not want what they considered to be "foreign intervention" in the region. "I participated in several Arab League meetings because we wanted a solution without any foreign intervention to our region", Davutoğlu (2012b) highlighted. The emphasis on "foreign intervention" and a "regional solution" signifies that Turkey gave more weight to its consultations with the Arab League than to other actors, such as the EU. In other words, right from the beginning, coordination with the Arab League was the priority. This was why when Turkish decision makers were not able to convince Assad to make reforms, they sought the support of the Arab League and frequently met the heads of Arab states to discuss the situation. As the international pressure on the Assad regime mounted and the "bilateral engagement" failed, the Turkish government, in coordination with the Arab league, changed its stance.

On 27 November 2011, attending the meeting after which the Arab League declared its sanctions, Davutoğlu stated that there was a "full agreement" between Turkey and the Arab League on Syria and that Turkey planned to impose sanctions "parallel" in nature (NTV, 2011). Three days after the Arab League's decision, on 30 November, Turkey finally imposed similar economic sanctions (BBC, 2011). Indeed, as with every decision, it is difficult to say whether it was only one factor (the Arab League's decision in this case) that shaped the Turkish decision. It is possible that the positions of other actors, such as the US, played a role too, particularly because it would have been difficult and costly for the Turkish government to avoid imposing sanctions at a time when the international pressure on the Assad regime was mounting. Nevertheless, the strong Turkish emphasis on a "regional initiative", the timing of Turkish sanctions, and the fact that the Turkish sanctions were parallel in nature with those of the Arab League suggest that the Turkish government followed the steps of the Arab League, as it openly stated that it was intending to do. As a result, it is possible to see the Arab League as a major driver of a change in Turkish policy, that is, from a cautious approach to an actively critical approach.

In terms of interactions with the EU, the information exchange also continued after the announcement of Turkish sanctions, but it did not reach the degree of "consultation" for the reasons discussed. After the regional initiative with the Arab League, the Turkish government voiced opposition to the Syrian regime and urged the UNSC to act, as explained by Foreign Minister Davutoğlu (2012b). It is possible to claim that during this stage of Turkish reaction, the Turkish government mainly prioritised dialogue with UNSC members. So, for the Turkish government, individual EU member states in the UNSC were at the forefront in terms of the actors that the Turkish government was urging. The bottom line here is that, again, the EU as an actor was not seen as much worthy of cooperation.

In sum, the Turkish government did not immediately impose sanctions or call Assad to step aside, but the EU did. The question for both actors around potential cooperation was whether to criticise Assad and impose sanctions. The key question for this analysis was whether there was any consultation with the EU when the Turkish government decided to impose sanctions and become critical of the Assad regime. Detailed and repeated discussions between EU and Turkish officials took place, and there was information exchange both before and after the public announcement of the Turkish decision to impose sanctions on 30 November 2011. However, there is no evidence that the Turkish government sought EU feedback on Turkish policy, requested the EU position, or even reached out to the EU to inform it in advance about its positions. Therefore, it is hardly possible to say that substantial "consultation" took place. The interaction did not reach the "unilateral information" point either. The meetings with the EU, both bilateral and international, indicate that the EU was able to present its take on the crisis and that there was mutual information exchange throughout the CO. Therefore, the interaction was a step further than "unilateral information".

Overall, rationalism better explains Turkish motivations – both considering Turkey's reaction to the crisis and its attitude to cooperation with the EU. The three-stage strategy Davutoğlu outlined was essentially a strategic adjustment of policy based on Turkish interests in Syria. Even though Turkish decision makers did not want to jeopardise their relationship with Assad, the ongoing crisis compelled them to eventually take a critical stance, which was particularly a result of the failure of the "bilateral engagement with Assad" that they had attempted and the monumental increase in the costs of not joining states that were imposing economic sanctions.

Seeking a higher level of cooperation would have been costly, especially because of policy divergence from the EU and differences of views with regard to how to approach the crisis. "Co-decision" with the EU would have been particularly costly because the EU held different preferences on the issue of sanctions and it had voiced criticism earlier than the Turkish government, whereas the Syrian regime had a greater strategic value for the Turkish government. However, cooperation took place regardless. It is not possible to claim any substantial "consultation" took place because the Turkish government did not specifically aim for holding consultation or reaching out to request the EU's opinion. Yet, there was information exchange, which was not costly. Moreover, this is another example in which the EU wanted Turkish cooperation more rather than the other way around, which explains the absence of "consultation" and the nature of information exchange that involved the EU side from time to time, making the effort to ascertain the Turkish positions.

Turkish reaction to the creation of the "Friends of Syria Group"

After Russia and China vetoed a UNSC resolution on 4 February 2012, which would have backed an Arab League plan urging Assad to resign, France, with the support of the US, proposed creating a "Group of Friends of the Syrian People" (hereafter "Friends of Syria Group" [FSG]) in order to establish a coalition of the willing in reaction to the failure of the UNSC to act. According to Davutoğlu (2012b), after the first two policy options in Figure 6.1 – "bilateral engagement with the Assad regime" and "regional initiative with the Arab League" – did not work, the Turkish strategy was to "make it an international issue" through encouraging a collective response in the UNSC to put an end to the conflict. To this end, cooperation could potentially have taken place with the EU. This CO specifically concerns the third stage in the Turkish response and whether cooperation with the EU took place when the Turkish government decided to join the international coalition. This section will examine the motivations of Turkish decision makers as well as the interactions with the EU in order to assess the degree of cooperation with the EU.

The Turkish decision to participate in the coalition was part of the three-stage strategy, and it was based on costs and benefits of action with regard to the crisis, as discussed in the previous section. When they joined the wider international community, Turkish decision makers became vocally critical of Assad, claiming that there was an "ethical responsibility" (Davutoğlu, 2012b) of Turkey to end the violence, and made arguments based on democracy promotion, which was not the kind of approach they had previously had towards the region prior to the Arab Spring (Öniş, 2012). Again, rationalism better explains why they had to adjust their policy: because giving support to the Assad regime in the face of international pressure against the regime was no longer viable, and there were now benefits of joining the wider international community too. For example, the Turkish government could play a leading role because of its proximity to the turmoil, and Turkish decision makers could demonstrate how they had made Turkey an influential actor in matters of global importance.

When urging the UNSC did not work, there was an opportunity for cooperation with the EU regarding the international stance against the Assad regime. Similar to the previous CO, there was frequent information exchange but no substantial "consultation" or "co-decision". Turkish decision makers saw themselves in a position of strength and as key players in the solution of the conflict and therefore did not see it necessary to approach the EU for consultation. If anything, the EU was the party that approached the Turkish government for information. The Friends of Syria Group is a specific example of a forum in which the EU sought consultation with the Turkish government, especially because it hosted the Syrian opposition, which was an essential actor in the crisis. Overall, this CO was an opportunity for the Turkish government to demonstrate to the EU that it was a valuable asset in the region for EU foreign policy.

The creation of the international coalition against the Syrian regime, the Friends of Syria Group, was a reaction to the inability of the UNSC to act. Western allies, particularly France, led the initiative with Arab states to create the coalition right after the Russian and Chinese veto. On the day of the veto, 4 February 2012, it was reported that the French President said he was consulting with the Arab and European countries to create a contact group on Syria to find a solution to the crisis (Irish, 2012). Turkey would also be a part of this group, along with more than 60 other states. On 9 February 2012, expressing his disappointment following the Russian and Chinese veto, Davutoğlu (2012b) made it clear that the Turkish government would also participate in this group. He argued that "an international platform to support Syrian people and reforms" was needed and then added, "We are currently reassessing this with the Arab League and with several colleagues in Europe. The nature of this platform will be specified after consultations" (ibid.).

So, it is possible to say that "consultation" took place more with individual EU member states, primarily with France, in order to create this coalition, rather than with the EU as an actor.

However, it is still possible to point to meetings between the EU and Turkey during this period in which the issue was discussed. There are two prominent examples of high-level official foreign policy interaction with the EU during this period. During Davutoğlu's meetings in Washington on 10 February 2012, HR Ashton telephoned Davutoğlu about developments in Syria. It was reported that she requested the conversation, after which she invited him to the next EU Foreign Affairs Council (*Sabah*, 2012). Also between 18 and 20 February 2012, during the G20 Ministerial Meetings in Mexico, Davutoğlu discussed the issue of Syria with several leaders, including HR Ashton (Ministry of Foreign Affairs of Turkey, 2012c). So, there was not only close contact – Ashton and Davutoğlu frequently having chances to talk and to update each other – but also instances in which the EU side took the initiative to reach out to the Turkish government to talk about the crisis in Syria.

After the creation of the group, the close contact continued. The Syrian conflict, as well as the reaction of the international community, was a major item on the agenda when high-level Turkish and EU officials met. For instance, a week before the second meeting of the FSG, which was held in Istanbul on 1 April 2012, the EU High Representative, Commissioner for Enlargement, Turkish Foreign Minister, and Turkish EU Minister met in Brussels for a Political Dialogue meeting to discuss membership negotiations, as well as the situation in Syria (*Today's Zaman*, 2012).

The way in which there were frequent and detailed meetings with the EU both before and after the Turkish government participated in the FSG means that there was more than just "unilateral information". The EU was able to present its view on the crisis, and the Turkish government was providing information about its own position.

However, the Turkish government was not specifically seeking EU feedback on its policy with regard to the creation of FSG, or requesting meetings with the EU to discuss its policy, which means that the interaction did not reach the "consultation" level. It is not a straightforward case of "consultation" because there is no evidence suggesting that there was a will from the Turkish government to seek the EU opinion on the matter or indicating that Turkish officials reached out to the EU for consultation. Two points need to be highlighted here. First, as mentioned earlier, this is an instance in which the EU desired Turkish cooperation because of Turkey's position as a key player in hosting the opposition and its proximity to the crisis. The EU consulted the Turkish government, especially regarding matters concerning the Syrian opposition, which became an important issue, particularly in FSG meetings. An EU diplomat claimed that the EU had "a lot to learn from Turkey", particularly because Turkey hosted the Syrian opposition and the EU was passing messages to the opposition, for instance, about the need to be more inclusive, which was "a big message of the EU in the beginning" (Interview EU06). Confirming these claims and emphasising the importance of dialogue with

Turkey, HR Ashton's Turkey advisor at the time claimed that Turkey had "networks" and "niche contacts" in the Middle East that the EU didn't have, and this was one of the main reasons why the EU wanted Turkey's cooperation (Interview EU04). This is important information because it suggests that the EU was the side that was asking favours from the Turkish government and requesting cooperation rather than the other way around, which could be one of the explanations as to why there is no conclusive evidence indicating that the Turkish government approached the EU.

In addition, there is evidence indicating that the EU was not seen as an actor with which the Turkish government should have a consultation and therefore not much importance was given to EU preferences. This attitude is evident from the comments of Turkish decision makers about the role of the EU during the uprising. For example, when asked about Syria and interactions with the EU at the time, the EU minister and chief negotiator of Turkey, Bağış, claimed that the EU was a "weak" actor and not capable of acting (Interview TR01). He even argued that Turkey was the actor influencing the EU position: "Our initiatives and policies especially regarding the Friends of Syria Group meetings had a major impact on the Syria policies of other important actors including the EU" (Interview TR01). Similarly, when asked about discussions with the EU about Syria at the time, Çavuşoğlu, the deputy chairman of AKP in charge of foreign relations (later on minister for EU Affairs, then foreign minister since 2015), argued that the EU had "no influence" on Turkish policy during talks because the EU had "no vision" and "no policy" (Interview TR11). Whether or not Turkish positions actually made any impact on EU policies is a different issue. The main point here is that the Turkish leadership was somewhat reluctant to consult the EU because it saw it as ineffective with respect to the conflict, which might also explain why the Turkish government prioritised cooperation with certain individual EU member states that they thought were influential, such as France. This point brings us to the question of why there was then any cooperation in the first place.

Arguably, in the third stage of the response of the Turkish government, pushing the international community about the crisis in Syria, Turkish policy makers cooperated with the EU mainly because they wanted international support. Although they did not really believe that the EU could make any significant difference, they agreed to get together with EU officials bilaterally to talk about the FSG and the international response to the crisis in Syria in general. For them, presumably the only area in which EU opinion could be useful was if it backed Turkish positions so that the Turkish position could be internationally accepted. The third stage of the Turkish reaction was making the issue international, and having meetings with the EU was a part of this policy. The key point here is that through these meetings, the Turkish government was not so much seeking EU opinion or feedback on Turkish policy; rather it was following the third stage of its policy, which was based on urging the international community to increase the pressure on the Syrian regime. Therefore, cooperation with the EU involved a projection of Turkish interests with regard to the crisis in general.

Again, rationalism better explains the Turkish behaviour since it was an extension of the strategic adjustment of behaviour after bilateral engagement with the Assad regime had not worked. It was beneficial for the Turkish government to explain itself to the international community, and to the EU, which in return might have allowed them to play a leading role in the international coalition, which planned to shape the movement of change in Syria. The Turkish government did not believe the EU could be a significant actor, which explains the lack of substantial consultation, but still wanted to sit together with the EU, as to do so was a part of its policy of making the issue international.

When the FSG was created, the desire of the Turkish government was to be able to play an influential role and to be recognised as an important actor in the region. To this end, cooperation with the EU took place. As for specific explanatory factors determining the costs and benefits of cooperation with the EU, it could be claimed that achieving recognition as a key actor in the international response was the main benefit of having information exchange and meetings with the EU. It was not beneficial to have a higher degree of cooperation because the EU was not seen as a relevant actor that could make a change with regard to the solution of the crisis.

Turkish reaction to the record refugee influx 6–8 April 2012

This CO is embedded in the broader Syrian refugee crisis and the Turkish reaction thereto. This analysis only addresses the initial period, when a high number of refugees started to arrive in Turkey. The initial Turkish reaction and attitude towards the resolution of the problem typify the overall Turkish approach to cooperation with the EU during the broader refugee crisis.

Cooperation with the EU during this CO could have taken place with the aim of finding a solution to the Syrian refugee crisis. It should, however, be noted that initially, the EU did not need Turkish cooperation so much, but this changed later when the refugee crisis started to affect EU member states due to irregular migration. Although cooperation with the EU could potentially help the Turkish government regarding the management of refugees, Turkish decision makers believed they did not need any help, mainly because they thought the crisis would be over soon.

Ankara was alarmed on the weekend of 6–8 April 2012 due to a record increase in the number of Syrians fleeing to Turkey as a consequence of violence escalating in Syria. The total number of Syrian refugees rapidly reached nearly 25,000, which, coupled with shots being fired from Syria on refugee camps in Turkey on 9 April 2012, made the refugee issue one that needed urgent attention from the Turkish government. The crisis presented an opportunity for cooperation with the EU. The Turkish government had the chance to consult the EU and include the EU in its decision-making process while formulating a response in order to address this foreign policy issue.

Similar to the previous case, there was no substantial "consultation". The main difference with this CO was that the EU offered help to the Turkish government specifically on the issue of Syrian refugees, but the Turkish government turned it down. There is clear evidence that "consultation" was avoided, since EU help would have required closer coordination involving the use of EU funds to help Syrian refugees. This analysis first examines the reaction and motivation of the Turkish government, then goes on to analyse the extent of cooperation with the EU and interactions between the EU and Turkish officials regarding this CO and the refugee crisis in general.

The Turkish reaction to the crisis at the border is important to analyse because it shows how the Turkish government behaved and the kind of attitude it displayed toward the EU while making policy. Since the beginning of the Syrian uprising, Turkey kept its borders open to civilians fleeing from Syria and created refugee camps. When a record number of people crossed the border, after which shots were fired toward Turkey, the government wanted to resolve the issue of refugees once and for all before it got out of hand. When numbers rapidly increased, Davutoğlu called UN Secretary General Ban Ki-moon and asked for humanitarian aid (Daily Sabah, 2012). It was reported that Davutoğlu said, "Come to our border and see for yourself what is transpiring. It is now time you intervene", and, after the conversation, UN observers headed for the Turkish border (ibid.). After shots were fired, the Turkish government immediately began to lobby members of the UNSC to encourage the formulation of a collective response including the condemnation of Assad (Anadolu Ajansı, 2012a). Among those Davutoğlu called were the French and British foreign ministers (ibid.). On the same day, Erdoğan made a statement emphasising the urgency of the matter and expressing concerns. He said:

> Up until today we have taken nearly 25,000 people as temporary asylum seekers. Where would this number reach? 100,000? More? We cannot close these doors. . . . At the moment, the total cost of them for us is 150,000,000 dollars. . . . We will want UN intervention.
>
> (*Hürriyet*, 2012c)

In these statements the Turkish government clearly urges the international community to intervene. As pointed out earlier, when there is an issue threatening border security, it is generally more beneficial for Turkey to bring in the international community and specifically to use the NATO framework for encouraging a collective response. It is therefore costly for the Turkish government to consult actors that it does not believe are capable of acting. Here, the Turkish government did not see the EU as a capable actor in terms of initiating a military response for the solution of the crisis. What the Turkish government essentially wanted, and voiced in various international meetings, was the creation of a buffer zone enforced by military force with the help of the international community (Habertürk, 2012). When the violence escalated and the number of refugees dramatically increased, the refugee crisis started to become a security issue for the Turkish government. The important point here is that the Turkish government wanted an international intervention similar to the one in the case of Libya and stressed the point that it was not only the problem of Turkey but also an international problem and that the UN and NATO needed to act. Arguably, the Turkish government believed it was possible for the international community to intervene and for the regime to change soon with the help of intervention. For this reason, the states that the Turkish government approached were the ones that it believed could initiate international action, such as the NATO and UNSC allies, primarily the UK, France, and the US. Therefore, the EU was not the first organisation the Turkish government preferred to approach to discuss the situation.

Although the Turkish government did not prioritise consultation with the EU, Davutoğlu was in touch with EU officials in bilateral and international meetings, and the issue of Syria was frequently on the agenda. According to HR Ashton's Turkey advisor, Ashton was one of the people to whom Davutoğlu frequently spoke (Interview EU04). To give a specific example, on 11 April 2012, right after the record refugee influx, Foreign Minister Davutoğlu addressed a G8 meeting via video conference and exchanged views with ministers at the meeting where Ashton was also present (Anadolu Ajansı, 2012b; EU Council Press, 2012). Responding to a question on cooperation with Turkey on Syrian refugees, Ashton herself at the time stated, "The EU and Turkey are in close contact on developments in Syria. We appreciate Turkey's role in Syria and in particular the hosting in Turkey of tens of thousands of Syrian refugees and part of the Syrian opposition" and indicated that the EU was determined to work together with Turkey and support its efforts regarding the Syrian refugees (Interview EU10). Davutoğlu also frequently made similar emphasis on "close contact", stating, for instance, that he was in "constant" contact with Ashton on Syria – "Sometimes we see each other a couple of times in one week . . . perhaps we are the only two ministers who meet most frequently", he said (Davutoğlu, 2012a).

Evidence suggests that there was more than "unilateral information" because there was a mutual information exchange in which the EU also had a chance to present its views on the issue of refugees. However, as discussed earlier, because the Turkish government did not reach out to the EU to seek its view or feedback on the Turkish policy and prioritised talking to allies who were capable of initiating an international response, which the Turkish government wanted, it is hardly possible to say that there was substantial "consultation" with the EU. In fact, as this analysis will highlight, the Turkish government turned down an EU offer at the time of this CO which could have helped the Turkish government to deal with the issue more effectively and have led to more consultation with regard to the use of EU funds. The Turkish attitude to the EU offer signifies that consultation with the EU was not desired and the Turkish government thought they would handle the situation without help.

It should be noted that information exchange also continued after the Turkish action with regard to this CO, and there were several layers to the interaction. Over the course of the Syrian refugee crisis, the EU member states and the Commission supported Turkey's initiative with regard to Syrian refugees and provided financial aid (European Commission, 2014). Again, this is an area in which the EU needed Turkish cooperation because over time the large numbers of refugees crossing borders to reach the EU became a concern and most notably a €3bn refugee deal was made between the EU and the Turkish government to tackle the refugee crisis and curb irregular migration to the EU in 2015. The interaction not only took place at the top political level, but it also took place on the ground. For instance, the European Commission's Humanitarian Aid and Civil Protection Department (ECHO) sent personnel to Turkey as the number of Syrians was rising in late 2012, to be permanently present in Turkey. Having an office also in Gaziantep near the Syrian border, ECHO's mission was to assist Syrian refugees in Turkey as well as to carry out operations in the region, while "discussing and negotiating with Turkish authorities and actors" (Interview EU09). So, there were various layers to the interaction, and close communication continued throughout the crisis.

However, the narrative provided by most of the public speeches at the time of this CO – the EU helping Turkey and Turkey working closely with the EU – rather reflects what was at the surface of the EU-Turkey relationship regarding Syrian refugees. In fact, as a Turkish diplomat claimed (Interview TR09), especially until the recent deal in 2015, there was considerable tension and resentment toward the EU with the Turkish side believing that the EU was not helpful, which brings us to the question of what kind of help the Turkish government would have expected.

An example of this resentment can be found in a speech by the Turkish President in 2015, in which he accused the world, including the EU, of being merely spectators to the crisis. He said: "There are 1,700,000 Syrians in Turkey. The total expenditure has been 5.5 billion dollars. The total financial contribution around the world is about 250 million dollars" (BBC, 2015). So, the main Turkish criticism was that, although Turkey hosted so many Syrian refugees, it had to bear a heavy financial burden on its own. In other words, what the Turkish government expected was either more financial help or some distribution of refugees to decrease the total cost to the Turkish government. The issue, however, is not so straightforward, and a particular incident between the Turkish government and the EU that took place around the time of this CO sheds light on the Turkish behaviour as well as on the underlying reason why there was no substantial "consultation" with the EU.

According to HR Ashton's Turkey advisor and a senior Turkish diplomat, the EU offered financial help at the time of this CO, but the Turkish government did not want it (Interviews TR09 and EU04). HR Ashton's Turkey advisor explains in the following way:

> We offered financial support when there were 20–30,000 refugees in Turkey. And that offer was turned down by Turkey. So, you could say that that was a missed opportunity. Now we find that there is 1.5 million and possibly near 2 million in Turkey and there is great resentment from Turkey that the EU and the West hasn't supported it. The offer wasn't accepted when this was a much smaller problem. Now, it's a massive problem.
>
> (Interview EU04)

This was a missed opportunity because it could have potentially helped the Turkish government deal with the problem more effectively before it got out of control and presumably allowed more consultation between the EU and Turkey.

The official reason for rejecting the offer was because the EU would have transferred the money through the international NGOs and UN organisations with which it was working, but the Turkish government was not keen to register these groups. According to a retired officer who worked at the UN High Commissioner for Refugees (UNHCR), the Turkish government essentially said, "Thank you but we have the capacity to deal with this" (T24, 2013). Commenting on why it was turned down, the Turkey advisor to the HR explained:

> So, I think what Turkey basically wanted from the EU was a cheque, a cheque written to the government in Ankara saying here is X million to spend on your camps. That's not the way we do it. We give our money to international NGOs, like UNHCR or the Red Cross.
>
> (Interview EU04)

Similarly, a former EU ambassador to Turkey commented:

> Back then the EU offered assistance to Turkey and Turkey refused. The official reason for refusing was that the EU was used to working with international NGOs and UN organizations; Turkey was not. Turkey said 'you just have to write blank cheques to AFAD' – the emergency agency – and that would be it. Of course, the EU cannot do that. So, whether the reason was genuine whether they had other things to hide, the question is open, but it didn't happen.
>
> (Interview EU03)

A senior Turkish diplomat involved in EU-Turkey negotiations admitted that "the main issue was that the government thought they wouldn't need any EU help and that the crisis wouldn't last so long, reaching millions of refugees" (Interview TR09). It is therefore possible to claim that the fundamental reason why the Turkish government turned down the offer was that it thought the humanitarian crisis would soon be over and President Assad would be removed from power, similarly to Gaddafi in Libya. The Turkish government would then have ideally taken the credit for hosting Syrians without needing any support.

This example is important for this analysis because it helps explain the Turkish attitude towards cooperation with the EU during the time of this CO. The key issue of cooperation, as discussed, was how to respond to the record refugee influx, and this analysis has examined whether consultation with the EU took place during the Turkish foreign policy decision-making process. The Turkish action was to consult allies that it believed were capable of initiating an international action that might resolve the issue of the refugees. Examining the Turkish action, it is possible to claim that the EU was not particularly an actor that the Turkish government approached for consultation. Information exchange took place between EU and Turkish officials and they were in regular contact, which indicates that there was more than "unilateral information"; however, the way in which the Turkish government prioritised its UNSC and NATO allies while turning down the EU offer for help indicates that there was no substantial "consultation". In fact, as the example makes clear, the Turkish government avoided consultation with the EU, thought they would be able to handle the situation without EU help, and even asked the EU to transfer money directly, knowing that this was incompatible with the way the EU worked.

In sum, there was no benefit of substantial "consultation" with the EU because it was seen as a weak actor that could not help resolve the refugee crisis, whereas prioritising consultations with NATO and UNSC allies was more beneficial. Nevertheless, regular contacts continued, which indicates that the Turkish government valued its foreign policy dialogue with the EU, although it was resentful, as the refugee crisis did not end as Turkish decision makers had expected.

Turkish reactions to the Syrian downing of Turkish plane on 22 June 2012 and to the Akçakale shelling on 3 October 2012

Two important incidents, the Syrian downing of a Turkish plane on 22 June 2012 and the Akçakale shelling on 3 October 2012, will be discussed together here because they concern a similar issue: does Turkey retaliate militarily to attacks on its territory and planes? The main issue around potential cooperation was the extent to which the EU view was taken into account when the Turkish government consulted allies in the international community and whether any consultation with the EU took place.

This is an example of a CO in which there was only "unilateral information". The EU was not seen as a capable actor that would help Turkey achieve what it wanted: a buffer zone and more international engagement in the conflict. It should also be noted that these are hard security issues, which explains why the Turkish government directly engaged in consultations with NATO allies while the EU was only informed about Turkish action. This analysis finds that "unilateral information" took place mainly aimed at asking for expressions of solidarity from the EU. Therefore, a rationalist approach that underlines security concerns and urgency of action would better explain the interaction with the EU that was at the "unilateral information" point, rather than an approach that explains cooperation taking place as a result of norms or identities.

On 22 June 2012, the Syrian army shot down a Turkish jet killing the jet's pilots and greatly escalating tension between the two countries. The main Turkish preference at this point was to urge an international reaction that would help facilitate the creation of a buffer zone enforced by military force, and the escalation of tension with Syria was one of the main reasons why the Turkish government sought international support. The main difference between Turkish and EU preferences was that the EU, although concerned, was disengaged and more averse to military conflict since there was no direct threat to itself. The potential for cooperation concerned whether the Turkish government also reached out to the EU when they were formulating their response in the aftermath of the incident. Therefore, examining Turkish behaviour over the following days is important to assess the nature of Turkey's interaction with the EU.

The Turkish government did not reach out to the EU for consultation on the matter. However, it informed the EU for the purpose of asking for expressions of solidarity. The first official Turkish statement read that PM Erdoğan had gathered ministers and generals for an emergency security meeting and that Turkey would take the necessary steps after all the information about the incident had been gathered (Bostan, 2012). There were immediately talks and a public debate on whether Turkey should take the issue to NATO in order to make it an Article 5 case and retaliate together with NATO allies, or at least to intimidate the Syrian regime (ibid.). On the same day, a spokesperson for the US government made a statement saying that the issue had not yet been brought to NATO and that if there was a request they would help with search and rescue efforts (ibid.). As a result of the emergency meeting in Ankara, the Turkish government declared that the downing of the plane had been a "hostile" act and requested consultations under Article 4 of the NATO charter in order to discuss its response to the shooting down of its warplane (BBC, 2012a). As a result, it was not an Article 5 case, but NATO strongly condemned the attack and expressed that it stood together with Turkey (BBC, 2012b). As a reaction to the attack, the Turkish policy was to warn the Syrian regime and change its rules of engagement so that any Syrian troops approaching the Turkish border would be seen as a military threat (ibid.).

Due to the incident being a hard security issue, the Turkish government prioritised consultation with its allies in NATO. The EU was informed about Turkish policy and was asked to express solidarity with Turkey; however, the main strategy of the Turkish government was to secure the backing of the NATO alliance because of the strategic value of consultation with NATO being high when considering how to respond. The Turkish government consulted individual members of the EU in NATO, such as the UK and France, but the EU as a body was only informed about how Turkish policy would take shape. A first counsellor at the EU Delegation in Ankara explained the interaction with Turkish officials at that time in the following way:

> What they did was to have a collective briefing during the Syria crisis regarding the plane incident. It was a mix of mainly EU and US ambassadors. They invited the EU ambassador, the head of the EU delegation, as well as the ambassadors of all EU states. All EU members were briefed. They wanted solidarity from partners and then they also explained the policy that they decided to follow.
>
> (Interview EU06)

So, this is only "unilateral information", because they had made up their mind about their policy, which was based on seeing the downing as a hostile act and changing the rules of engagement. When asked about the nature of the meeting and whether, for instance, the EU was able to make comments or offer feedback at all, including before and after the meeting, the interviewee explained that the interaction between the EU and Turkey was only based on the Turkish government explaining the policy that it had already formed and asking the EU to express solidarity. The interviewee also said:

> No [there was no opportunity to provide feedback] it was more a meeting where Turkey explained its policy and took some questions for if we needed any clarification and that was it. They wanted us to express solidarity when the plane was shot down, before Turkish position. They explained what kind of a reaction Turkey would give. They had already formed their position on their side when they informed us – so it was just about informing us about their position. They were in consultation with NATO when the briefing happened.
>
> (Interview EU06)

What is important here is that although the Turkish government did not hold consultations with the EU to discuss its response, as it did with NATO members, the EU was still a part of the Turkish strategy because the government valued EU support. They were interested in the EU making a statement of solidarity, backing the Turkish response, and, to this end, they informed the EU. The ad hoc meeting mentioned in this example was indeed in addition to the Davutoğlu-Ashton dialogue, which, according to interviewees, also continued on this matter (Interviews EU06 and EU02).

The day after Turkey requested consultations under Article 4, the EU Council issued a statement in support of Turkey, "condemning" the shooting down of the plane, and declared that it "once more reinforced EU sanctions against the Syrian regime" in response to the escalation of violence (The Council of the European Union, 2012). So, the Turkish government soon received the expression of solidarity for which it was asking. As a result, it is possible to make the assessment that, with regard to this incident, the relationship was based on "unilateral information" aimed at securing EU support for Turkish action. The exchange of information took place based on the fact that there were informal conversations between Ashton and Davutoğlu after the Turkish action was clear and considering that the EU, through its policies, backed the Turkish position.

The Akçakale shelling can be seen as an escalation in the conflict between Turkey and Syria. Similarly, there was "unilateral information" and EU support was sought for Turkish action. On 3 October 2012, Syrian shells hit the Turkish town of Akçakale, killing five civilians and bringing Turkey and Syria to the edge of war. Cooperation with the EU, again, would have ideally involved consultation with the EU about a Turkish response. This incident was also a hard security issue for Turkey, and it confirms the findings discussed in the plane incident – when the Turkish government feels a security threat, it immediately turns to its NATO allies and interaction with the EU stays at the information point mainly in requesting expressions of solidarity. Consultation with NATO then becomes the top priority because the Turkish government entertains the idea that it could be an Article 5 case. Even if it does not end up being an Article 5 case, consulting NATO has symbolic value intended to intimidate the aggressor. In this case, the EU was, again, informed about what the Turkish response would be, and it was asked to show solidarity with Turkey. This is, once more, important, as it shows that the EU was a part of Turkish strategy to gain international support.

An immediate reaction came from the Turkish Deputy PM, who stated, "Turkey will retaliate. This last incident was the final straw" (*Radikal*, 2012). Referring to the obligations of NATO members under Article 5, he urged NATO to act (ibid.). Once information was obtained from the Turkish General Staff and from the governor of the city in which Akçakale was located, Davutoğlu telephoned the UN Secretary General to pass on information (*Hürriyet*, 2012b). The government then requested NATO consultations under Article 4 and began to lobby its NATO partners for a collective response, which meant retaliation under the NATO framework that could pave the way for an international intervention or a creation of a buffer zone. As was also the case in the downing of the plane, there was a debate in policy circles as to whether it could qualify as an Article 5 case (T24, 2012). Condemning the incident and supporting Turkey, NATO gathered for consultation but agreed it was not (yet) an Article 5 case (NATO, 2012; T24, 2012). So, once again, it did not qualify as an Article 5 case. It was reported that NATO allies had "no appetite" for being dragged into the conflict, although Turkey was pushing for a more muscular response from the alliance, including a military intervention (Traynor, 2012). However, the Turkish government was able to gather support for its action, which was military retaliation.

In a short time, Turkey moved tanks and anti-craft missiles into Akçakale and began bombing targets in Syria belonging to the Syrian army in retaliation based on the rules of engagement, which the Turkish government had changed in the previous incident concerning the Turkish plane. At this stage, FM Davutoğlu was reaching out to allies to gather expressions of support for the action. It was reported that the US Secretary of State "promised" Davutoğlu that he had "full US backing" for military retaliation (*Hürriyet Daily News*, 2012). He also personally called the British Foreign Secretary and received a similar message of support (*Hürriyet*, 2012a). Here, looking at the Turkish behaviour, it could be claimed that the response was based on consultation with NATO allies, especially the US and UK, whose support was essential. In addition, the Turkish government sought to ensure that its response was legitimate through informing the UN and discussing it with the UN Secretary General, while at the same time seeking support from the international community. It should also be noted that as part of the Turkish response, a day after the incident, the Turkish Parliament passed a motion authorising military ground troops to enter "foreign countries" for operations, which was more of a symbolic gesture to intimidate the Syrian government, as it was not expected to be carried out (Peker and Malas, 2012).

The Turkish government also made sure the EU was informed about its response and asked the EU to express support for the Turkish policy. Because the intention of the government was mainly to inform the EU of its response, cooperation was limited to information only, as in the previous incident. In the immediate aftermath of the shelling, a spokesperson for HR Ashton made a statement, saying, "We are in touch with our delegation in Turkey. We are evaluating the information about the incident that happened recently" (Aktan, 2012). A diplomat at the EU Mission to Turkey who was present at the delegation at the time explained exactly what happened while they were gathering information for Brussels from Turkish counterparts. As the interviewee explained, the Turkish government invited the EU for an ad hoc meeting, similar to the one that had taken place after the plane incident, in order to inform the EU about the policy the government would follow, while asking for expressions of solidarity (Interview EU06). The interviewee also pointed out that the Turkish government would rather inform "partners like the US and UK" than the EU about military matters (e.g., the same kind of briefing did not happen for the EU after the Operation Shah Euphrates in February 2015 (Interview EU02, EU06)). Yet, what is important here in this case is that the government reached out to the EU to inform and also ask for support.

Expressing support for Turkey, Ashton released a statement on the day following the incident and condemned the shelling. Expressing solidarity with Turkey, she said, "such violations of Turkey's sovereignty cannot be tolerated" (Ashton, 2012). She also publicly stated that she was "in contact with Foreign Minister Davutoğlu", which indicates that, in addition to the EU Delegation being briefed in Ankara, ministers were also in touch (ibid).

In sum, the interaction was at the "unilateral information" point because the Turkish government had already decided when it informed the EU about the action it was going to take. The information was aimed at securing EU support for Turkish policy, which was a part of a broader Turkish strategy to lobby actors in the international arena. After the Turkish action, the Turkish government and the EU stayed in touch, and the EU expressed its support for the Turkish action. The interaction lacked "consultation" because the Turkish government did not discuss its position with the EU or provide an opportunity for the EU to comment: it only briefed the EU.

As an explanation of the degree of cooperation, it can be claimed that it was not beneficial to cooperate with the EU for a number of reasons. First, the EU was not seen as a capable actor that could help the Turkish government obtain what it wanted, which was a muscular international response involving military elements and presumably leading to the creation of a buffer zone between the Syrian and Turkish borders. The main way in which cooperation with the EU could be beneficial for the Turkish government was if it gave support and expressed solidarity with Turkey, which explains why the Turkish interaction with the EU was based on only informing the EU.

Second, as mentioned, these were hard security issues, and it is generally costlier for the Turkish government to consult actors than to proceed with unilateral action because of the urgency of action. Here, the Turkish government did not proceed with unilateral action and consulted NATO allies, but the aim was to secure support so that Turkey would have international backing while retaliating.

Third, the EU was averse to being drawn into a military conflict. For this reason, consultation or co-decision with the EU would have been costly. As it turned out, the NATO allies were also reluctant to engage militarily, and they had concerns about the possible consequences of a NATO action. For instance, the

NATO Secretary General expressed "great concern" about the Akçakale shelling but mentioned that Syria was a "very, very complex society" and that "foreign military interventions could have broader impacts" (Traynor, 2012). The main point here is that bringing it to the attention of NATO was still beneficial because it had symbolic value. It legitimised the Turkish retaliation, since the allies were informed and offered support, and sent a strong intimidating message that the country that had been attacked was a NATO ally that would not hesitate to bring the NATO bloc into the crisis if necessary.

Conclusion

The broader pattern regarding the COs discussed in this chapter is that there is a lack of conclusive evidence that the Turkish government incorporated EU preferences, gave the EU opportunity to provide feedback on its policy, or adjusted its behaviour based on discussion with the EU. Therefore, cooperation never reached the "consultation" point.

Examining the COs individually, it is possible to claim that there is a certain degree of variation with regard to the outcomes in terms of cooperation. In the first CO of this chapter, which concerned the initial Turkish response and Turkish decision to impose sanctions, there was more than "unilateral information" because the EU and Turkish officials met in international and bilateral settings in which Syria was on the agenda. The EU had a chance to present its view on the crisis, which was different from the Turkish government's views. The Turkish government was reluctant to criticise the Syrian regime at first because its strategic importance to the Turkish government was high and it would have been a costly action to become hostile to the regime right away without seeing whether Assad would comply with Turkish requests for reform. Examining the timing of the Turkish decision to impose sanctions, it is possible to claim that the Arab League was highly influential. Following the steps of the Arab League was in fact consistent with Davutoğlu's three-stage strategy. To put it briefly, the Turkish government became critical of the Assad regime when the costs of being critical decreased after the international pressure against the regime increased and they were not able to keep appearing to support an oppressive regime.

With regard to Turkish participation in the FSG, there was more than "unilateral information" because there was mutual information exchange with the EU but no substantial consultation or coordination. Turkish decision makers saw themselves in a position of strength and as key players in the solution of the conflict and therefore did not see it necessary to approach the EU for consultation.

Potentially, the EU was able to present its view to the Turkish government, especially during the first two COs, through formal and informal communication. So, it could be claimed that there were some elements of consultation. Most importantly, the informal dialogue between Davutoğlu and Ashton, which was also based on personal friendship, provided an opportunity for consultation and helped the EU and Turkey to develop a mutual understanding of each other's policy. It is important for this analysis of cooperation that the foreign policy dialogue continued despite differences of views, which demonstrates that both were willing to work closely during the course of uprisings in the region.

Again, rationalism better explains Turkish behaviour since it was an extension of the strategic adjustment of behaviour after bilateral engagement with the Assad regime had failed. Dialogue with the EU was a part of Turkish policy to explain itself to the international community, which in return might have allowed them to play a leading role in the international coalition that planned to shape the movement of change in Syria.

The Turkish reaction to the record refugee influx and shots fired on camps in Turkey was another case of a lack of substantial consultation. It would have been costly to have conducted substantial "consultation" with the EU because it was seen as a weak actor that could not help resolve the refugee crisis, whereas prioritising consultations with NATO and UNSC allies was more beneficial. A key finding in this CO concerned the Turkish government turning down EU financial help, thinking that it would be able to handle the situation on its own, which shows the general Turkish attitude towards cooperation with the EU.

The CO concerning the Turkish reactions to the plane downing and shelling incidents was an example of "unilateral information". The Turkish government formulated its policy, which was based on military retaliation, without discussing it with the EU. It prioritised NATO allies because it wanted a military intervention and a buffer zone to be established. The EU was briefed only because the Turkish government wanted expressions of solidarity from the EU. It was costly to consult the EU not just because the EU was reluctant with regard to military intervention but also because it was seen as incapable of acting. The beneficial course of action in this case was to inform the NATO allies, see whether these allies could come in and intervene, and request expressions of solidarity. This was one of the main reasons why the EU was never the first actor that the Turkish government sought to be in coordination with while formulating foreign policy, and it explains why there was no substantial cooperation in the form of "consultation" with the EU.

In the first three COs, there was more than "unilateral information", mainly because the EU and the Turkish government had time to meet in bilateral and international settings and exchanged information on Syria. The key overall finding is that the Turkish government did not wish for substantial consultation with the EU. It was not interested in reaching out to the EU to request feedback on its policy, primarily because it saw the EU as an actor that could not make much of a difference to the crisis. This was the case even with regard to refugees. This was a particular area in which EU help, which presumably would have led to consultation, could have been useful to the Turkish government in handling the situation more effectively. However, the Turkish government avoided consultation with the EU, mainly because Turkish decision makers thought that there would be an international intervention and that the crisis would not last long or turn into a complex civil war.

The final CO was, however, significantly different from the others because there was only "unilateral information". Again, a rationalist approach better helps explain the degree of cooperation. Since the plane downing and shelling incidents were hard security issues, it was less costly to proceed with unilateral information. The Turkish government only consulted NATO allies because they were the actors that could initiate an international military offensive, and it was beneficial to bring the issue to the attention of NATO. Because the EU was incapable of acting, it was only informed in order to request an expression of support for Turkish military retaliation. Overall, across the COs the Turkish reaction was based more on interests than identity or norms of appropriate behaviour.

In terms of specific explanatory factors, it could be claimed that, across the COs, the urgency of action and hard security matters caused variation in the sense that they lowered the degree of cooperation, as was the case with the shooting down of the Turkish plane and the shelling of the Turkish town. Examining COs individually, a variation of power politics and economic reasons were influential factors when the Turkish government delayed criticising Assad. With regard to the FSG, the Turkish government wanted to play a leading role in the international community for strategic reasons, but the EU was not seen as an actor that could help. So, power politics was also relevant in this CO as an aspect of the behaviour of the Turkish government. The EU was also not seen as a capable actor in the last two COs that could help the Turkish government to influence the international community, which made cooperation non-beneficial.

Overall, the Syrian uprising is an important case study for examining cooperation between Turkey and the EU. It allows us to see the ways in which Turkish and EU decision makers were frequently in touch even though their policies did not always converge. Informal information exchange between EU and Turkish officials, especially between the EU High Representative and the Turkish Foreign Minister, became a norm as the uprising progressed into a complex civil war. The successors of Foreign Minister Davutoğlu and High Representative Ashton – Foreign Minister Mevlüt Çavuşoğlu and High Representative Federica Mogherini – have continued to stay in close contact to discuss developments in the region. Top issues on the agenda in Political Dialogue meetings have typically included cooperation regarding irregular migration, counter-terrorism, and the civil war in Syria. Turkey has continued to play an important role in the EU's security policy, especially because of its involvement in the Syrian conflict, and Turkish foreign policy makers have often emphasised that Turkey should be regarded as an asset to EU foreign policy. For example, President Erdoğan has repeatedly said, "if European countries are living in peace today, it is thanks to Turkey for hosting 4 million refugees" (Anadolu Ajansı, 2019b) and claimed that "Europe owes its safety to Turkey's sacrifices" (Anadolu Ajansı, 2019a).

References

Aktan, S. (2012) "AB'den İlk Açıklama" ["The First Statement from the EU"], *İhlas Haber Ajansı*, 3 October, www.iha.com.tr/haber-abde-ilk-aciklama-245738.

Anadolu Ajansı. (2019a) "Europe Owes Its Safety to Turkey's Sacrifices: Erdogan", *Anadolu Ajansı*, 23 February, www.aa.com.tr/en/politics/europe-owes-its-safety-to-turkey-s-sacrifices-erdogan/1400992.

————. (2019b) "Europe in Peace Thanks to Turkey: Erdogan", *Anadolu Ajansı*, 3 May, www.aa.com.tr/en/europe/europe-in-peace-thanks-to-turkey-erdogan/1469285.

————. (2012a) "Davutoglu Phones FMs of Countries in UN Security Council", *Anadolu Ajansı*, 10 April, http://aa.com.tr/en/turkey/davutoglu-phones-fms-of-countries-in-un-security-council/373854.

————. (2012b) "Turkish FM Set to Address G8 Counterparts Via Video Conference", *Anadolu Ajansı*, 11 April, http://aa.com.tr/en/world/turkish-fm-set-to-address-g8-counterparts-via-video-conference/373598.

Ashton, C. (2012) "Statement by EU High Representative Catherine Ashton Following the Shelling of the Turkish Town of Akçakale", Brussels, Belgium, 4 October, www.consilium.europa.eu/uedocs/cms_Data/docs/pressdata/EN/foraff/132709.pdf.

————. (2011a) "Declaration by the High Representative, Catherine Ashton, on Behalf of the European Union on EU Action Following the Escalation of Violent Repression in Syria", Brussels, Belgium, 18 August, http://europa.eu/rapid/press-release_PESC-11-282_en.htm.

————. (2011b) "Parliamentary Questions: Answer Given by High Representative/Vice-President Ashton on Behalf of the Commission", European Parliament, Brussels, Belgium, 15 November, www.europarl.europa.eu/sides/getAllAnswers.do?reference=E-2011-008727&language=EN.

Balcı, B. (2012) "The Syrian Dilemma: Turkey's Response to the Crisis", *Carnegie Europe*, 10 February, http://carnegieendowment.org/2012/02/10/syrian-dilemma-turkey-s-response-to-crisis/9jxj.

BBC. (2015) "Erdoğan: Türkiye AB kapısında dilenmez" ["Erdogan: Turkey Will Not Beg the EU"], *BBC*, 24 January, www.bbc.com/turkce/haberler/2015/01/150124_erdogan_ab.

————. (2012a) "Turkey Calls Nato Meeting on Warplane Downed by Syria", *BBC*, 24 June, www.bbc.com/news/world-middle-east-18568207.

————. (2012b) "Turkey PM Erdogan Issues Syria Border Warning", *BBC*, 26 June, www.bbc.co.uk/news/world-middle-east-18584872.

————. (2011) "Turkey Imposes Economic Sanctions on Syria", *BBC*, 30 November, www.bbc.co.uk/news/world-europe-15959770.

Bostan, Y. (2012) "Suriye Türk Jetini Vurdu" ["Syria Shot Down Turkish Jet"], *Sabah*, 23 June, www.sabah.com.tr/gundem/2012/06/23/suriye-turk-jetini-vurdu.

CNN Türk. (2009) "Türkiye ile Suriye Arasında Vize Kalktı" ["Visas Lifted Between Turkey and Syria"], *CNN Turk*, 17 September, www.cnnturk.com/2009/turkiye/09/16/turkiye.ile.suriye.arasinda.vize.kalkti/543804.0/index.html.

The Council of the European Union. (2012) "3179th Council Meeting: Foreign Affairs", Luxembourg, 25 June, www.consilium.europa.eu/uedocs/cms_data/docs/pressdata/EN/foraff/131188.pdf.

————. (2011) "Council Regulation (EU) No 442/2011 of 9 May 2011 Concerning Restrictive Measures in View of the Situation in Syria", *Official Journal of the European Union*, 10 May, https://eur-lex.europa.eu/LexUriServ/LexUriServ.do?uri=OJ:L:2011:12 1:0001:0010:EN:PDF.

Daily Sabah. (2012) "Turkey's Emergency Call to the UN", *Daily Sabah*, 7 April, www.dailysabah.com/nation/2012/04/07/turkeys-emergency-call-to-the-un.

Davutoğlu, A. (2012a) "Speech in Turkey-EU Political Dialogue Meeting", Istanbul, Turkey, 7 June.

————. (2012b) "Address on Turkish Foreign Policy", George Washington University, Washington, DC, 3 April, www.youtube.com/watch?v=Se6ynRCqlb4.

————. (2010) "Joint Press Conference with Syrian Foreign Minister Walid Muallem", Ankara, Turkey, 9 December.

————. (2001) *Stratejik Derinlik* [*The Strategic Depth*], Istanbul: Küre Yayınları.

The Economist. (2012) "Turkey and Its Neighbours: Delicate Balance", *The Economist*, 7 July, www.economist.com/node/21558279.

Elci, Z. (2009) "Syria Says to Hold Military Exercises with Turkey", *Reuters*, 13 October, www.reuters.com/article/idUSLD314946.

Eligür, B. (2012) "Crisis in Turkish – Israeli Relations (December 2008–June 2011): From Partnership to Enmity", *Middle Eastern Studies* 48(3): 429–59.

Erdoğan, R.T. (2010) "Gaziantep Mitingi" ["Gaziantep Rally"], Gaziantep, Turkey, 15 August.

Ergan, U., and Özkaya, S. (2011) "Çırağan'da kader zirvesi" ["Critical Summit at Çırağan"], *Hürriyet*, 15 July, www.hurriyet.com.tr/ciraganda-kader-zirvesi-18259861.

EU Council Press. (2012) "Newsroom Schedule", 12 April, www.eucouncilpress.eu/?date=2012-04-12.

European Commission. (2014) "Violence Raging in Syria", European Commission, Brussels, 24 September, http://ec.europa.eu/commission_2010-2014/georgieva/hot_topics/violence_raging_syria_en.htm.

————. (2011) *Turkey 2011 Progress Report*, Brussels, Belgium: European Commission.

European External Action Service. (2015a) "The European Union and Syria", www.eeas.europa.eu/statements/docs/2013/131018_01_en.pdf.

————. (2015b) "European-Syrian Cooperation Agreement", http://eeas.europa.eu/delegations/syria/eu_syria/political_relations/agreements/index_en.htm.

————. (2011) "Frequently Asked Questions on EU Restrictive Measures Against the Syrian Regime", 13 September, www.eeas.europa.eu/archives/docs/syria/docs/faq_en.pdf.

Gül, A. (2009) "Suriye Ziyareti, 15 Mayis 2009" ["Visit to Syria, 15 May 2009"], www.youtube.com/watch?v=uWdaCRrx0cY.

Habertürk. (2012) "Annan olmazsa tampon! İşte Suriye İçin B Planı" ["Buffer Zone If Annan Doesn't Work"], *Haberturk*, 7 April, www.haberturk.com/dunya/haber/731896-annan-olmazsa-tampon.

Hague, W. (2011) "Written Ministerial Statements", UK Parliament, 12 September, https://publications.parliament.uk/pa/cm201011/cmhansrd/cm110912/wmstext/110912m0001.htm.

Hale, W. (2013) *Turkish Foreign Policy Since 1774* (3rd edition), London, UK: Routledge.

Hürriyet. (2012a) "Clegg: Türkiye'nin askeri harekatını destekliyoruz", *Hürriyet*, 4 October, www.hurriyet.com.tr/clegg-turkiyenin-askeri-harekatini-destekliyoruz-21621074.

————. (2012b) "Türkiye olayı dünyaya anlatıyor" ["Turkey Is Telling the Incident to the World"], *Hürriyet*, 3 October, www.hurriyet.com.tr/turkiye-olayi-dunyaya-anlatiyor-21615661.

————. (2012c) "Erdoğan: Sınır ihlali olmuştur. Gereken adımları atacağız" ["Erdoğan: There Have Been Illegal Border Crossings, We Will Take Necessary Steps"], *Hürriyet*, 10 April, www.hurriyet.com.tr/erdogan-sinir-ihlali-olmustur-gereken-adimlari-atacagiz-20310178.

————. (2011a) "Arap Birliği'nden Suriye'ye son bir şans daha" ["A Final Chance from the Arab League to Syria"], *Hürriyet*, 25 November, www.hurriyet.com.tr/arap-birliginden-suriyeye-son-bir-sans-daha-19324491.

————. (2011b) "Türkiye'den Esad'a bir hafta süre" ["A Week of Time from Turkey to Assad"], *Hürriyet*, 20 June, www.hurriyet.com.tr/turkiyeden-esada-bir-hafta-sure-18071245.

————. (2011c) "Erdoğan'dan Esad'a telefon" ["Phone Call from Erdogan to Assad"], *Hürriyet*, 27 May, www.hurriyet.com.tr/erdogandan-esada-telefon-17893494.

————. (2011d) "Erdoğan Beşar Esad'la görüştü" ["Erdoğan Talked to Assad"], *Hürriyet*, 14 June, www.hurriyet.com.tr/erdogan-besar-esadla-gorustu-18030795.

————. (2011e) "Erdoğan'dan Esad ailesine sert mesaj" ["Harsh Message from Erdogan to Assad Family"], *Hürriyet*, 10 June, www.hurriyet.com.tr/turkiyenin-sambuyukelciliginde-protesto-gosterisi-18017916.

————. (2011f) "Esad'ın istifasını istemek için erken" ["It Is too Early to Call for Assad's Resignation"], *Hürriyet*, 19 August, www.hurriyet.com.tr/esadin-istifasini-istemek-icin-henuz-erken-18528917.

————. (2011g) "Davutoğlu: Bizim Suriye konusunda mesajımız açık" ["Davutoğlu: Our Message Regarding Syria Is Clear"], *Hürriyet*, 16 June, www.hurriyet.com.tr/davutoglu-bizim-suriye-konusunda-mesajimiz-acik-18046686.

Hürriyet Daily News. (2012) "US Slams Syria for 'Depraved' Shelling of Turkish Town", *Hürriyet Daily News*, 4 October, www.hurriyetdailynews.com/us-slams-syria-for-depraved-shelling-of-turkish-town.aspx?pageID=238&nID=31640&NewsCatID=359.

İHA. (2008) "Bodrum'da Erdoğan-Esad buluşması" ["Erdoğan-Assad Meeting in Bodrum"], *İHA*, 5 August, www.iha.com.tr/haber-bodrumda-erdogan-esad-bulusmasi-30877/.

Irish, J. (2012) "France, Partners Planning Syria Crisis Group: Sarkozy", *Reuters*, 4 February, www.reuters.com/article/us-syria-france-idUSTRE8130QV20120204.

Keinon, H. (2009) "Syria: We Held Exercise with Turkey", *The Jerusalem Post*, 13 October, www.jpost.com/Middle-East/Syria-We-held-exercise-with-Turkey.

Kohen, S. (2012) "Ortadoğu politikasındaki terslikler ve nedenleri" ["Misfortunes in the Middle East Policy and Its Reasons"], *Milliyet*, 15 August, www.milliyet.com.tr/ortadogu-politikasindaki-terslikler-ve-nedenleri-2-/dunya/dunyayazardetay/15.08.2012/1581219/default.htm.

McDonald-Gibson, C. (2013) "Divided Europe Imperils Syrian Arms Embargo", *Independent*, 25 May, www.independent.co.uk/news/world/europe/divided-europe-imperils-syrian-arms-embargo-8632376.html.

Ministry of Foreign Affairs of Turkey. (2012a) "Turkey-Syria Economic and Trade Relations", www.mfa.gov.tr/turkey_s-commercial-and-economic-relations-with-syria.en.mfa.

————. (2012b) "Relations Between Turkey–Syria", www.mfa.gov.tr/relations-between-turkey%E2%80%93syria.en.mfa.

————. (2012c) "Foreign Minister Ahmet Davutoğlu, at the G20 Meeting Emphasized the Importance of Adopting New Approaches in the Global System", www.mfa.gov.tr/foreign-minister-ahmet-davutoglu-at-the-g20-meeting-emphasized-the-importance-of-adopting-new-approaches-in-the-global-system.en.mfa.

NATO. (2012) "North Atlantic Council Statement on Developments on the Turkish-Syrian Border", Brussels, 3 October, www.nato.int/cps/en/natohq/news_90447.htm.

NTV. (2011) "Arap Birliği Suriye'ye yaptırımları onayladı" ["Arab League Approves Syrian Sanctions"], *NTV*, 27 November, www.ntv.com.tr/dunya/arap-birligi-suriyeye-yaptirimlari-onayladi,Dj7BKFt5aUyzK51ikL8ymg.

Öniş, Z. (2012) "Turkey and the Arab Spring: Between Ethics and Self-Interest", *Insight Turkey* 14(3): 45–63.

Oweiss, K.Y. (2011) "EU Agrees Oil Embargo as Syrians March Against Assad", *Reuters*, 2 September, www.reuters.com/article/syria-idUSL5E7K22C920110902.

Özdil, Y. (2012) "Akepe deme Ak de Esad deme Esed de" ["Don't Say AKP, Say Ak Don't Say Esad Say Esed"], *Hürriyet*, 26 March, www.hurriyet.com.tr/akepe-deme-ak-de-esad-deme-esed-de-20212376.

Peker, E., and Malas, N. (2012) "Turkey Strikes Syria, Adds War Powers", *The Wall Street Journal*, 5 October, www.wsj.com/articles/SB100008723963904436354045780358223 73395226.

Radikal. (2012) "Arınç: Bardağı taşıran son damla!" ["Arınç: The Last Straw!"] *Radikal*, 3 October, www.radikal.com.tr/politika/arinc-bardagi-tasiran-son-damla-1102651/.

Sabah. (2012) "Foreign Affairs Minister Davutoğlu Shares Turkey's Stance with the U.S.", *Sabah*, 10 February, http://english.sabah.com.tr/National/2012/02/10/ foreign-affairs-minister-davutoglu-shares-turkeys-stance-with-the-us.

Shadid, A. (2011) "Turkey Calls for Syrian Reforms on Order of 'Shock Therapy'", *The New York Times*, 25 May, www.nytimes.com/2011/05/26/world/europe/26turkey. html?pagewanted=1&_r=2.

T24. (2013) "Türkiye, Suriyelilere BM Yardımını Hiçbir Zaman Kabul Etmedi" ["Turkey Never Accepted UN Help for Syrians"], *T24*, 6 November, http://t24.com.tr/haber/ turkiye-suriyelilere-bm-yardimini-hicbir-zaman-kabul-etmedi,243322.

———. (2012) "Türkiye'den NATO'ya olağanüstü toplantı çağrısı" ["Turkey Calls for Extraordinary Meeting with NATO"], *T24*, 3 October, http://t24.com.tr/haber/ turkiyeden-natoya-olaganustu-toplanti-cagrisi,214443.

TBMM. (2011) "Türkiye Cumhuriyeti Hükümeti ile Suriye Arap Cumhuriyeti Hükümeti Arasında Terör ve Terör Örgütlerine Karşı Ortak İşbirliği Anlaşmasının Onaylanmasının Uygun Bulunduğuna Dair Kanun Tasarısı ve Dışişleri Komisyonu Raporu (1/1009)" ["Report of the Foreign Affairs Committee of the Turkish Parliament on the Counter-terrorism Agreement Between the Turkish and Syrian Governments"], 9 February, www. tbmm.gov.tr/sirasayi/donem23/yil01/ss713.pdf.

Today's Zaman. (2012) "Turkey Rebukes EU for Double Talk on Visa Liberalization", *Today's Zaman*, 24 March, www.todayszaman.com/diplomacy_turkey-rebukes-eu-for-double-talk-on-visa-liberalization_275250.html.

———. (2009) "Turkey and Syria Conduct Military Drill, Israel Disturbed", *Today's Zaman*, 29 April, www.todayszaman.com/diplomacy_turkey-and-syria-conduct-military-drill-israel-disturbed_173723.html.

Traynor, I. (2012) "Syrian Shelling of Turkish Village Condemned by NATO and Pentagon", *The Guardian*, 4 October, www.guardian.com/world/2012/oct/03/nato-pentagon-shelling-turkish-village.

Ülgen, S. (2011a) "Turkey's Zero 'Problems' Problem", *Carnegie Europe*, 15 November, http://carnegieeurope.eu/publications/?fa=45985.

———. (2011b) "How Successful Is a 'Zero Problem with Neighbors' Policy Declared by Turkish Government", *Carnegie Europe*, 18 November, http://carnegieeurope.eu/ publications/?fa=46280.

7   Turkey's foreign policy cooperation with the EU in post-uprising Egypt

After Hosni Mubarak was overthrown in 2011, Mohamed Morsi was elected as president in 2012. Following the protests against his rule in June 2013, a coup d'état took place and General Abdel Fattah el-Sisi took office. Considering that leaders were ousted twice in Egypt, it is useful to extend this analysis to examine cooperative opportunities (COs) in the post-Mubarak era. Specifically, this chapter focuses on the protests against Morsi and the coup to replace him. As in the previous cases, this chapter makes an assessment of Turkish behaviour with regard to foreign policy cooperation with the EU and examines whether there was consultation with the EU before and after the public announcement of Turkish positions.

This chapter focuses on the way in which the EU and Turkey had differences of views regarding the turmoil in Egypt and how they were reflected in their policies. The different approaches of the EU and Turkey are important for an analysis of their foreign policy cooperation mainly because these differences led to tension, especially due to the Turkish government's accusations that the EU was "silent" regarding the coup in Egypt. However, as the chapter finds, despite Turkey's harsh criticism of the EU, there was regular communication through formal and informal channels. Most significantly, the Davutoğlu-Ashton dialogue continued regardless of Turkey's harsh criticism of the EU.

Interests and reactions after the overthrow of Mubarak

A discussion of the preferences and positions of Turkey and the EU with regard to Morsi is useful for the examination of the COs in this chapter. The main points are that the Turkish government preferred to support Morsi, even though his policies were leading to further polarisation, and that there was a significant difference of views between Turkey and the EU regarding Morsi. The next section examines the Turkish reaction to the killings in Port Said on 26 January 2013 as an extension of the Turkish reaction to the anti-Morsi protests and as a CO in which there was potential for cooperation, and the interactions between the Turkish government and the EU.

Tens of thousands of protesters gathered in Tahrir Square in Cairo to voice their opposition to President Morsi on 22 November 2012. The main reasons behind

Table 7.1 Cooperative opportunities after Mubarak

	Turkish government preference	*Turkish government action*	*EU preference*	*Outcome in terms of cooperation*
CO9: Turkish reaction to the killings in Port Said on 26 January 2013	Support for Morsi to restore stability in Egypt	Issued statements that see killings as a natural consequence of Morsi's struggle to restore order	Strong condemnation of violence	A step further than "unilateral information" but no "consultation" Information exchange took place
CO10: Turkish reaction to the removal of Morsi on 3 July 2013	The Turkish government pushes the EU and international actors to condemn Sisi	Condemned the removal of Morsi, pushed international actors including the EU to criticise Sisi	Prioritising stability in Egypt and keeping channels of dialogue open with the Sisi government	A step further than "unilateral information" but no "consultation" after the Turkish position was formed
CO11: Turkish reaction to the Rabaa massacre on 14 August 2013	Solidarity with Muslim Brotherhood supporters, urging international actors to take a stance against Sisi	Strongly condemned Sisi, urged the EU to adopt a harsher stance, and criticised the EU for not cutting ties	Condemned the violence but avoided using the term coup d'état	More than "unilateral information" No consultation, but information exchange took place

the unrest were that the president was not following democratic policies and that there were problems concerning minority rights and the separation of powers (Kirkpatrick and Sheikh, 2012). Shortly before protesters gathered in Tahrir Square, Morsi had declared unilaterally that he would give himself sweeping new powers to oversee his country's political transition: this was a last straw, leading people to see him as "Egypt's new Pharaoh" (Spencer, 2012). The number of protesters shortly reached hundreds of thousands, and the demonstrations that started on 22 November 2012 went on for more than seven months, ending with Morsi's deposition.

After the initial turmoil in Egypt leading to the fall of Mubarak, the new crisis of anti-Morsi unrest presented another opportunity for the EU and Turkey to cooperate. The main question around potential cooperation for these actors with regard to this specific CO concerned whether to support Morsi or to consider the demands of protesters and the criticisms of Morsi when responding to the crisis. In order to make an assessment, the empirical investigation presented here will focus on what the policies and preferences of Turkey and the EU were and then examine the interactions between these two actors.

To begin the analysis, it is useful to examine the EU's relations with Egypt after Morsi had been elected. In line with the EU's overall policy and preferences regarding Egypt, which were discussed previously in Chapter 4, the EU sought to enhance its "close partnership" with Egypt after the revolution. This included, for instance, making funds available as financial support for Egypt's democratic transition. There was, however, a certain uneasiness on the part of the EU about the idea of a government dominated by the Muslim Brotherhood. The main concern was whether the Muslim Brotherhood's policies would undermine human rights and democracy, leading to a further polarisation of the society (Interview EU02).

As for Turkey's relationship with Egypt under Morsi, it is possible to say that the Turkish government had established a very close relationship with Morsi, which was again consistent with the government's overall approach to the Middle East, characterised by a desire to make Turkey a regional leader. The desire to become a regional leader remained the same in the Sisi period after Morsi. The main aspect of the relationship with Morsi was the ideological and political proximity of the Turkish government to the new government in Egypt. In other words, the political affinity between the Muslim Brotherhood in Egypt and the Islamist-rooted AKP government in Turkey had enabled a close friendship to develop. Indeed, as a report by the Turkish Economic and Social Studies Foundation (TESEV) pointed out, for this reason, the Turkey-Egypt relationship had its "golden age" when Morsi was in power (Akgün and Gündoğar, 2014: 4). Moreover, with the Muslim Brotherhood in power, the Turkish government believed they would be able to use a foreign policy rhetoric based on religion and culture (or "Turkey's geo-cultural potential", as Davutoğlu would put it) more effectively, and therefore they were pleased with Morsi's coming to power.

For example, shortly before the start of the protests against Morsi, Erdoğan and Morsi met and reiterated the importance of working closely in the Middle East. During Morsi's visit to Turkey in September 2012, Erdoğan and Morsi declared that they shared the same views regarding the situation in Syria. During Erdoğan's visit to Egypt just a few days before the start of the protests in Egypt, on 19 November 2012, Erdoğan and Morsi in a joint press conference "warned" Israel, referring to it as a "terrorist state" (Peker, 2012). In addition, they signed 27 new bilateral agreements, committed to increasing the volume of trade between Turkey and Egypt, which had been deemed "insufficient", and made frequent references to the cultural and religious affinity between Turkey and Egypt (TRT, 2012). For instance, in order to make the point that Turkish people and Egyptian people were "brothers" in his speech, Erdoğan described Cairo as a "City of Qur'an, just like Istanbul and Mecca" (*Hürriyet*, 2012). One columnist writing in a popular daily newspaper, the *Hürriyet*, noted that Erdoğan was establishing a very close alliance with the Muslim Brotherhood in Egypt, gradually taking a side against the West, which complemented the Turkish government's preference to position itself within the bloc of Arab states, especially after the Davos incident in 2009 (Ergin, 2012).

Both Turkey and the EU wanted to establish a close relationship with Egypt under Morsi, both wishing to contribute to Egypt's democratic transition. Yet, there were increasing tensions in the domestic arena in Egypt due to the polarising policies that Morsi was implementing. After Morsi's constitutional declaration on 22 November 2012, which caused great concern among Egyptian judges and drew condemnation from various organisations due to the way in which it concentrated power in the hands of Morsi, demonstrations and, consequently, clashes between opponents and proponents of Morsi began (Spencer, 2012). The clashes eventually required attention from the EU and Turkey and created a situation in which Turkey and the EU could act in cooperation.

At this point, considering the approaches of the EU and Turkey regarding Egypt under Morsi, it is important to analyse how they reacted in the aftermath of the protests. It is possible to say that the Turkish government was reluctant to be critical of Morsi, whereas the EU gradually emphasised restraint. It is essential to establish that the Turkish government clearly sided with the Muslim Brotherhood in Egypt. Then, based on this empirical analysis, it is possible to make the claim that the Turkish behaviour was in line with its strategic interests in Egypt because the Turkish government saw the Muslim Brotherhood as an ally in the region that would side with Turkey and help Turkey to gain more influence in regional matters. So, to some degree, there was also a strategic dimension to supporting Morsi, although the strategic dimension alone does not fully explain why the Turkish government supported the Muslim Brotherhood when it was clear that the Muslim Brotherhood would not be able to retain power.

When the clashes began, the EEAS issued a statement on 5 December, and EU High Representative Ashton expressed her concerns about the clashes, urging "calm and restraint on all sides" (Ashton, 2012a). Similarly, on 10 December, in another statement, Ashton called on both sides to "try and work together" to stop the tension for the sake of the democratic transition, peace, and security in Egypt (Ashton, 2012b). She stated:

> We had the Task Force to demonstrate our commitment to the economic recovery in Egypt, and also to the political process, dialogue with civil society, issues that are so important, like human rights, and of course this broader question of inclusivity. We've been saying the same consistent message: we will support the people of Egypt through the transition and in any way that we can.
>
> (ibid.)

Therefore, the EU's position directly after the start of the protests was based on support for Egypt's democratic transition, while acknowledging problems with democracy in Egypt and calling for restraint from both sides. The EU did not directly express criticism but signalled that it would start to adopt a critical stance against the Morsi government. In fact, the EU had criticised the Morsi government even before the demonstrations. For instance, following the crackdown on civil society in Egypt, Ashton issued a statement on 1 February 2012 urging the

Egyptian authorities to "respect" the rights of civil society organisations in Egypt (Ashton, 2012c). So, the EU already had ongoing concerns about the course of democratic transition and had acknowledged them even before the clashes. However, with the start of anti-Morsi demonstrations and clashes, the situation deteriorated, and the EU did not hesitate to call on all sides, including the Egyptian authorities, to reduce tension.

The Turkish government, on the other hand, was reluctant to direct any criticism at Morsi and even supported his policies, openly dismissing the claims that he was concentrating power. One clear example of this is the reply PM Erdoğan gave on 28 November (almost a week after the protests had begun) in response to a journalist asking him what he thought about the situation in Egypt and specifically with regard to criticisms voiced against Morsi as an increasingly authoritarian leader. Erdoğan replied:

> Some events in Egypt upset us too. Actually, it is not like there is a concentration of power [by Morsi]. He [Morsi] is going through the similar troubles that we [the AKP] have gone through. You need to take legal steps to assure freedom. The regulations [referring to the changes in regulations Morsi had made] consist of 6–7 articles. I regard the criticisms being presented as if Morsi is concentrating power, as attempts to cast suspicion on his authority.
>
> (Demir, 2012)

So, whereas the EU was urging calm and promoting negotiation, mindful of the problems with democracy in Egypt, while supporting democratic transition, the Turkish government saw the crisis as a normal occurrence, and essentially a challenge that Morsi needed to overcome. In other words, there was a fundamental divergence between the approaches of the EU and Turkey because the EU did not defend Morsi's policies: on the contrary, it viewed his policies as polarising; whereas, the Turkish government supported Morsi, even referring to criticisms directed at him as attempts to cast suspicion on his authority.

Based on these divergent preferences of the EU and the Turkish government, it could be claimed that cooperation would have been costly to a degree that would have meant an adjustment of behaviour for the Turkish side. A constructivist approach underlining the cultural affinity between the AKP and the Muslim Brotherhood also has explanatory potential to understand why there was divergence and a lack of cooperation in the first place. In order to make an assessment, this analysis proceeds to focus on the Turkish behaviour following the killings in Port Said on 26 January 2013 and interactions with the EU.

Turkish reaction to the killings in Port Said on 26 January 2013 as a part of the Turkish reaction to the anti-Morsi protests starting on 22 November 2012

More than 70 people were killed and at least 1000 people were injured in Port Said on the second anniversary of the beginning of the 2011 revolution in clashes between protesters and security forces (Fahmy and Lee, 2012). The violence escalated as troops were deployed, and shortly thereafter localised protests grew into widespread civil unrest that led Morsi to cancel a trip to Addis Ababa. Again, the main question for the EU and the Turkish government was whether to appear supportive of Morsi or not. This analysis focuses on to what extent consultation or information exchange took place before these actors took a stance publicly. This chapter finds that there were exchanges of views between Turkey and the EU, although they remained largely as a matter of formality without any substantial cooperation involving consultation.

There is no conclusive evidence that the Turkish government specifically reached out to the EU to inform it about its actions before publicly adopting a position, nor is there any evidence that it consulted the EU on its actions. However, there was dialogue on foreign policy that included information exchange on Egypt at different levels: the Turkish Foreign Minister and the EU High Representative talked informally in addition to the communication on the ground between the EU delegation and the Turkish mission in Egypt. So, there was more than "unilateral information" since the EU presumably could convey its view on the crisis through formal diplomatic channels as well as through informal channels.

The Turkish government saw the killings as a natural occurrence and an inevitable consequence of Morsi's struggle to restore order. Based on Turkish preferences favouring Morsi, constructivism has explanatory potential when considering the reaction that the Turkish government displayed to the killings. Constructivism explains why there was a fundamental divergence between the Turkish government and the EU. However, this is not a straightforward case because siding with Morsi also had a strategic aspect since it was an indicator that the Turkish government was positioning itself within the Islamist bloc. For this reason, it is not completely accurate to claim that Turkish support for Morsi was solely an appropriate action. This section proceeds to make a detailed analysis following an examination of empirical evidence.

HR Ashton on behalf of the EU, as well as individual member states, condemned the violence, urging the authorities to restore peace. The UK, for instance, expressed concern and called for "all sides to exercise maximum restraint" (Foreign and Commonwealth Office, 2013). The Foreign Office Minister for the Middle East, Alastair Burt, said:

> [The violence] cannot help the process of dialogue which we encourage as vital for Egypt today, and we must condemn the violence in the strongest terms. . . . We remain committed as a strong friend of Egypt and the Egyptian people to support the aim of strengthening true democracy. . . . The right to peaceful freedom of expression and assembly is an essential part of this, but the violence we have seen [Saturday] can have no place in a truly democratic Egypt.
>
> (ibid.)

Similarly, Ashton condemned the violence, saying that it was "with great concern" that she had received the news and urged "the Egyptian authorities to restore calm and order", calling "all sides to show restraint" (Ashton, 2013). The Turkish government, on the other hand, did not want to appear overly critical and jeopardise its relations with Morsi due to its strategic interests.

The Turkish Ministry of Foreign Affairs issued a basic statement expressing condolences to the families of victims, emphasising the need for dialogue and peace in Egypt and reiterating support for the democratisation of Egypt as a "friend and brother to Turkey" (Ministry of Foreign Affairs of Turkey, 2013b). The killings received considerable attention in Turkey, prompting journalists to ask about the government's position at a press conference at the Ministry of Foreign Affairs on 31 January 2013. The reply given by the ministry spokesperson was again based on a general reiteration that Turkey wished for the well-being of Egypt, its "brother and friend" (Ministry of Foreign Affairs of Turkey, 2013c). The final remarks of the spokesperson, however, included signs of how the government perceived the killings. He said: "Naturally, in the aftermath of regime changes, it takes some time to put things in order. As it happens in other countries, there are some political developments in Egypt" (ibid.).

Therefore, the EU had a more critical attitude, especially towards the Egyptian authorities; whereas, the Turkish government saw the killings as a natural consequence of Morsi's effort to restore order. In addition, as evident in Erdoğan's remarks mentioned earlier, the Turkish government sympathised with Morsi, dismissing anti-Morsi criticisms in Egypt as attempts to challenge Morsi's power (Demir, 2012). In this way, the Turkish government hoped to be able to strengthen its relationship with Egypt under Morsi even further.

The Turkish attitude continued in the aftermath of the deadly clashes. Turkish decision makers not only avoided criticising Morsi but also sought to strengthen their relationships with him. To give an example, just a few days after the killings in Port Said, Turkish President Gül visited Egypt to attend a meeting of the Organization of Islamic Cooperation on 7 February 2013. The Turkish President received a state welcome, and he did not hesitate to pose with the Egyptian President, smiling to the cameras and holding hands together in the air. The main message Gül gave in the press conference was: "We [Turkey] support Egypt in every area" (*Hürriyet*, 2013f). He emphasised the importance of developing the economic relationship between Turkey and Egypt, referred to his conversation with Morsi about doubling the existing trade volume, and claimed that Israel was the greatest obstacle to peace and stability in the Middle East (Presidency of the Republic of Turkey, 2013). Here, again, it is possible to identify the economic and cultural dimensions of the Turkish approach to Morsi: furthering economic interdependence and developing Muslim solidarity against Israel.

Gül's comments in response to a question asked by a journalist from the Anadolu Agency made the perspective of Turkish decision makers clear:

AA: [Referring to protests and clashes] How do you see the events that increasingly happen in Egypt and the demands made in this context?

GÜL: We appreciate the accomplishments of Egypt in their democratic transition. It is of historical importance that the country is governed by the first democratically elected president. . . . The struggle for democracy is a struggle that requires long-term patience and effort (*Hürriyet*, 2013f).

Here, when the Turkish President talked about democracy, he put emphasis on the fact that Morsi was the first democratically elected head of state in Egypt. He avoided appearing critical despite the turmoil in Egypt, with a view he shared with PM Erdoğan and FM Davutoğlu that the violence was a natural consequence of the political transformation. Gül's comments, in fact, encapsulate the Turkish approach of turning a blind eye to what was happening in Egypt.

There is no specific evidence that the Turkish government wanted to come to a mutual understanding with the EU on democratisation in Egypt or at least make any effort to reconcile the Turkish and EU approaches regarding democratisation. The variation in the interpretation of the term, democratisation, was the main divergence between the EU and the Turkish government. Both expressed support for democracy in Egypt and issued statements to this effect. However, the nuance here is that when the EU expressed its support for democracy, it also condemned the authorities for using violence and urged the Egyptian government to respect the rights and freedom of people in Egypt; whereas, when the Turkish government expressed support for democracy, it supported Morsi, highlighting the fact that he had been democratically elected.

The Turkish emphasis on Morsi's democratic mandate gained more importance after the Gezi Park protests in June 2013. There were parallelisms between the unrests in Turkey and Egypt, which made the Turkish government especially concerned about its own political survival. As a result, the Turkish government was extremely sensitive to anyone who made comparisons or who came across to the Turkish government as having such a view. An evident example is the tension between President Erdoğan and the Doğan Media Group later in 2015. The *Hürriyet*, a popular newspaper in Turkey, announced on its website on 16 June 2015 that Morsi had been given a death sentence. Their headline read: "The world is shocked: Death sentence to the president who got 52% of votes".[1] A few hours later, Erdoğan lashed out at the media group, accusing it of plotting against the Turkish government and saying that he would not end up in the same position as Morsi (Al Jazeera, 2015). Later, the *Hürriyet* denied having made any implication and stated that the headline had quoted Erdoğan's own words about Morsi (*Hürriyet*, 2015a). Whether the *Hürriyet* had intended to allude to Erdoğan is not relevant for this analysis; however, a key point is that the Turkish government was becoming sensitive. Unease with Erdoğan's policies in Turkey could be regarded as another reason why the Turkish government vehemently opposed criticising Morsi, underlined by the fact that Morsi had been democratically elected, and regarded the unrests in Egypt as normal.

It is important to analyse the impact of potential cooperation not only on the formation of Turkish preferences but also on Turkish behaviour once these preferences had been formed. This implies that there is a question about the extent to which Turkey communicated with the EU after the public announcement of its policies. Although the Turkish government did not specifically reach out to the EU to inform or consult concerning their divergent positions beforehand, there was foreign policy dialogue involving policy makers and diplomats exchanging information in order to keep each other updated. When the anti-Morsi protests began,

Turkey-EU relations were at a low point. Turkish decision makers were upset with EU policies, and the existing tension limited potential cooperation. However, as this analysis will explain, despite the tension, the EU and the Turkish government were in touch, especially through informal channels of communication.

At the time when the anti-Morsi protests started, Turkey-EU relations had deteriorated because the Turkish government had frozen relations with the EU as a reaction to the Republic of Cyprus's presidency of the Council (July to December 2012). For the Turkish government, the Republic of Cyprus's presidency was a sensitive issue, and it had announced a year before that it would freeze relations with the bloc if the Republic of Cyprus were to assume the presidency. In September 2011, the Deputy PM of Turkey had stated, "if the EU gives its presidency to southern Cyprus, the real crisis will be between the EU and Turkey. . . . we will then freeze our relations with the EU. . . . we have made this decision" (*Hürriyet*, 2011).

The prevalent view among Turkish decision makers was that the EU did not genuinely want to accept Turkey as a full member, and the presidency of the Republic of Cyprus fuelled this sentiment. The Turkish government had made it clear in the accession talks that it wanted nothing less than full membership, dismissing other proposals such as giving Turkey a "privileged partner" status. For instance, Turkish EU Minister and Chief Negotiator Bağış claimed, "the EU membership is like pregnancy. You're either pregnant or not. There is no other option" (Interview TR01). There was a view among Turkish elites that the EU was, in fact, surreptitiously rejecting Turkey. For example, PM Erdoğan stated, "the EU is trying to forget us but it refrains [from saying it]. Yet, it would be a relief for us if they [the EU] declared. They should declare instead of wasting our time so that we can move on" (*Hürriyet*, 2013b). During this CO, especially due to the presidency of the Republic of Cyprus, the relationship between Turkey and the EU was at its lowest point since the opening of negotiations in 2005. The implication this had regarding cooperation was that Turkish decision makers were resentful towards the EU due to the slow momentum of negotiations. As the Turkish leadership lost trust in the EU, it became harder to achieve a higher degree of cooperation, such as co-decision. So, essentially, the deterioration of relations could be why there was no particular desire from the Turkish leadership to seek consultations with the EU during this CO.

There were initiatives aimed at keeping the relationship moving, such as the Positive Agenda between the EU and Turkey (to be precise, among the Commission, the EEAS, and the Turkish government) launched earlier in May 2012. However, the Turkish government overall adopted a resentful attitude towards the EU, which consequently made any kind of formal interaction (e.g., in the form of leaders or high-level officials meeting) difficult to maintain. In fact, this resentful attitude can be seen in the public statements of Turkish decision makers. To demonstrate the negative sentiments that the Turkish government had, for example, Erdoğan very clearly stated that he wanted Turkey to join the Shanghai Cooperation Organisation (SCO), and if they were to take Turkey in, then Turkey would "bid good-bye to the EU" (*Hürriyet*, 2013b). He said, "since it [Turkey's membership bid] is going so negative, as the prime minister of 75 million, you inevitably begin to look for alternatives" and even argued that the SCO would be a "better" option for Turkey because it was "more powerful" than the EU (ibid.). Some commentators in Turkey, at that time, argued that Erdoğan was toughening his position because of his frustration with the deadlock regarding Turkey's membership (Ergin, 2013). This statement was an indicator that the Turkish government no longer saw EU membership as a primary goal, and inevitably reflected on the prospects of cooperation in a negative manner. Moreover, the discontent of the Turkish government and the freezing of relations did not help foreign policy cooperation because maintaining formal relations, including in the area of foreign policy, became increasingly difficult.

Although Turkey-EU relations were at a low point, interviews with diplomats in the Turkish Ministry of Foreign Affairs and the EEAS confirmed that the Davutoğlu-Ashton dialogue continued without interruption. This suggests that there were potentially information exchange and ongoing dialogue, which were not always made public due to the relations being frozen. It is hardly possible to say there was any substantial cooperation in which, for instance, the Turkish government consulted the EU or offered the EU a chance to give feedback on its position because the Turkish government displayed an attitude of indifference to the EU. Moreover, the Turkish leadership had strong preferences with regard to relations with Egypt under Morsi. This meant that interactions with the EU mattered neither during the preference formation nor after Turkey's position was made public.

Furthermore, despite the low point in relations, interaction in the area of foreign policy continued between Turkish and EU diplomats. For example, in addition to the EU Delegation in Ankara finding out more about Turkey's positions (e.g., the EU ambassador liaising with Turkish ministers) and the Turkish Delegation in Brussels doing the same, Turkish and EU embassies were in touch on the ground (Interviews EU05, EU06, and EU02). This meant that they gathered, exchanged views, and evaluated the situation in the conflict zone. A senior diplomat at the EU Delegation in Ankara explained: "it was agreed that the delegation and Turkish embassies in the countries of the Arab Spring would meet and exchange information on the ground" and described this as a "concrete" decision (Interview EU02). This was not a "systematic" dialogue, and it "depended on the ambassadors" on the ground (Interview EU02). With regard to the time of this CO, Turkey's ambassador to Cairo at the time (who was declared persona non grata later on in November 2013) confirmed that there was dialogue with the EU Delegation in Cairo (Interview TR12). The EU ambassador would invite Turkish diplomats for consultation as well as for social events. However, these were informal gatherings rather than structured or ad hoc meetings. Still, the existence of continuing diplomatic contact, even on the ground, indicates that there was communication between the EU and Turkey, which eventually helped them to understand each other's positions better.

As a result, there was no "consultation" because the Turkish government did not reach out to the EU to request its opinion specifically before or after this CO;

however, there was information exchange because EU and Turkish officials kept each other updated. It is highly likely that the Turkish position on the killings did not catch the EU by surprise, considering the information exchange and the general Turkish position on Morsi's restoration of order in Egypt. Therefore, there was more than "unilateral information" during this CO.

Turkish reaction to the removal of Morsi on 3 July 2013

Anti-Morsi protests continued until the removal of Morsi by General Sisi after the intervention of the Egyptian military on 3 July 2013. The military arrested Morsi and Muslim Brotherhood leaders, assumed power, and declared Adly Mansour, the Chief Justice of the Supreme Constitutional Court, as the Interim President. The decision sparked a counter-reaction. Morsi supporters began demonstrating, and there were clashes between the supporters and opponents of the move, which dragged the country into another episode of crisis. The main question around potential cooperation for the EU and Turkey concerned how harshly to criticise the coup and whether to establish relations with Sisi in view of the turmoil in the country.

This section examines the policy choices of the Turkish government and the EU regarding the removal of Morsi as a result of the coup d'état and focuses on their interactions in order to evaluate the extent to which cooperation took place. The Turkish government sided with the Muslim Brotherhood despite costs attached to cutting all ties with the government in Cairo. There was a shift from the earlier strategic behaviour in the sense that persisting with support for Morsi after the military had consolidated power was not instrumentally efficient, which means that constructivism has explanatory potential since it points to the cultural and political affinity between the AKP and the Muslim Brotherhood as a motivation for policy action. In terms of concrete policy choices, Turkish decision makers continued to regard Morsi as the only legitimate leader in Egypt and often criticised the EU for its relationship with Sisi. The policy divergence was one of the main reasons why there was no high-degree cooperation between the EU and Turkey. However, the information exchange continued, and there was still more than "unilateral information" during this CO.

The main difference between the policies of the EU and the Turkish government was that the EU prioritised restoring peace and stability in Egypt and keeping the channels of dialogue open with the post-Morsi administration, but the Turkish government refused to recognise Sisi as a legitimate leader. As previously highlighted, cooperation does not necessarily mean convergence. There could well have been some degree of cooperation in the absence of convergence if, for instance, Turkey had held consultations with the EU, informed it about its policy, or if they had agreed to disagree on how to deal with Egypt. "Consultation" with the EU could have been achieved if Turkey had discussed with the EU the events in Egypt both prior to and after the formulation of its position. The empirical evidence does not suggest that the Turkish government specifically sought the EU opinion on their policy; however, it does suggest that a degree of information exchange took place. This analysis unpacks the different emphasises in the Turkish and EU responses as a factor limiting cooperation, addresses the question of whether Turkish foreign policy followed a Sunni agenda, which is highly important in order to understand if constructivism came into play, and assesses the degree of cooperation during this CO.

Different emphasises in the approaches of the EU and Turkey

The EU diplomats interviewed both in Ankara and Brussels frequently used the phrase "different emphasises" when they described the different policies the Turkish government and the EU followed regarding Sisi. The main underlying reason for this expression was the EU's effort to underline its disapproval, in principle, of coup d'état. By saying they had "different emphasises", the EU officials pointed out that they actually had similar approaches in essence. In other words, they wished to convey that they were not supportive of the Egyptian army led by Sisi and did not approve of the means by which Morsi was removed, contrary to Turkish claims and accusations. "Nobody in Europe ever said that Sisi came to power in a democratic way", a former EU ambassador to Turkey explained (Interview EU03). Another senior EU diplomat in Ankara said, "I am not saying we have differences; we have different attentions when considering the events. Our objectives are similar" (Interview EU06). Another claimed: "On principle, we are on the same line. When Sisi took power, we always said that democratic principles should be the aim of this process. We are also making statements to condemn, for example, the death penalty based on principles in the EU" (Interview EU02).

"Different emphasises" is a useful term here because essentially the divergence concerned Turkey and the EU having different perspectives in response to events in Egypt. Otherwise, they both declared support for Egypt's democratic transformation, although they had different understandings of it as discussed in the previous section, regarding anti-Morsi protests. After the removal of Morsi, they reacted differently and chose distinct ways to deal with the crisis. The Turkish response needs to be examined first in order to understand what exactly was different and how the views diverged.

The Turkish government strongly preferred to see Morsi as the legitimate leader. Erdoğan's speech two days after the removal of Morsi on 5 July summarised the Turkish position:

> [In Egypt] there is a president who was elected on 52% of the votes. There is a president that was elected by the will of people. After one year suddenly there are some groups saying, 'We don't like it' and the military intervenes. . . . Criticisms saying, 'Morsi had faults' are not honest. Every politician, every leader may make mistakes. I, too, might have made mistakes. It is not the duty of some powers to punish this, removing [Morsi] from politics. That can only happen with the will of people.
>
> (NTV, 2013)

According to an interviewee at the EU delegation in Ankara, the EU found out about Turkish policy through diplomatic channels; however, no prior information or consultation took place (Interview EU06). It is still unlikely that the Turkish position caught the EU by surprise, considering the informal communication between HR Ashton and FM Davutoğlu during the Morsi era.

The Turkish government emerged as one of the biggest opponents of the military intervention in Egypt by condemning the removal of Morsi at the risk of burning its bridges with the government in Egypt. It sided with the Muslim Brotherhood, saw Morsi as the legitimate leader, and urged the world to condemn the event in the same way. Its harsh attitude was perceived as being hostile by the government in Cairo, and the Turkish ambassador had to leave Egypt after being declared persona non grata. The Turkish government also began to push international actors to display similar reactions towards Sisi and criticised those who formed relations with him.

A simple example was Erdoğan's attitude towards a lunch event in New York hosted by UN Secretary General Ban Ki-moon. He was invited to sit at the "main" table of the event with Ban Ki-moon, US President Obama, and Spanish King Felipe IV among others. Then he discovered that Sisi had been invited too and that South African President Zuma was supposed to sit between him and Sisi. Erdoğan, then, refused to attend the event, saying that he would not sit at the same table as Sisi because it would legitimise Sisi and those who carried out the coup in Egypt. He also criticised the UN and coupists in his speech at the UN General Assembly:

> While in Egypt, the president who was elected by the will of people is removed by a coup and thousands of innocent people who stand by their votes are massacred, in the UN, democratic states only watch. And the person who carried out the coup is being legitimised. If we care about democracy, we need to respect the ballot box. If not, and if we will defend those who come to power with a coup then I wonder why the UN exists.
>
> (Berber, 2014)

Again, PM Erdoğan underlined that Morsi had been democratically elected and that there was a need to "respect the ballot box" and the will of people. The Turkish government rationalised its support for Morsi based on the argument that coup d'états were unacceptable in democracies and Morsi was a democratically elected leader, which made him the only legitimate leader, and, therefore, support for democracy should be translated into support for Morsi. The Turkish government's criticism was directed at the international arena, not specifically at the EU. However, as will be discussed, the Turkish government also pushed the EU to criticise Sisi. This example demonstrates that the Turkish government fiercely refused to recognise the Sisi government to the extent that Erdoğan even refused to attend the same event as Sisi and criticised the UN, questioning the purposes of the organisation and accusing states of being merely spectators.

The EU, on the other hand, had an approach that prioritised the restoration of stability in Egypt. The fundamental difference between the approaches of Turkey and the EU concerned the Turkish government's cutting of all ties with the Sisi government. The Turkish government wanted to see the EU take a similar step. EU HR Ashton's advisor described the difference clearly in the following way:

> The approach of Davutoğlu and the approach of Ashton were very different with Davutoğlu believing that we should cut all ties really and that we should declare what had happened a coup d'état and that the EU should stand on its principles and not engage with those who had ousted Morsi. Cathy Ashton adopted a very different approach, which was about trying to keep the channels of communication open with all sides and trying to set out a roadmap of where she expected Egypt to get to.
>
> (Interview EU04)

In Ankara, however, this difference was presented as the Turkish government standing up for democratic principles and the EU being self-seeking. A clear example of how the Turkish government pushed the EU to take further steps was when Morsi was given a death sentence in May 2015. Speaking in a public rally on 17 May 2015, Erdoğan urged the EU to impose sanctions on Egypt, saying, "Hey, Europe! Hey, West! Isn't the death penalty prohibited there? So why are you silent? Why do you side with Sisi? I call on the entire world, international institutions: Why don't you impose sanctions?" (Erdoğan, 2015b). A few days later on 20 May, he repeated, "[Referring to the death sentence] I am calling out to EU states, to those who call themselves democrats, why are you silent?" (Erdoğan, 2015a). A month later in an interview, he repeated that the world had failed to defend democracy in Egypt (*Sabah*, 2015). So, the bottom line is, again, that the Turkish discourse was based on the democracy argument, that is, that Turkey was defending the democratic rights of the Egyptian people. Indeed, the main reason for using this argument in a determined way was to legitimise the Turkish government's policy of support for the Muslim Brotherhood, which will be discussed later.

It should be noted that the Turkish government's emphasis on democracy promotion significantly differed from its earlier approach to the Middle East and North Africa in the pre-Arab Spring period. As discussed in Chapter 2, before the uprisings began, the AKP government had emphasised developing economic interdependence and cultural affinity: an approach that had enabled the AKP to form strong bonds with authoritarian regimes in Syria, Libya, and Egypt. A central paradox that can be highlighted here is that when the Turkish government perceived itself as a democracy promoter, the EU remained relatively passive (e.g., compared to the role it had played in post-communist democratic transitions in eastern Europe following the Cold War) and even avoided the term "coup d'état".

While the Turkish government was conveying its defence of democracy in Egypt, it also criticised the EU for not cutting all ties with Egypt and for being self-seeking. For instance, a senior Turkish diplomat explained the Turkish position and the Turkish view on the EU position very clearly:

> They [the EU] maintained relations [with Sisi] and looked at the situation in a self-seeking way, prioritising their interests. Our government looked at it more emotionally. Now, I am not entirely sure if that was a democratic perspective because at one time there was an emphasis on democracy, at another time in another area there was not, so it is not possible to talk of a real democratic perspective [referring to the position of the Turkish government]. The government had certain red lines and Muslim Brotherhood was one of them. The EU had a more interest-based approach, which is understandable since it cannot easily function [referring to the slow nature of the EU foreign policy decision-making process]. Yet, they [the EU] make criticisms and declarations like 'we are concerned about the anti-democratic etc.' Then they sweep it aside and continue trade and relations with Egypt. This is life.
>
> (Interview TR13)

A couple of points can be drawn from this statement. First, it confirms that the democracy argument was used as a tool to support the Muslim Brotherhood; the real issue was that the Muslim Brotherhood in Egypt was a "red line" issue for the Turkish government, which will be discussed further in the next subsection. Second, it shows that there were different voices in the Turkish Ministry of Foreign Affairs that disagreed with the government's position. This diplomat, for instance, claimed the Ministry of Foreign Affairs had a difficult time advocating the Turkish government's position, implying that Turkey was not in a place to teach democracy and that the democracy argument was used inconsistently, in the sense that it was used on one issue, the removal of Morsi and the crisis around the Muslim Brotherhood, but not on other issues. The government was "emotional", which the diplomat used as opposed to "rational". This will be discussed shortly as well. Third, there is the argument that the Turkish government wanted to present itself as a defender of democracy while regarding the EU as a "hypocrite" in the sense that the EU made only superficial statements and, contrary to such statements, that business-as-usual would prevail. Indeed, it should be noted that it was not only the Turkish government who thought this way. Various EU analysts at the time also argued that the EU was prioritising its short-term interests while being ineffective at criticising Sisi. For example, an analysis in the *EUobserver* declared that the EU Neighbourhood Policy was in a "coma" and the EU was just "paying lip service to human rights, democracy and the well-being of the Egyptian people" while prioritising its immediate interests (Tubiana, 2014). Fourth, and above all, the statement of the diplomat shows that the Turkish government had a significantly different view on the issue.

Having established that the EU and Turkey adopted different positions, stemming from different possible motivations, the key question is whether there were Turkish attempts at information exchange or consultation prior to the declarations of these different positions. An EU diplomat in Ankara stated that they were in touch with the Ministry of Foreign Affairs to gain an understanding of Turkish positions and they were up-to-date during the CO, but there was no specific attempt from the Turkish side to inform the EU about its divergent position prior to it being stated publicly (Interview EU05). However, it is hardly possible to say that the EU was caught by surprise because of the generally supportive Turkish attitude towards Morsi and the probable informal communication between HR Ashton and FM Davutoğlu.

A Sunni narrative in Turkish foreign policy?

A significant question that needs to be addressed is why the Turkish government sided with the Muslim Brotherhood and what this meant for the motivation of the Turkish government when determining the Turkish position. Having established an understanding that the EU and Turkey had fundamentally different "emphasises", it is essential to examine why the Turkish government emphasised support for the Brotherhood in its approach.

As touched upon, the real issue with the critical position that the Turkish government had was that the government wanted to keep its support for the Muslim Brotherhood in Egypt. The Muslim Brotherhood was an essential ally for the Turkish government particularly because of the cultural and political affinity between them and the AKP. Morsi was also seen as a natural partner to the AKP in regional affairs: for example, with regard to the Israeli-Palestinian conflict because by partnering with Morsi, the AKP would be able to carry out Turkish foreign policy based on Muslim solidarity.

The key point here is that strategic motives alone do not explain why the Turkish government continued to advocate for Morsi when it was clear that the military had seized power. Cutting all ties with the government in Egypt was a costly action. Disapproving of the removal of Morsi did not necessarily mean hostility towards Sisi, and the Turkish government had the choice of being neutral, especially after it was clear that Sisi would lead Egypt. This is the point where identity comes into play. To some extent, constructivism has explanatory potential because it is possible to claim that shared Muslim (and Sunni) identity was an important aspect of the continuous Turkish support for Morsi. Among the actors in Egypt, the Muslim Brotherhood was the closest to the AKP in terms of their Sunni Islamist religious, political, and social preferences, which was the main reason why the Turkish government continued to see Morsi as the legitimate leader and pushed international actors to cut off their relations with Sisi.

The question of whether the Turkish government purposefully planned and pursued a foreign policy favouring Sunni actors throughout the Arab Spring from the beginning is a different issue. However, in the case of Morsi and Sisi, it could be argued that the policy was based on favouring the actor with a Sunni Islamist agenda. Again, the question of whether Turkish foreign policy deliberately followed a Sunni agenda is a different question, yet it is useful to point out that this question made it into both academic and popular debate. For instance, Yetkin

(2015), a columnist in a popular newspaper, argued that the "AKP established its Middle East policy on the cooperation of Sunni powers in the triangle of Ankara-Cairo-Damascus". Özel (2012), an academic and journalist, believed that Erdoğan had not had a particularly Sunni policy before, but, after the start of the Arab uprisings, he sided with the Muslim Brotherhood, who he thought were the closest to him, positioning himself in the Sunni bloc. On the other hand, Öniş (2014: 10–11), an academic, emphasised that the AKP found itself in the Sunni bloc as a consequence of its increased engagement with the region, not particularly because it had purposefully followed a Sunni agenda since the beginning of its involvement. He contended that "there is evidence to support the claim that Turkey is siding with Sunni Muslims in a number of ongoing conflicts within key Arab States. . . . In the Egyptian context, a similar tendency is apparent given the strong support of the AKP for the Muslim Brotherhood at the expense of other groups within the country's broad political coalition" (ibid.). But he also claimed that Turkey had been "drawn into" the Sunni bloc:

> Turkey has found itself in the awkward position of being part of the Sunni axis in the Middle East represented by countries like Saudi Arabia and Qatar, with established authoritarian regimes, which so far have been quite resilient to the spreading effects of the Arab revolutions. Being drawn into this kind of coalition on sectarian lines is highly inconsistent with Turkey's image as a force for democracy promotion in the Arab world.
>
> (ibid.:11)

Evidence from the fieldwork presented here also supports that the Turkish position was based on identity. As mentioned earlier, one diplomat interviewed used the word "emotional" as opposed to "rational" to describe the Turkish position regarding continued support for Morsi. Similarly, another diplomat involved in EU-Turkey relations claimed, "We no longer have a rational foreign policy" (Interview TR09). Upon being asked to elaborate, the diplomat commented: "Our policy towards the Muslim Brotherhood is sentimental and ideological. It reflects the government's ideology and political views" (ibid.). Another official at the Ministry of Foreign Affairs claimed that the government had "blindly" followed the Muslim Brotherhood (Interview TR07). A senior diplomat criticised the government and argued that the government had followed a clearly sectarian policy with regard to Egypt, despite their denial of this, and he elaborated on the foreign policy decision-making process in Ankara: "It [the government's policy] is clearly sectarian. Since the establishment of the Republic [of Turkey], the Ministry of Foreign Affairs had not seen anything like this or been asked to implement such a policy. We were astonished too" (Interview TR13).

This data is important for two main reasons. First, it demonstrates that the Turkish government prioritised solidarity with the Muslim Brotherhood because of its identity. From a theoretical perspective, constructivism works better to describe such a motivation since it can be said that identity was the main factor shaping Turkish preference, that is, the support for Morsi. Second, this is a good example to catch a glimpse of the decision-making process in Ankara. Clearly, the diplomats here disagreed with the government's position since they claim it was not a rational position but rather an emotional one, which again shows that the Turkish policy is more a direct reflection of the preferences of AKP elites with regard to Turkey's place in the region instead of being a policy formed as a result of a cost-benefit calculation with many inputs. This evidence, then, supports the argument that continued support for Morsi was of little strategic value.

Interactions with the EU

Having discussed the Turkish policy regarding Morsi, this subsection focuses on the interactions between the Turkish government and the EU. Before proceeding with an examination of interactions during this CO, it should be highlighted that the context of interaction was one in which there was an interest from both sides in closer cooperation. This is evident from the statements after the 51st Meeting of the EU-Turkey Association Council held in Brussels on 27 May 2013, about a month before the coup took place. In his statement, FM Davutoğlu clearly stated:

> In view of the Arab transformations, which are at a critical juncture, the urgency for a genuine partnership between the EU and Turkey has become even more manifest. . . . Therefore, it is only natural for Turkey and the EU to join strengths to bring about a real and positive change in our shared neighbourhood. . . . Foreign and defence policy is a specific field of close dialogue and cooperation. Turkey could indeed bring in substantial contributions to the EU once a meaningful and honest dialogue could be established and reinforced by a set of institutional coordination mechanisms. Prerequisite for such a mutually rewarding cooperation is the abolishment of institutional impediments stemming from the EU's own rules and regulations that pose limitations on our strategic dialogue.
>
> (Davutoğlu, 2013b)

Restating the main points from the previous year's meeting, Foreign Minister Davutoğlu once again underlined the added value of cooperation in the face of instability in the region. To some extent, this could also have been an attempt to portray Turkey as a strategic asset for the EU and may not have stemmed from a genuine will to cooperate with the EU, but, still, there was an emphasis that Turkey and the EU needed to achieve closer cooperation due to the Arab uprisings.

Expressing disappointment with institutional impediments limiting dialogue, FM Davutoğlu argued that Turkey could contribute to EU foreign policy and that coordination would be mutually beneficial. Yet, he repeated that "full coordination and joint action between Turkey and the EU" would become "practicable only when Turkey becomes a part of the EU decision making as a full member" (Davutoğlu, 2013b). Therefore, what is important to note here is that, almost a month before the crisis, the Turkish government reaffirmed its willingness to coordinate and to be a part of the EU decision-making mechanism. This indicates that the Turkish government saw the EU as an important actor in the region, at least in their official statements, just before the removal of Morsi.

Similarly, the EU side also stated that they were "committed to further enhance political dialogue on foreign policy issues of common interest", such as developments in the Middle East. Speaking after his meeting with PM Erdoğan on 23 May 2013, the President of the European Council, Herman Van Rompuy, underlined that cooperation was essential and claimed, "Turkey is a key international partner and ally for the European Union. Its regional role and active involvement in its wider neighbourhood deserve special acknowledgement and is irreplaceable" (European Council, 2013). This means, again, that in their statements, both the EU and Turkish leaders reaffirmed that coordination would be mutually beneficial. In this context, about a month later, Morsi was removed and the crisis presented an opportunity for cooperation in practice.

When Morsi was removed, it is possible to say straight away that the EU had no impact on the Turkish position because the Turkish government declared its position, support for Morsi, immediately. There was not even basic cooperation because the EU was not specifically informed. A higher degree of cooperation could not have taken place anyway because the EU had no position when the Turkish government immediately reacted by condemning Sisi. This analysis will also highlight that in this instance the Turkish government was the actor that pushed the EU to adopt a certain stance and criticise Sisi.

After the Egyptian Army removed Morsi from office on 3 July 2013, the Turkish government immediately reacted and condemned the move. FM Davutoğlu was at the ASEAN Summit in Singapore when he received the news, and his first reaction was to make calls to various foreign ministers around the world. Then, he interrupted his work at the Summit and returned to Istanbul the day after to evaluate the situation with PM Erdoğan. The position of the Turkish government was clear: the removal of Morsi was "unacceptable" (Davutoğlu, 2013a). On the day of the event, before leaving Singapore, Davutoğlu telephoned and urged foreign ministers around the world to stand up against the coup as Turkey did (*Hürriyet*, 2013e). It was reported that telephone calls were made to the foreign ministers of the US, UK, France, Germany, and Qatar (ibid.). At the very beginning of the crisis, the Turkish government had already decided on its position. Meanwhile, on Twitter, the Minister for EU Affairs and Chief Negotiator of Turkey, Bağış (2013b), expressed support for Morsi and said, "We must oppose a coup under any circumstances". So, there was at least "unilateral information" after the Turkish reaction. An interviewed EU diplomat in Ankara also confirmed that they found out about the position of the Turkish government from the Ministry of Foreign Affairs once it was clear, and the overall tone was one in which Turkey called on the international community to criticise Sisi's move (Interview EU05). This is a good example in which the Turkish government pushed the EU to align with itself and to make statements condemning the coup.

While Davutoğlu was making telephone calls to foreign ministers around the world, Bağış took charge of contacting the EU. It was reported that among the people that he telephoned were the EU High Representative, the Commissioner for Enlargement, the President of the European Parliament, and the Foreign Minister of Lithuania (because of its presidency of the EU Council) (*Hürriyet*, 2013e). With regard to these contacts, it was reported that Bağış sent a message of "we must oppose the coup together" (ibid.). The Turkish government immediately formed its response on the day of the coup, and these messages indicate that this is one of the clear instances in which the government urged the EU to act and expected support.

The Turkish government especially expected a condemnation from the EU, which included referring to what had happened specifically as a coup d'état. On the day of the event on 3 July, the EU High Representative issued a statement, which said that the EU had a "deep concern" and expressed support for democracy in Egypt. The statement did not include the phrase "coup d'état", nor did the subsequent statements released by the EEAS on 7 and 8 July. It was reported on 4 July that an EU diplomat had commented that the EEAS thought the army had gone "too far", but at the same time it was an "awkward" situation because nobody wanted to appear to back Morsi (Rettman, 2013). A spokesperson for the EEAS was asked whether events in Egypt could be described as a "coup d'état". He responded, "We are, of course, not in favour of military interventions" but added, "It's interesting the army has said it intervened in order to avoid a bloodbath" (ibid.).

What the Turkish government wanted to see from the EU was a clear message describing the events particularly as a coup d'état, and, as the EU avoided using this specific term, the Turkish government very quickly became critical of the EU's attitude. For instance, on 5 July, on Twitter, Turkey's EU Minister Bağış posted a tweet, targeting the EU:

> Those who cannot even say 'coup d'état' to a coup d'état should not anymore lecture the world on democracy and human rights. They would be ridiculed – even the African Union would laugh. :)
>
> (Bağış, 2013c)

Then, on 7 July, he wrote another message in English in a more formal manner without the smiley: "The coup d'état in Egypt can lead to undesired consequences. . . . It is essential for the EU to call for immediate restoration of democracy" (ibid.). Therefore, the Turkish government was pushing the EU to take a stance recognising the events as a coup d'état and to make converging statements.

There was a dialogue with the EU in the immediate aftermath of the events, in the sense that EU and Turkish high-level officials were on the telephone discussing the events as they happened. However, this was a part of the broader lobbying strategy of the Turkish government. Many ministers and high-level officials around the world were telephoned, including EU officials. So, this was not cooperation with the EU per se. That being said, the fact that the EU officials (and not only the High Representative) were called indicates that the Turkish government gave importance to the EU position after all; by making the telephone calls, the

Turkish government took the initiative to communicate the Turkish position. In the conversations, the EU also had a chance to communicate its position, and, for this reason, it could be claimed that it was a step further than "unilateral information". Though, it should be distinguished that the main purpose for the telephone calls was not to consult the EU or ask for feedback on the Turkish position; the main purpose of the calls was to urge the EU to align with the Turkish position, which had already been determined. And the Turkish government immediately became critical of the EU as soon as the EU avoided the term "coup d'état". So, there was hardly any substantial cooperation; rather there was pressure from the Turkish side on the EU to act in a certain way.

Moving on from the initial Turkish reaction to potential cooperation after the preferences had been formed, it could be argued that there was even less cooperation between the EU and Turkey because the Turkish leadership was upset with the EU over the avoidance of the term "coup d'état" and accused the EU of hypocrisy. The tension then limited the potential for EU and Turkish leaders to liaise. Yet, information exchange continued.

The Turkish government continued to intensify its criticism of Sisi and the EU. As a consequence, this created a situation in which, on one hand, the Turkish government was constantly criticising the EU for "failing" to react appropriately, and, on the other hand, as explained by a former EU ambassador to Turkey, nobody in the EU wanted to sit at the same table with the Turkish government, knowing that the Turkish leadership was blasting the EU at every opportunity and constantly "lecturing" about how to behave (Interview EU03). That being said, information exchange with regard to this CO continued; the EU and Turkey did not stop discussing foreign policy issues altogether. Egypt was indeed an item on the agenda, for example, when the EU High Representative and Turkish FM met in international meetings. However, the main point here is that, especially after the Turkish government started to criticise the EU fiercely, there was no political will from either side to cooperate. The Turkish attitude significantly limited any kind of potential cooperation that could have taken place with regard to Egypt.

It is essential to clarify how the deterioration of Turkey-Egypt diplomatic relations and the critical Turkish attitude towards the EU reflected on cooperation in the area of foreign policy. The Turkish government defended its position fiercely to the extent that it burned its bridges with the government in Cairo. Officially, the Turkish Ministry of Foreign Affairs stated that Turkey was advocating for the well-being of Egyptian people but that the Egyptian administration had "adopted a negative attitude and criticised Turkey's principled and pro-democracy stance" (Ministry of Foreign Affairs of Turkey, 2015). What actually happened was that the Turkish government became so much involved in the political situation in Egypt that it came across as hostile and provocative. On 23 November 2013, Egypt expelled Turkey's ambassador to Cairo, declaring him persona non grata. Justifying this act, the Egyptian Foreign Ministry spokesperson referred to the remarks of the Turkish PM on the overthrow of Morsi and said, "Turkey was provocative and interfering in Egypt's internal affairs" (Al Jazeera, 2013). Diplomatic relations were subsequently downgraded. As a result, the Turkish government sided with the Muslim Brotherhood under the pretext of supporting democracy for the Egyptian people so much that it caused a serious crisis between Turkey and Egypt.

After this point, the Turkish government became even more critical of the EU because the EU maintained its links to Sisi, whereas, the Turkish government wanted the EU to cut all ties too, as HR Ashton's advisor explained (Interview EU04). Former EU ambassador to Turkey Pierini described after this point in the following way, which also sheds light on the EU perspective:

> Nobody in Europe has said that Sisi has come to power democratically. The first objective is to restore stability in Egypt, so this is the realpolitik attitude of the West to deal with Sisi. As you can see Sisi has been received by a number of EU countries recently France and Italy. That's something that Turkey totally disagrees with and Erdoğan keeps blasting.
>
> (Interview EU03)

Then, with regard to whether consultations took place, he explained:

> You have episodes like Erdoğan blasting the entire Western world about Morsi or about not defending Morsi and supporting generals who made coup d'états. Then, you're not in a rational mode anymore. The methodology followed by Turkey became more and more difficult to coordinate.
>
> (ibid)

On the way in which the Turkish Ministry of Foreign Affairs brought up establishing coordination with the EU (e.g., the proposals made to establish institutionalised cooperation mechanisms across various platforms, such as through the EU-Turkey Association Council meetings), Pierini claimed that even though the Ministry of Foreign Affairs was willing, the government's policy did not allow anything of that sort. He stated:

> That [attempts by MFA bureaucracy] was contradicted by the political level. No politician wants to be lectured. So, what's the point of having high officials sit and discuss the situation in Egypt if suddenly the [Turkish] political leadership blasts the EU. Yes, indeed the MFA was very willing but the political conditions were not there.
>
> (ibid.)

About the issue of the Turkish government "lecturing" the EU, which was mentioned in Chapters 4 and 6, Egypt was one of the issues on which FM Davutoğlu adopted an attitude perceived as being "lecturing". In addition to the various EU diplomats mentioned earlier, a Turkish bureaucrat at the EU Ministry also cautiously confirmed the claim, saying some Turkey-EU meetings "might have turned into having more of an academic tone than a diplomatic one" (Interview TR02). This kind of behaviour also limited potential cooperation because, as another EU diplomat claimed, it was not possible to talk to the Turkish government about Egypt after a certain point because they had a "know-it-all attitude" (Interview EU05).

Various EU diplomats also confirmed Pierini's claim that the position of the Turkish government limited interactions. For example, an interviewee at the EU Delegation in Ankara explained: "Erdoğan said the EU had a wrong assessment of Egypt. Harsh anti-Western statements of course do not help cooperation" and gave a very specific example in which the Turkish attitude towards the EU limited interaction:

> During the Gezi Park protests [started in May 2013] there was a visit of the European Parliament Foreign Committee foreseen and they had adopted a resolution on this event, which was critical. There was one paragraph pointing at PM Erdoğan and he didn't like the resolution. So, the visit was cancelled. So, the public statement you're making [referring to anti-Western comments of the Turkish leadership] can have an impact on both sides.
>
> (Interview EU06)

It should also be pointed out that the beginning of the Sisi period coincided with the Gezi Park protests in Turkey. There were some parallels with the situation in Egypt in the sense that the government was dealing with public unrest, which was one of the reasons why the situation in Egypt was particularly salient for the AKP government.

Furthermore, the government accused the West of being behind the unrest in Turkey, which led to anti-Western statements by government officials. In addition, various EU foreign ministers backed Germany's proposal to temporarily block EU negotiation talks due to the protests. The point here is that the aftermath of the coup was not particularly a good time for EU-Turkey relations in general. And, as indicated, this reflects on the foreign policy relationship too. Both the accusations of the Turkish government that the EU was backing the generals that carried out the coup and anti-Western sentiments in public statements made by Turkish elites significantly limited EU-Turkey interactions.

With regard to the anti-Western comments of the Turkish leadership, Pierini very clearly pointed to the problem with maintaining a working relationship with the Turkish government:

> Where it becomes totally incomprehensible for the EU is when the Turkish leadership uses conspiracy theories [referring to claims that the West was behind the Gezi Park protests (e.g., an AKP official openly accused Germany)]. That works perfectly fine, or almost, within Turkey but outside it is either ridiculous or insulting.
>
> (Interview EU03)

Then, he added, "And that is when you suddenly have a split", after which it is not possible to move the relationship further (ibid).

In short, the EU and the Turkish government had different reactions to the coup. The Turkish behaviour was based on supporting the Muslim Brotherhood at the expense of cutting relations with Egypt. The government pushed the EU to adopt a similar stance and stop talking to Sisi. The EU left the channel of dialogue open with Sisi, which upset the Turkish government, who began to fiercely criticise the EU. There were anti-Western sentiments in Turkish behaviour, portraying Europe as supporting coups or being behind unrest in Turkey. The Turkish government sided with the Muslim Brotherhood and criticised those who did not share the same position to a degree that it limited interactions with the EU.

In terms of cooperation, there was no cooperation when the Turkish preferences were formed because the Turkish government immediately reacted by condemning the move of Sisi. Overall, there was information exchange because, after the public announcement of the Turkish position, Turkish decision makers stayed in touch with the EU, mainly to push them to adopt a similar stance. As the EU kept dialogue open with Sisi, the Turkish government began to criticise the EU and accuse it of hypocrisy, which increased the tension with the EU even more to a degree that it was not possible to have a high level of cooperation. However, throughout this CO, after the Turkish reaction, there was information exchange, which indicates that there was more than "unilateral information".

Support for the Muslim Brotherhood did not derive from a purely rationalist cost-benefit calculus aimed to advance Turkey's strategic interests in Egypt. So, it is not a clear-cut case in which rationalism might explain Turkish behaviour. However, it is possible to say that the fundamental divergence from the EU regarding Sisi made it costly for the Turkish government to have a high degree of cooperation with the EU, which explains not only why there was merely informative exchange but also why the Turkish government pushed the EU to take a similar stance.

Turkish reaction to the Rabaa massacre on 14 August 2013

On 14 August 2013, security forces raided protest camps of Brotherhood supporters, leaving behind more than 800 dead. It became known as the Rabaa massacre, as one of the larger camps was in Rabaa Square. An examination of Turkish behaviour in the aftermath of the removal of Morsi would be incomplete without touching upon the Turkish reaction to the Rabaa massacre. This CO is similar to the previous one since it is also about whether to support Morsi or Sisi; however it has a different quality because it is not simply about how legitimately the power was obtained but also how it was exercised. In this sense, it is similar to the case of Port Said (CO9), but under the Sisi government. So, it provides us with a chance to assess whether the need for consistency in the responses of the EU and the Turkish government provided an opportunity to engage in cooperation.

Considering the importance of Egypt both for the EU and Turkey, cooperation was possible to tackle the crisis and growing regional instability. Turkey, who reacted immediately to the bloodshed, could have displayed cooperative behaviour in its response, which, again, as in the previous cases, would have ideally involved an exchange of assessments of the situation and consultation. What happened was that, in line with its policy of support for the Brotherhood, the Turkish government immediately became one of the biggest opponents of the Sisi regime as well as one of the biggest critics of the EU due to the latter's persistent reluctance to refer to the intervention as a "coup d'état" and due to the way in which the EU continued to maintain open channels of dialogue with the Sisi government.

This CO confirms the findings discussed so far that there was no consultation but only information exchange because, first, there was a serious divergence between the approaches of the EU and the Turkish government. In the aftermath of the incident, the EEAS issued statements condemning the violence and expressing concern but still avoiding the term "coup d'état", whereas Turkey emerged as one of the harshest critics of Sisi, urging the international community to take steps against the regime and refusing to recognise Sisi as legitimate. There were even insults traded between the Egyptian and Turkish authorities. For instance, urging Turkey not to interfere in Egypt's domestic affairs, the Egyptian authorities called PM Erdoğan a "Western agent" that should not lecture Egypt on what to do (*Hürriyet*, 2013c). Consequently, diplomatic relations worsened between Turkey and Egypt, with the Egyptian ambassador in Ankara being recalled on 18 August and the Egyptian Foreign Minister arguing that Turkey clearly showed a "hostile" attitude, not only with speeches given by the Turkish government but also with its international moves (*Hürriyet*, 2013a, 2013d). Therefore, the essential difference was that the EU emphasised the need to end violence, and the restoration of stability, whereas the Turkish government emerged as an opponent of the Sisi regime at the risk of cutting off its relations with Egypt.

Second, as described previously, the Turkish government was very critical of the EU for avoiding the term "coup d'état", and this criticism can also be seen right after the Rabaa massacre as well. Before the massacre, PM Erdoğan was already critical, for instance, on 5 July, when referring to the EU, he said: "They haven't been able to call it a coup d'état. West, why are you silent? Why don't you talk? Those who cannot openly say 'coup d'état' to a coup d'état are supportive of coup d'état" (Erdoğan, 2013b). After the Rabaa massacre, he again claimed that the EU should be "ashamed" for being silent (Erdoğan, 2013a). Similarly, the Minister for EU Affairs tweeted that the EU needed to "wake up" and not be "quiet during the slaughter" (Bağış, 2013a).

Third, the reaction of the Turkish government after the Rabaa massacre exemplifies how identity elements could be found in Turkish foreign policy discourse. Speaking in the Turkish city of Bursa, PM Erdoğan harshly criticised the West and expressed support for the Muslim Brotherhood on the grounds of shared culture and history with Egypt. The following excerpt summarises the Turkish position and attitude towards the EU:

> Personally, I called all the UNSC permanent members. My foreign minister called most of the foreign ministers of the EU. . . . Even if everyone remains silent, we are not going to be silent. Because we know this: those who stay silent in the face of unfairness are evil. We are not going to be evil . . . I will open the pages of history now. What Skopje, Sarajevo, Pristina and Prizren mean to us is what Cairo means to us. . . . If we let Egypt down, then we cannot come into the presence of Orhan Gazi[2] in Bursa. . . . When Sarajevo cries,

Bursa sheds tears. When Cairo cries, Bursa cries as well. . . . When we turn to the direction of Qibla[3] we would like to have peace of mind. When we look ourselves in the mirror, we would like to see a reflection that is not ashamed and fulfilled its duty to its history and the heritage of our ancestors. . . . The EU cannot dare to look itself in the mirror.[4] When people who want justice are being shot down in Egypt, those who are silently approving and encouraging [the violence] have blood on their hands to the extent that they cannot even listen to their conscience. And I must say this openly: Those who are silent with regard to Egypt today cannot lecture anybody on democracy tomorrow. Those who cannot say 'coup' to a coup cannot raise their voices tomorrow for another country. They will play the same game that they play in Egypt today in another Muslim country tomorrow. . . . Maybe they will want to involve another country or Turkey because they do not want a strong Turkey. They do not want a stable, developed country in this region.

(Erdoğan, 2013a)

PM Erdoğan's words are a reflection of the Turkish approach. There is very harsh criticism of the EU to an extent that the EU is accused of giving support to violence due to its silence. There is the idea that it is "evil", whereas Turkey is not. There are many elements that are about identity; namely there are references to the Ottoman history and the idea that Cairo is similar to Bursa, as Sarajevo, Pristina, Skopje, and Prizren all are (all share Muslim identity). And the important point is that the support for the Muslim Brotherhood is based on these identity-related arguments, for example, the idea that Turkey has a moral and historical duty to stand by the people of Cairo, which then, according to PM Erdoğan, means support for the Muslim Brotherhood. The remarks towards the end of the quote show the kind of anti-Western sentiments that are used in the foreign policy discourse of the Turkish government. There is the idea that "they" play a "game" – "they" referring to the idea that there are Western powers plotting against Turkey. "They" play this game in the Islamic world, and because Erdoğan places Turkey in the Islamic world, he states that, and this is also a method for the rationalisation of support for the Muslim Brotherhood, what is happening to Morsi today can happen to "us" tomorrow.

Furthermore, another clear indication of how much the Turkish government was "emotionally" engaged in Egypt (as a Turkish diplomat claimed (Interview TR13)) and supported Morsi, is the way in which the Turkish government embraced the Rabaa hand sign.[5] The hand sign emerged right after the massacre and became a symbol of it, and one of the people who used it a lot was PM Erdoğan. In fact, it was reported (e.g., by Voice of America, 2013) that PM Erdoğan might have invented the hand sign, although its origin remains unclear. PM, and later President, Erdoğan regularly used the hand sign in conferences and speeches. Shortly, many AKP decision makers started to use the hand sign when making speeches, and there was even a suggestion to rename one of the squares in Istanbul "Rabia Square" (Serbest, 2013). President Erdoğan kept on using the hand sign, and it was reported in November 2015 that he had a statue of the Rabaa sign on his study desk. This was revealed because, on his social media account, the chief advisor to President Erdoğan shared a photo of the president sitting in his office, with the caption: "Our President called President Obama and discussed regional affairs" (*Milliyet*, 2015). On the desk, there was a statue of a hand doing the Rabaa sign, and on the statue it was written, "One Nation, One Flag, One Motherland, One State. – Recep Tayyip Erdoğan", which was a line that he used in speeches in order to give messages of unity (*Hürriyet*, 2015b). The statue of the Rabaa sign and the way in which the Turkish government embraced and used the hand sign generally (and possibly invented it) demonstrate the kind of intimate connection the Turkish government felt with the Muslim Brotherhood.

Lastly, in terms of cooperation with the EU it can again be argued that this is an example of a case in which there was no substantial consultation with the EU. After the Rabaa massacre, the immediate reaction of the Turkish government on the day of the massacre was to urge UN members, especially the P5, to take action, which was mentioned in Erdoğan's remarks in Bursa. Consequently, the Prime Minister's office and the Ministry of Foreign Affairs urged the international community, primarily the UNSC, to react (Ministry of Foreign Affairs of Turkey, 2013a). For this reason, especially the US Secretary of State was telephoned by FM Davutoğlu personally right after the incident (*Hürriyet*, 2013g). Therefore, as was the case in previous COs, the EU was not the first point of contact; instead, the UNSC was prioritised. This is relevant more generally to the way in which the Turkish government prioritises cooperation with the UNSC or NATO when it requires a firm response/action (as also happened in the cases of Libya and Syria). It could also be claimed that this was another low point in Turkey-EU relations due to the Turkish accusations and attitude towards the EU, one clear indicator of this being a meeting between Erdoğan and President Putin on 23 November 2013 in which Erdoğan reiterated his desire for Turkey to join the Shanghai Cooperation Organisation. It was reported that Erdoğan, resentful of the EU, said to Putin, "Take us into the Shanghai Cooperation Organisation and save us from this [the EU] trouble" (Çetin, 2013).

There is also evidence from the interviews of this research that informal communication continued for this CO, as during the Sisi period, in general (Interview EU04). However, EU diplomats mentioned that dialogue with the Turkish government was particularly difficult when the Turkish government blamed the EU for supporting a coup and accused it of hypocrisy (Interviews EU06, EU02).

So, regarding the aftermath of the Rabaa massacre, there is no conclusive evidence that consultation took place, and there is no indication that there was a political will to engage in cooperative behaviour involving consultation. It is, however, highly unlikely that the Turkish position caught the EU by surprise, considering the general attitude of the Turkish government towards support for Morsi and the fact that the EU was updated about Turkish actions and even was urged to take a critical stance through diplomatic channels.

Conclusion

In this chapter, the preferences of the EU and the Turkish government were mostly opposed. Nevertheless, cooperation still took place in the form of information exchange. The Turkish government kept in touch with the EU, although it did not completely believe the EU was an influential actor, and the EU was informed about Turkish behaviour generally after Turkish decisions had been made.

The key aspect of the Turkish reaction to the post-uprising disorder was that the Turkish government regarded the killings as a consequence of Morsi's efforts to restore order in the country. The EU harshly criticised Morsi, whereas the Turkish government continued to show support for Muslim Brotherhood policies. The support of the Turkish government for the Muslim Brotherhood contained elements of religion and identity, in the sense that the AKP in Turkey and the Muslim Brotherhood in Egypt had a shared political and cultural orientation. However, the continuous support of the Turkish government can also be explained by a cost-benefit calculation pointing to the way in which the Turkish government expected the Muslim Brotherhood to become a strategic ally in the region who could support the Turkish government on issues of regional importance, such as the Israeli-Palestinian conflict. Therefore, the strategic importance of cooperation with the Morsi government was higher than cooperation with the EU, which Turkish decision makers did not see as a capable actor in the region. This also meant that a higher degree of cooperation with the EU or criticising Morsi would have been costly.

The second CO in this chapter concerned the removal of Morsi on 3 July 2013, after which there was potential for cooperation with the EU. The Turkish government immediately condemned Sisi's action and pushed international actors to recognise it as a coup d'état. There was again a divergence between Turkey and the EU because the EU avoided using the term coup d'état and prioritised the restoration of stability with the military in power. The EU kept channels of dialogue open with Sisi, whereas the Turkish government did not recognise him as a legitimate leader, regarding instead Morsi as the sole legitimate leader. The Turkish government gave continuous support to the Muslim Brotherhood even after it had become clearer that Morsi would not be able to retain power and that the military would stay. The Turkish government defended Morsi even at the expense of cutting all ties with the government in Cairo. At this point, it is possible to say that the logic of appropriateness has explanatory potential because the Turkish behaviour of cutting ties with Egypt is difficult to explain as a strategic action.

In terms of Turkish interaction with the EU, the divergence made it costly to seek a higher degree of cooperation. The Turkish leadership often accused the EU of hypocrisy for not referring to what had happened as a coup d'état, which led to the deterioration of Turkey-EU relations and limited potential cooperation. Despite all, information exchange continued, which again indicates that there was more than unilateral information.

The third CO in this chapter focused on the Rabaa massacre in August 2013. The massacre was another instance in which there was a possibility for cooperation with the EU. However, there is no conclusive evidence that the Turkish government reached out to the EU for its opinion on their strong condemnation of Sisi. In fact, during this CO, the Turkish government fiercely criticised the international community for being silent on a coup d'état. This CO confirms the finding of the previous one in the sense that there was more than unilateral action and the Turkish government's behaviours cannot be fully explained by strategic action. Although support for Morsi had strategic aspects, support for Morsi after it was clear that Sisi would stay is difficult to explain as purely strategic, because completely cutting ties with Egypt was a costly action.

Notes

1 It should be noted that the AKP also received the overwhelming majority of votes in Turkey, as Morsi did in Egypt.
2 The second Ottoman sultan and son of Osman Gazi, the founder of the Ottoman Empire.
3 Turning to the direction of Mecca for prayer.
4 In the sense that it is ashamed of itself.
5 Raising four fingers because *Rabia* in Arabic means "fourth" (feminine). It was used to express solidarity with the victims of the massacre.

References

Akgün, M., and Gündoğar, S.S. (2014) *Mısır-Türkiye ilişkilerinde daha iyi bir geleceğe doğru*, TESEV Foreign Policy Bulletin, Istanbul, Turkey: TESEV.
Al Jazeera. (2015) "Erdoğan'dan Doğan Grubu'na: Avucunu daha çok yalarsın" ["From Erdoğan to Doğan Media Group: Not on Your Life"], *Al Jazeera*, 17 May, www.alja zeera.com.tr/haber/erdogandan-dogan-grubuna-avucunu-daha-cok-yalarsin.
———. (2013) "Egypt Expels Turkey's Ambassador", *Al Jezeera*, 6 June, www. aljazeera.com/news/middleeast/2013/11/egypt-asks-turkey-ambassador-leave-2013112310229476406.html.
Ashton, C. (2013) "Statement by the Spokesperson of the High Representative Catherine Ashton on the Killings in Port Said", Brussels, Belgium, 25 January, www.consilium. europa.eu/uedocs/cms_Data/docs/pressdata/EN/foraff/135034.pdf.
———. (2012a) "Statement by EU High Representative Catherine Ashton on the Situation in Egypt", Brussels, Belgium, 5 December, www.consilium.europa.eu/uedocs/ cms_Data/docs/pressdata/EN/foraff/134065.pdf.
———. (2012b) "Remarks by High Representative Catherine Ashton Upon Arrival at the Foreign Affairs Council", Brussels, Belgium, 10 December, www.consilium.europa.eu/ uedocs/cms_Data/docs/pressdata/EN/foraff/134131.pdf.
———. (2012c) "Statement by the Spokesperson of High Representative Catherine Ashton on the Continued Crackdown on Civil Society in Egypt", Brussels, www.consilium. europa.eu/uedocs/cms_Data/docs/pressdata/EN/foraff/127777.pdf.
Bağış, E. (2013a) "UN, EU, OIC & Others Must Wake Up! There Is a Clear Attempt to Start a Bloody Civil War in Egypt. We Can't Keep Quiet During This Slaughter", *Tweet*, 14 August, 2.55 AM, https://twitter.com/EgemenBagis/status/367585272785272832.
———. (2013b) "Mursi'nin darbe çığırtkanlarına dik duruşunu takdirle karşılayıp, darbenin her türlüsüne her yerde karşı çıkmalıyız" ["We Must Oppose a Coup Under Any Circumstances and Applaud Morsi's Stance Against Coupists"], *Tweet*, 3 July, 8.09 AM, https://twitter.com/EgemenBagis/status/352443890063785985.

———. (2013c) "Darbeye darbe bile diyemeyenler artık dünyaya demokrasi ve insan hakları ahkamı kesmesin. Komik duruma düşerler – Afrika Birliği bile güler" ["Those Who Cannot Even Say 'Coup d'état' to a Coup d'état Should Not Anymore Lecture the World on Democracy and Human Rights. They Would Be Ridiculed – Even the African Union Would Laugh"], *Tweet*, 5 July, 7.39 AM, https://twitter.com/egemenbagis/status/353161128521633792+&cd=8&hl=en&ct=clnk&gl=uk.

Berber, M.A. (2014) "Darbecilerle aynı masaya oturmam" ["I Won't Sit at the Same Table as a Coupist"], *Sabah*, 26 September, www.sabah.com.tr/gundem/2014/09/26/darbeciyle-ayni-masaya-oturmam.

Çetin, Ü. (2013) "Şangay'a Alın AB'den Kurtarın" ["Let Us in Shanghai, Save Us from the EU"], *Milliyet*, 23 November, www.hurriyet.com.tr/sanghaya-alin-abden-kurtarin-25186657.

Davutoğlu, A. (2013a) "Press Conference Regarding Egypt", Prime Minister's Office in Dolmabahçe, Istanbul, Turkey, 4 July, www.mfa.gov.tr/disisleri-bakani-davutoglu-misirda-yasanan-son-gelismeleri-degerlendirdi.tr.mfa.

———. (2013b) "Statement at the 51st Session of the EU-Turkey Association Council", Brussels, Belgium, 27 May.

Demir, M. (2012) "Taksim'e de cami yapılacak" ["A Mosque Will Be Built at Taksim Too"], *Hürriyet*, 28 November, www.hurriyet.com.tr/taksim-e-de-cami-yapilacak-22028461.

Erdoğan, R.T. (2015a) "Press Conference with the Chairman of the Presidency of Bosnia and Herzegovina Mladen Ivanic", Bosnia and Herzegovina, 20 May.

———. (2015b) "Kayseri Toplu Açılış Töreni Konuşması" ["Opening Ceremony Speech in Kayseri"], Kayseri, Turkey, 17 May.

———. (2013a) "Bursa Kentsel Dönüşüm Töreni Konuşması" ["Bursa Urban Transformation Meeting Speech"], Bursa, Turkey, 18 August.

———. (2013b) "Tübitak Kurultayı Kapanış Oturumu" ["Tübitak Council Closing Speech"], The Scientific and Technological Research Council of Turkey, Ankara, Turkey, 5 July.

Ergin, S. (2013) "Şanghay Beşlisi'ne Doğru: Erdoğan'ın Batı'ya Tavrı Sertleşiyor" ["Towards the Shanghai Five: Erdoğan Toughens Tone on the West"], *Hürriyet*, 30 January, www.hurriyet.com.tr/sanghay-beslisi-ne-dogru-2-erdogan-in-bati-ya-tavri-sertlesiyor-22475982.

———. (2012) "Erdoğan ve Dış Politika Popülarite çok iyi, ya sonuç?" ["Erdoğan and Foreign Policy: Popularity Is Good, and the Result?"] *Hürriyet*, 24 November, www.hurriyet.com.tr/yazarlar/22001320.asp.

European Council. (2013) "Remarks by President of the European Council Herman Van Rompuy After His Meeting with Prime Minister of Turkey Recep Tayyip Erdoğan" [EUCO 121/13], Ankara, Turkey, http://europa.eu/rapid/press-release_PRES-13-209_en.htm?locale=EN.

Fahmy, M.F., and Lee, I. (2012) "Anger Flares in Egypt After 79 Die in Soccer Riot", *CNN*, 2 February, http://edition.cnn.com/2012/02/02/world/africa/egypt-soccer-deaths/index.html?hpt=hp_t1.

Foreign and Commonwealth Office. (2013) "FCO Minister Condemns Egyptian Violence in Strongest Terms", Foreign and Commonwealth Office, London, UK, 26 January, www.gov.uk/government/news/fco-minister-condemns-egyptian-violence-in-strongest-terms.

Hürriyet. (2015a) "Sayın Cumhurbaşkanı'na Sesleniyoruz" ["To Mr President"], *Hürriyet*, 19 May, www.hurriyet.com.tr/sayin-cumhurbaskani-na-sesleniyoruz-29042781.

———. (2015b) "Cumhurbaşkanı Erdoğan'ın Masasındaki Heykel", *Hürriyet*, 10 November, www.hurriyet.com.tr/cumhurbaskani-erdoganin-masasindaki-heykel-40012295.

———. (2013a) "Mısır'dan Türkiye'ye Ağır Suçlama" ["Egypt's Accusation Against Turkey"], *Hürriyet*, 19 August, www.hurriyet.com.tr/misirdan-turkiyeye-agir-suclama-24541236.

————. (2013b) "Şangay Beşlisi'ne Alın AB'yi Unutalım" ["Accept Us to the Shanghai Five and We Will Forget the EU"], *Hürriyet*, 26 January, www.hurriyet.com.tr/sangay-beslisine-alin-abyi-unutalim-22448548.

————. (2013c) "Mısır'dan Türkiye'ye Orantısız Tepki" ["Overreaction by Egypt"], *Hürriyet*, 21 August, www.hurriyet.com.tr/misirdan-turkiyeye-orantisiz-tepki-24562238.

————. (2013d) "Mısır'ın Ankara Büyükelçisi ülkesine gitti" ["Egyptian Ambassador to Ankara Returned to His Country"], *Hürriyet*, 18 August, www.hurriyet.com.tr/misirin-ankara-buyukelcisi-ulkesine-gitti-24534163.

————. (2013e) "Türkiye'den Dünyaya Mısır Telefonu" ["Turkey's Telephone Calls Regarding Egypt"], *Hürriyet*, 3 July, www.hurriyet.com.tr/turkiyeden-dunyaya-misir-telefonu-23647504.

————. (2013f) "Mısır'ı Her Alanda Destekleriz" ["We Support Egypt in Every Area"], *Hürriyet*, 7 February, www.hurriyet.com.tr/misir-i-her-alanda-destekleriz-22540273.

————. (2013g) "Davutoğlu Kerry ile Mısır'ı Görüştü" ["Davutoğlu Talked to Kerry on Egypt"], *Hürriyet*, 14 August, www.hurriyet.com.tr/davutoglu-kerry-ile-misiri-gorustu-24521550.

————. (2012) "Erdoğan: İsrail'den hesabı sorulacak" ["Erdoğan: Israel Will Pay"], *Hürriyet*, 18 November, www.hurriyet.com.tr/planet/21951746.asp.

————. (2011) "AB'ye Kıbrıs Ultimatomu: Iliskileri Dondururuz" ["The Cyprus Ultimatum to the EU: We Will Freeze Relations"], *Hürriyet*, 19 September, www.hurriyet.com.tr/ab-ye-kibris-ultimatomu-iliskileri-dondururuz-18765571.

Kirkpatrick, D.D., and Sheikh, M.E. (2012) "Citing Deadlock, Egypt's Leader Seizes New Power and Plans Mubarak Retrial", *New York Times*, 22 November, www.nytimes.com/2012/11/23/world/middleeast/egypts-president-morsi-gives-himself-new-powers.html?_r=0.

Milliyet. (2015) "Erdoğan'ın Masasında Dikkat Çeken Ayrıntı" ["Interesting Detail Regarding Erdoğan's Desk"], *Milliyet*, 10 November, www.milliyet.com.tr/erdogan-in-masasinda-dikkat-ceken/siyaset/detay/2145852/default.htm.

Ministry of Foreign Affairs of Turkey. (2015) "Relations Between Turkey and Egypt", Ankara, Turkey, www.mfa.gov.tr/relations-between-turkey-egypt.en.mfa.

————. (2013a) "Mısır'daki Kanlı Müdahale Başbakanlık Tarafından Yapılan Açıklamayla Kınandı" ["Crackdown in Egypt Condemned by Prime Ministry"], Ankara, Turkey, 14 August, www.mfa.gov.tr/misirdaki-kanli-mudahale-basbakanlik-tarafindan-yapilan-aciklamayla-kinandi.tr.mfa.

————. (2013b) "Mısır'da Yaşanan Olaylar Hk. Press Release No 22" ["Regarding Events Taking Place in Egypt"], Ankara, Turkey, 27 January, www.mfa.gov.tr/no_22_-27-ocak-2013_-misir_da-yasanan-olaylar-hk_.tr.mfa.

————. (2013c) "Dışişleri Bakanlığı Sözcüsü Elçi Selçuk Ünal'ın Son Basın Toplantısı" ["MFA Spokesperson Ambassador Selçuk Ünal's Final Press Conference"], 31 January, www.mfa.gov.tr/disisleri-bakanligi-sozcusu-elci-selcuk-unal_in-son-basin-toplantisi_-disisleri-bakanligi_-taha-carim-salonu_-31-ocak-2013_-pers.tr.mfa.

NTV. (2013) "Erdoğan'dan Mursi açıklaması" ["Erdoğan's Statement on Morsi"], *NTV*, 5 July, www.ntv.com.tr/turkiye/erdogandan-mursi-aciklamasi,0ykobTXaI0Ozq7ZGhFQCPA.

Öniş, Z. (2014) "Turkey and the Arab Revolutions: Boundaries of Regional Power Influence in a Turbulent Middle East", *Mediterranean Politics* 19(2): 203–19.

Özel, S. (2012) "Arap İsyanları AKP'nin Ayarını Bozdu" ["Arab Uprisings Disorientated the AKP"], *Taraf*, 6 July, http://arsiv.taraf.com.tr/haber-yazdir-96766.html.

Peker, E. (2012) "Turkey Labels Israel a 'Terrorist State'", *The Wall Street Journal*, 19 November, www.wsj.com/articles/SB10001424127887323353204578128880612421650.

Presidency of the Republic of Turkey. (2013) "Cumhurbaşkanı Gülden İslam Dünyasına Dört Öneri" ["Four Suggestions from President Gül to the Islamic World"], Ankara, Turkey, 7 February, www.tccb.gov.tr/haberler-abdullah-g220l/1726/10761/cumhurbaskani-gulden-islam-dunyasina-dort-oneri.html.

Rettman, A. (2013) "EU Reaction to Egypt Coup: 'Awkward. Disturbing'", *EUObserver*, 4 July, https://euobserver.com/foreign/120766.

Sabah. (2015) "Erdoğan: Batı'nın sicili Mısır'da Suriye'de bozuldu" ["Erdoğan: The West Failed in Egypt and Syria"], *Sabah*, 21 June, www.sabah.com.tr/gundem/2015/06/21/erdogan-batinin-sicili-misirda-suriyede-bozuldu.

Serbest, E. (2013) "Esenler Dörtyol Rabia Meydanı Olsun", *Hürriyet*, 20 August, www.hurriyet.com.tr/esenler-dortyol-rabia-meydani-olsun-24552617.

Spencer, R. (2012) "Mohammed Morsi Grants Himself Sweeping New Powers in Wake of Gaza", *The Telegraph*, 22 November, www.telegraph.co.uk/news/worldnews/africaandindianocean/egypt/9697347/Mohammed-Morsi-grants-himself-sweeping-new-powers-in-wake-of-Gaza.html.

TRT. (2012) "Erdoğan ve Mursi İsrail'I Uyardı" ["Erdoğan and Morsi Warned Israel"], *TRT*, 18 November, www.trthaber.com/m/?news=israilden-cevap-yok&news_id=63681&category_id=1.

Tubiana, M. (2014) "EU Foreign Policy in Coma", *EUObserver*, 7 November, https://euobserver.com/opinion/126422.

Voice of America. (2013) "Egyptians Defiant Over Use of 'Rabaa' Symbol", *Voice of America*, 29 November, www.voanews.com/a/egyptians-defiant-over-use-rabaa-symbol/1800249.html.

Yetkin, M. (2015) "Suriye ve Mısır Siyaseti Açmazda" ["Dead End in Syria and Egypt Policies"], *Radikal*, 17 March, www.radikal.com.tr/yazarlar/murat-yetkin/suriye-ve-misir-siyaseti-acmazda-1315020/.

8   Conclusion

The Arab Spring presented a critical juncture for the EU and Turkey. Both had interests in the countries where there were uprisings. These crises presented an opportunity for them to cooperate and tackle the growing instability in the region more effectively. Yet, there was a deadlock in Turkey-EU relations that created a challenge in terms of foreign policy cooperation.

The main questions that this book has asked were: "To what extent did the Turkish government cooperate with the EU regarding the uprisings, and why?" These questions are important because the analysis presented here not only sheds light on the dynamics of Turkey-EU relations during the Arab Spring but also makes a contribution to the literature that seeks to understand the foreign policy relationship between Turkey and the EU. The key point that has been made is that the foreign policy relationship is an ambiguous area of interaction that has been pushed slightly outside of the membership negotiations, which is precisely why it requires attention. Because the issue at hand is not exactly EU membership negotiations, the conventional literature that deals with Turkey-EU relations falls short of capturing the full picture due to its EU studies-centric analysis, which narrows down the area of interaction to the negotiation framework and presupposes a will from the Turkish side to enter the EU. The Arab Spring demonstrated that there was (and still is) a lot more to the Turkey-EU relationship, regardless of the momentum of membership negotiations. It is possible to consider the EU and Turkey as two actors, and allies, in a region in which they have mutual interests, rather than basing analyses on EU membership negotiations.

This book has focused on the uprisings in Egypt, Syria, and Libya and has analysed Turkey's foreign policy cooperation with the EU using an analytical framework that distinguished between different levels of cooperation: "no cooperation" (unilateral action without any information or consultation with the EU); "unilateral information" (only informing the EU about planned action without giving it an opportunity to express its views); "consultation" (reaching out to the EU to request feedback on planned policy); and "co-decision" (consulting the EU, and, if necessary, modifying behaviour according to feedback from the EU). Using this scale, the main objective of the empirical research was to identify the extent to which Turkish and EU officials consulted each other before and after the public announcement of Turkish positions. For analytical reasons, key moments during the crises were identified as cooperative opportunities in which there was a possibility for the Turkish government to take the initiative and to act in cooperation with the EU.

The empirical investigation concerning the extent to which the Turkish government cooperated with the EU was complemented by a theoretical investigation that aimed to assess the factors that explained the degree of Turkish cooperation with the EU. The main question here was whether cooperation was a result of a cost-benefit calculation or appropriate action. The theoretical framework (Chapter 2) outlined different motivations behind Turkish action with regard to cooperation and discussed rationalist and constructivist approaches that help explain potential factors influencing outcomes in terms of cooperation.

For the rationalist approach, the book used a neoliberal institutionalist and a realist approach, and distinguished between general and issue-specific costs of action regarding cooperation. Fundamentally, the neoliberal institutionalist approach prioritised welfare maximisation as the dominant motivation behind Turkish action and focused on the long-term benefits of action; whereas, the realist approach emphasised short-term gains of cooperative behaviour and security concerns as the main drivers of Turkish behaviour. Specifically, the theoretical framework identified a combination of high and low politics, mainly involving security concerns in the short term and economic interests in the long term, policy divergence from the EU, and urgency of action as key factors determining the costs and benefits of cooperation with the EU.

On the other hand, the constructivist approach regarded the degree of cooperation as a result of the Turkish government following appropriate behaviour and pointed to norms and identity as key factors that affected the decision-making process in Turkey. Specific factors were identified as political and cultural affinity affecting foreign policy behaviour, including attitude towards the EU, and identification with norms of appropriate behaviour prompting cooperation with the EU. The theoretical framework also clarified different notions of appropriateness relating to both the general appropriateness of cooperative action and the issue-specific considerations that the Turkish government might have taken into account.

Variation across cases

It is important to discuss the emerging pattern regarding the outcome of cooperation across different cases, and outline the factors that have contributed to this pattern. Figure 8.1 shows the variation across COs regarding outcomes in terms of cooperation. The emerging pattern is that the degree of cooperation never reached the point of "consultation", but, in most cases, there was more than merely "unilateral information". Therefore, cooperation was mostly between "unilateral information" and "consultation" points.

Overall, there was a lack of "consultation": no conclusive evidence suggests that the Turkish government reached out to consult the EU about its actions either before or after the public announcement of Turkish positions. EU feedback was

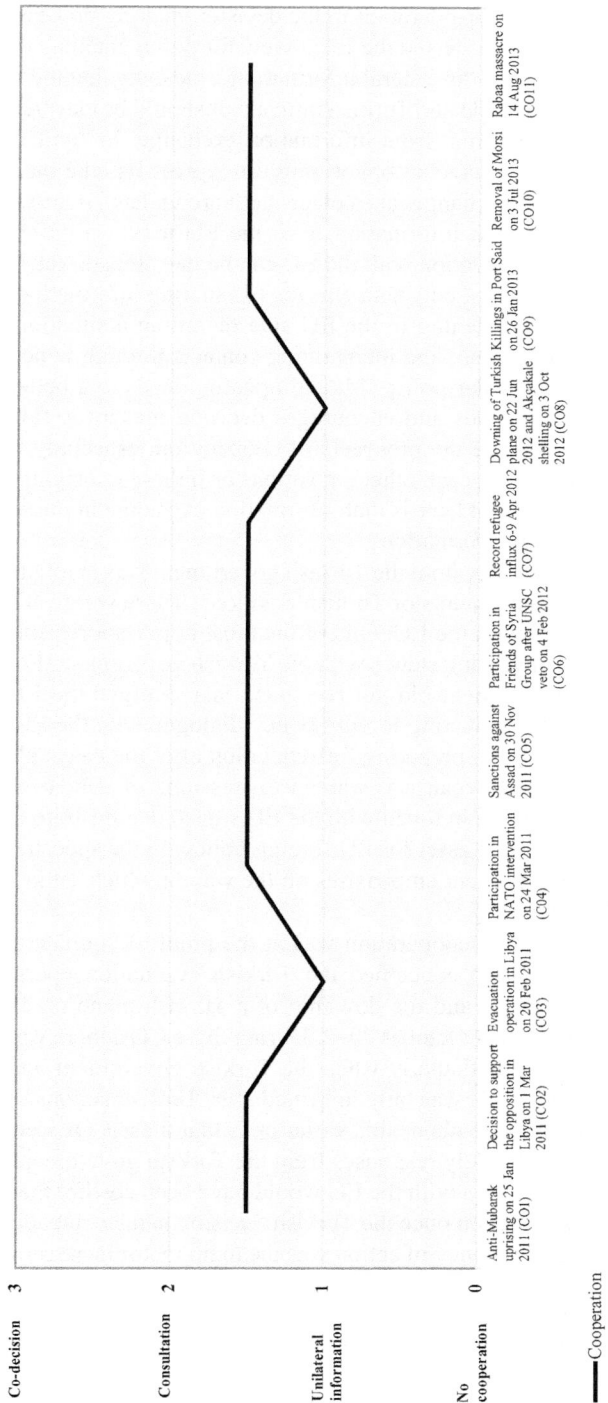

Co-decision 3

Consultation 2

Unilateral information 1

No cooperation 0

Anti-Mubarak uprising on 25 Jan 2011 (CO1)

Decision to support the opposition in Libya on 1 Mar 2011 (CO2)

Evacuation operation in Libya on 20 Feb 2011 (CO3)

Participation in NATO intervention on 24 Mar 2011 (CO4)

Sanctions against Assad on 30 Nov 2011 (CO5)

Participation in Friends of Syria Group after UNSC veto on 4 Feb 2012 (CO6)

Record refugee influx 6-9 Apr 2012 (CO7)

Downing of Turkish plane on 22 Jun 2012 and Akçakale shelling on 3 Oct 2012 (CO8)

Killings in Port Said on 26 Jan 2013 (CO9)

Removal of Morsi on 3 Jul 2013 (CO10)

Rabaa massacre on 14 Aug 2013 (CO11)

—— Cooperation

Figure 8.1 Degree of cooperation across cooperative opportunities

not sought after and not taken into consideration in the decision-making process, and the Turkish government never requested the EU's view for policy making.

In most cases, there was more than "unilateral information", meaning that there was information exchange between EU and Turkish officials. It should be clarified that "unilateral information" is different from information exchange. In "unilateral information", the EU does not have an opportunity to express its take on a situation, but when informational exchange takes place, both are updated on each other's policies. The extent to which information from the EU makes a difference to the degree of Turkey's cooperation with the EU can be questioned. Yet, it should be highlighted that the issue not only concerns the EU sharing information, but also the Turkish government listening to the EU side regarding a situation, keeping the channels of dialogue open, and maintaining contacts through which the EU is able to justify any particular policy. Mutual updating leads to a better understanding of each other's policies and encourages decision makers to talk more, which can potentially enhance the prospects of cooperation, especially if there is a lack of understanding about each other's positions or if there is a significant policy divergence. The key point here is that information exchange involves more cooperation than "unilateral information".

The EU was one of the actors with whom the Turkish government was in touch, especially after the public announcements of Turkish positions. There were various reasons for staying in touch with the EU. One of the most important reasons was to push the EU to take a converging stance with the Turkish government. For instance, when the Turkish government did not recognise Sisi, it urged the EU to take a similar stance through conducting foreign policy dialogue with the EU, or when the Turkish government was preparing for retaliation after the Akçakale shelling, it kept the EU informed because it wanted expressions of solidarity. Another important reason for staying in touch with the EU was to demonstrate to the EU that Turkey was an important asset for EU foreign policy. In the speeches of Turkish officials, there were frequent emphases on the way in which Turkey could contribute to EU foreign policy.

There are two instances in which cooperation was at the point of "unilateral information": CO3 and CO8. These concerned the Turkish evacuation operation in Libya on 20 February 2011, and the downing of a Turkish plane on 22 June 2012/the Akçakale shelling on 3 October 2012. During these COs, there was no specific contact with the EU, particularly when the Turkish government was formulating its responses, and the EU was only informed after Turkish actions so that it could express support. What explains this variation is that these COs were hard security issues that required timely responses from the Turkish government. Having a higher degree of cooperation with the EU would have been costlier than informing the EU about Turkish action once the Turkish decision had been made. Therefore, it can be claimed that urgency of action was the main factor increasing the costs of cooperation.

With regard to the Libyan evacuation operation, the violence in Libya started to become a threat to the Turkish government due to the large number of stranded Turkish citizens and the uncertainty of the turmoil. As this analysis has pointed out, the EU was informed about the decision after the operation had started. Therefore, there was only unilateral information after the Turkish action – the EU opinion was not sought whatsoever. Similarly, in the cases of the Turkish plane and the shelling, there was only "unilateral information" in the sense that the EU was briefed about the course of action the Turkish government had already decided to take. In these instances, the EU was contacted primarily for the purpose of mobilising international support for the Turkish retaliation, which had the potential to escalate violence near the Syrian border.

The other cases did not fully require immediate unilateral action. When the anti-Mubarak uprising (CO1) and the anti-Gaddafi uprising (CO2) started, the Turkish government waited for the international reaction and also did not want to jeopardise its relationships with the incumbent regimes. The decisions to contribute to NATO action in Libya (CO4), impose sanctions against the Syrian regime (CO5), participate in the Friends of Syria Group (CO6), and request international help for the record influx of Syrian refugees (CO7) were all made after observing the international reaction while exchanging information with the EU both before and after the declaration of Turkish policy. Similarly, after the killings in Port Said (CO9), the removal of Morsi (CO10), and the Rabaa massacre (CO11), the Turkish government not only informed the EU about Turkish policy but also urged the EU to take a similar action to condemn Sisi. Therefore, all COs, except the two hard security COs mentioned, involved exchange of information with the EU to one degree or another. Although the reason for information exchange was not to enact "consultation", there was a higher degree of cooperation than "unilateral information".

Strategic action or logic of appropriateness?

There is also the question of whether Turkish behaviour was based on the costs and benefits of action or the logic of appropriateness. Overall, it is possible to argue that the decisions the Turkish government took regarding the crises and regarding cooperation with the EU were based on minimising the costs of actions. To unpack this point, the rationalist approach has more explanatory potential in the sense that cooperation with the EU was limited when it would have been costly.

There were not only general but also issue-specific costs regarding cooperation with the EU. The EU was not seen as a significant actor in the region that was capable of acting or making a change, which meant that cooperation with the EU seemed of little benefit. For instance, Turkish decision makers often emphasised that the EU was divided and unable to make quick decisions, and used this to strengthen their arguments that EU foreign policy would be more effective with the help of Turkey. It was not, then, particularly preferable to consult the EU when making a decision, or especially when a decision was needed urgently. Moreover, in most cases, it was politically preferable to consult the US, given its super power status. When it came to hard security issues, Turkey opted to coordinate with its NATO allies or relied on its own army, rather than on the EU, which could not provide military support, making higher-degree cooperation with the EU a low priority in Turkey's foreign policy.

The issue-specific costs involved differences of opinions with the EU. Policy divergence from the EU, as a specific factor determining costs and benefits, was particularly important. Most notably with regard to how to react to the removal of Morsi, the EU and the Turkish government had fundamentally different opinions. The EU wanted to keep the channels of dialogue open with the Sisi government, whereas the Turkish government not only cut all ties but also condemned all, including the EU, who continued to talk to Sisi. Such radical divergence limited the prospects of a higher degree of cooperation, such as "co-decision", since Turkish decision makers would not entertain the thought of speaking to Sisi, as the EU was doing.

Regarding the removal of Morsi, the FPA literature was particularly useful in identifying issue-specific factors that qualified as costs of cooperation with the EU. Particularly in this case, the AKP was sensitive about domestic developments, such as the Gezi Park protests in Turkey, which in return contributed to the way in which the Turkish government strictly opposed military intervention in Egypt. FPA's focus on the domestic makes it possible to identify that the costs of cooperation with the EU were specific to what the AKP government in Turkey identified as costs. It is even possible to distinguish between the costs perceived by the AKP leadership and the bureaucracy, namely the Ministry of Foreign Affairs of Turkey. This research has found that the decision to cut all ties with the Sisi government was more a choice of the leadership rather than being a decision supported by different layers of the government.

The rationalist approach also has more explanatory potential in the case of Libya. There was a U-turn in Turkish policy with regard to the Gaddafi regime at a time when the costs of criticising the regime decreased. The Turkish government joined the international coalition against the Libyan regime when it was clear that Gaddafi was going to fall and when it was more beneficial for the Turkish government to join the international action. Similarly, in the case of Syria, the Turkish government hesitated to criticise Assad because Turkish decision makers were not sure whether he would follow Gaddafi's fate. When the international pressure increased, and when it was no longer possible to appear to support the Assad regime, Turkish decision makers strategically adjusted their policy and joined the wider international community.

Although rationalism better explains Turkish behaviour overall, there were instances for which rationalism could not fully account. Particularly in the case of Egypt, the continuous Turkish support for Morsi after it had become clear that Sisi would stay can hardly be explained as strategic behaviour alone. It is possible to say that support for the Muslim Brotherhood did indeed have its benefits when Morsi was in power. For example, Morsi was also seen as a key ally for the Turkish government in the region, especially on matters of regional importance, such as the Israeli-Palestinian conflict. When Morsi was removed, it was costly to cut all ties with the Egyptian government no matter who was leading Egypt because Egypt could still be, as it was before Morsi, a strategic ally for the

Turkish government. Therefore, continuing to support Morsi, that is, seeing him as the sole legitimate leader of Egypt at the expense of creating hostility towards Sisi, was the costly action. Considering the political and cultural affinity between the AKP and the Muslim Brotherhood, it is possible to say that there were also elements of religion and identity motivating the Turkish government to continue to side with Morsi. Therefore, the constructivist approach also has explanatory potential, especially in this case.

The continuous Turkish support for Morsi also shows that in some cases identity can be salient and affect the Turkish foreign policy decision-making process. As this book has discussed, identity may widen policy divergence between Turkey and the EU and limit prospects of cooperation, as it did in the case of Sisi. Although Turkish behaviour vis-à-vis cooperation with the EU was mostly based on costs and benefits, there were instances in which identity significantly affected Turkish behaviour and the preferences of the Turkish leadership.

Overall findings

There are three overall findings of this study based on the analyses of case studies. First, the correlation between policy divergence from the EU and the lack of a high degree of cooperation does not indicate a complete absence of cooperation between the EU and Turkey. Cooperation still exists even in periods when Turkish decision makers verbally attack the EU – for example, when they accused the EU of hypocrisy regarding its support for Sisi, or when they publicly claimed the EU was wasting their time and that the Shanghai Cooperation Organization was a better choice for Turkey.

To elaborate, divergence can take many forms. The most obvious one was when the Turkish government openly called what had happened in Egypt a coup d'état when the EU did not. Divergence can increase the costs of cooperation with the EU because it makes it difficult to incorporate EU inputs into Turkish decisions. There is also a practical aspect of the situation, which is that when leaders make openly critical statements about each other, it is difficult to have them in the same room to discuss foreign policy matters. Therefore, when there is divergence, it is generally costly to have a higher degree of cooperation, such as "co-decision" or "consultation".

However, this does not mean that there is a total absence of cooperation. This analysis has demonstrated that the EU-Turkey foreign policy relationship has many layers, which include formal and informal channels of communication between the EU and the Turkish government. Regardless of the degree of divergence, there was no instance in which there was "no cooperation"; there was at least "unilateral information" even when the Turkish government had to take urgent action. During the course of the uprisings, the Davutoğlu-Ashton dialogue particularly helped the EU and Turkey to talk to each other no matter how the formal relationship was progressing. In addition to that, the EU Delegation in Turkey was constantly in touch with officials in Ankara to learn of Turkish positions, and they were often informed by the Turkish government.

The implication this has is that, in one way or another, the EU was always attached to the Turkish decision-making process. There was no substantial consultation or co-decision, but none of the Turkish decisions caught the EU by total surprise because the EU was reasonably well informed. Sometimes, the purpose of giving information was to request expressions of support or to make the point that Turkey was a valuable asset in the region for the EU, but there was information nonetheless. It could be claimed that Turkish decision makers valued informing the EU despite statements that portrayed the EU as an incapable and weak actor.

The second overall finding is that the Arab uprisings marked a turning point in the foreign policy relationship because the EU frequently needed Turkish cooperation rather than the other way around, and Turkey was often in the driver's seat in the relationship. It was the EU that sought Turkish cooperation and used Turkish expertise in the region, which is a clear indicator of a shift in the balance of power between Turkey and the EU. For example, EU officials claimed that they trusted Turkey's expertise in the region because Turkey had niche connections with regional actors that the EU did not. When Turkey hosted the Syrian opposition, the EU used Turkey to pass its messages (e.g., the EU wanted to urge the opposition to be more inclusive). Similarly, in the case of Libya, EU member states, especially France, wanted to play a leading role in the intervention, but Turkish cooperation was needed to be able to use the NATO command structure.

Therefore, it is possible to argue that the uprisings mark an effective departure from the traditional power asymmetry. Indeed, it could also be argued that this is not new but started when the EU began to lose its leverage over Turkey after the rise in Euroscepticism in Turkey following the loss of momentum in the membership negotiations. However, the Arab Spring is a clear example of the way in which the roles became reversed, in the sense that the EU is now in the position of making requests to Turkey. This is particularly important considering the increasing role Turkey has played in European security policy in the post-Arab Spring era. Most notably, the 2016 refugee deal reaffirmed the status of Turkey as a vital strategic partner for EU member states.

The third overall finding here concerns Turkish behaviour regarding the uprisings. In all cases, initially the Turkish government was reluctant to criticise the incumbent regimes. The primary reason was persistence with the "zero problems with neighbours" policy that had been implemented before the Arab Spring. The Turkish government had established close ties with the governments in Libya, Syria, and Egypt, and the policy was seen as a success story of the AKP government. When the crises started, Turkish foreign policy decision makers did not want to give up on the policy, and they did not anticipate that the unrests would snowball into a broader democratic upheaval in the region.

Again, the domestic politics approach of FPA literature is particularly useful because Turkish behaviour can be seen as the result of the foreign policy vision of Turkish decision makers. Individuals such as Erdoğan and Davutoğlu were particularly influential not only because of their personal relationship with the incumbent leaders but also because they were personally invested in the "zero problems with neighbours" policy. As for concrete policy choices, this meant that they hesitated to criticise and impose sanctions against the regimes. An evident example was when Turkish decision makers personally called Assad to persuade him to implement certain reforms.

Implications for the literature

One of the key implications of the findings of this research is that the foreign policy relationship between the EU and Turkey is not limited to the membership negotiations. The membership negotiations involve the foreign policy relationship, but it does not necessarily cover all aspects of the interaction. The foreign policy relationship is therefore a somewhat separate area of interaction that requires further attention.

This research has demonstrated that informal foreign policy interaction continued, and therefore can continue, in the absence of progress in EU membership negotiations. This is particularly important at a time when foreign policy cooperation is gaining more importance, especially considering the foreign policy challenges that emerged in the aftermath of the uprisings, such as the threat posed by the so-called Islamic State, and politics around the Syrian refugee crisis. What this research has shown is that there is much more to the relationship than the framework of membership negotiations, as foreign policy cooperation is becoming the cornerstone of the EU-Turkey relationship.

This analysis has also shown how Turkey and the EU explored inventive ways of maintaining a complex working partnership despite the deadlock in the accession process. Informal dialogue between officials has been an important driver of the foreign policy relationship between Turkey and the EU.

Furthermore, the asymmetry of power that has traditionally been the case between the EU and Turkey has changed, considering the instances in which Turkey had leverage over the EU. This implies that there needs to be a new focus to understand the evolving nature of the EU-Turkey relationship and a departure from an EU studies-centric approach that sees Turkey solely as an actor seeking membership from the EU. An approach that acknowledges both the EU and Turkey as two independent actors in the region better suits the dynamics of the relationship in this context.

Appendix
List of interviews

Interview code	Interviewee position/affiliation at the time of the interview	Interview date[1]
EU01	Officer, Political Affairs, CFSP, EU Mission to Turkey	06.04.2015
EU02	Political Officer, Political Section, EU Mission to Turkey	07.04.2015
EU03	Visiting Scholar at Carnegie Europe Brussels, Former ambassador of the EU to Turkey (2006–2011)	02.12.2014
EU04	Turkey Advisor of the EU High Representative, European External Action Service	27.11.2014
EU05	Officer, Foreign Policy and CFSP, EU Mission to Turkey	10.04.2015
EU06	First Counsellor, Foreign Policy, EU Mission to Turkey	13.04.2015
EU07	Head of Unit, Turkey, Directorate-General for Neighbourhood and Enlargement Negotiations, European Commission	13.11.2014 (email interview)
EU08	Head of International Cooperation Department, The Directorate-General for European Civil Protection and Humanitarian Aid Operations (ECHO), European Commission	21.11.2014 (email interview)
EU09	The Directorate-General for European Civil Protection and Humanitarian Aid Operations (ECHO) Representative at the EU Delegation in Ankara	07.04.2015
EU10	The High Representative of the Union for Foreign Affairs and Security Policy (HR)	08.08.2012 (email interview)
TR01	Minister for EU Affairs and Chief Negotiator of Turkey	09.08.2012
TR02	Senior bureaucrat, the Ministry of EU Affairs of Turkey	09.04.2015

Interview code	Interviewee position/affiliation at the time of the interview	Interview date[1]
TR03	Bureaucrat, the Ministry for EU Affairs of Turkey	08.04.2015
TR04	Diplomat, Permanent Delegation of Turkey to the EU	25.11.2015
TR05	Officer, EU Section, Ministry of Foreign Affairs of Turkey	07.04.2015
TR06	Officer, Disaster and Emergency Management Presidency, Republic of Turkey Prime Ministry	16.04.2015 (email interview)
TR07	Officer, Middle East Section, Ministry of Foreign Affairs of Turkey, Ankara	24.04.2015
TR08	Vice Chairman for international relations, Republican People's Party (CHP), former ambassador to Paris (2005–2009)	23.08.2012 (email interview)
TR09	Diplomat, Ministry of Foreign Affairs of Turkey, Ankara	26.11.2015
TR10	Vice Chairperson in charge of foreign relations, Republican People's Party (CHP), former ambassador to Washington (2001–2005)	08.09.2012 (email interview)
TR11	Deputy Chairman of AKP in charge of foreign relations Foreign Minister of Turkey (since 2015)	18.04.2013
TR12	Ambassador, Permanent Delegation to UNESCO Former ambassador to Cairo (2009–2013)	04.08.2015 (email interview)
TR13	Senior Diplomat, Ministry of Foreign Affairs of Turkey, Ankara	10.04.2015

[1] Personal interviews, unless otherwise specified

Index